Communication and Aging

Creative Approaches to Improving the Quality of Life

Communication and Aging

Creative Approaches to Improving the Quality of Life

Linda S. Carozza, PhD, CCC-SLP

PLURAL
PUBLISHING
INC.

5521 Ruffin Road
San Diego, CA 92123

e-mail: info@pluralpublishing.com
Website: http://www.pluralpublishing.com

FSC
www.fsc.org
MIX
Paper from
responsible sources
FSC® C011935

Library of Congress Cataloging-in-Publication Data

Communication and aging (Carozza)
 Communication and aging : creative approaches to improving the quality of
life / [edited by] Linda S. Carozza.
    p. ; cm.
 Includes bibliographical references and index.
 ISBN 978-1-59756-612-4 (alk. paper)—ISBN 1-59756-612-8 (alk. paper)
 I. Carozza, Linda S., editor. II. Title.
 [DNLM: 1. Aging. 2. Aged. 3. Communication. 4. Quality of Life. 5. Sensory
Art Therapies. WT 104]
 RC423
 616.85'5065156—dc23
                         2015015196

Contents

Acknowledgments   *vii*

Contributors   *ix*

Part I.   **1**

Chapter 1.   Introduction   3
             Tanya Budilovskaya

Chapter 2.   Perspectives on Communication and Aging   13
             Noel Shafi and Linda S. Carozza

Chapter 3.   Cognitive Changes in Aging: Implications   25
             for Discourse Processing
             Tricia Olea Santos

Chapter 4.   The Effect of Aging and Neurogenic Conditions   67
             on Speech Production: Recent Advances
             Linda S. Carozza

Chapter 5.   Language Comprehension and Production   95
             in Dementia and Aphasia
             Linda S. Carozza

Chapter 6.   Hearing and Aging   121
             Abbey L. Berg and Yula C. Serpanos

Chapter 7.   Swallowing Functions Across the Lifespan   157
             Matina Balou

Chapter 8.   Social Language Enhancement in Dementia   175
             and Aphasia
             Linda S. Carozza with contribution by
             Noel Shafi

Part II.   **205**

Chapter 9.   Psychosocial and Creative Approaches   207
             to Dementia Care
             Lauren Volkmer

v

Chapter 10. Creating the Climate for Contact and Positive   233
            Change in the Social Adult Day Program
            Setting: An Interview with Elizabeth
            Hartowicz, Director of CARE Program at
            Lenox Hill Neighborhood House
            Elizabeth Hartowicz

Chapter 11. Color My Words: How Art Therapy Creates   247
            New Pathways of Communication
            Raquel Chapin Stephenson

Chapter 12. Music Therapy in Neurologic Dysfunction   269
            to Address Self-Expression, Language, and
            Communication: The Impact of Group
            Singing on Stroke Survivors and Caregivers
            *Joanne V. Loewy, Jamée Ard, and
            Naoko Mizutani*

Afterword by Linda S. Carozza   *301*
Index   *305*

Acknowledgments

The inspiration for this book came from many sources, both personal and professional. This book would not have been possible without the ongoing work and effort of my esteemed colleagues and contributors to enhance the quality of life for aged and disabled individuals in our society.

Along with that are the acknowledgments due to a special group of people who stood beside my goal of bringing this book to fruition: my family and close friends, and my dedicated associates chief among them, Abigail Marcus and Therese Capilli whose diligence, knowledge and shared vision helped make my dream of this contribution into a reality; and also to Mr. Alex Radison for his help and support.

And finally, my day-to-day coworkers and patients and their families are owed the greatest debt of gratitude for sharing the goal of long-term care and quality rehabilitation for all.

Contributors

Jamée Ard, MS, DMA, MT-BC
Music Therapist
Hospice of New York
New York, New York
Chapter 12

Matina Balou, PhD, CCC-SLP, BCS-S
Assistant Professor
Department of Otolaryngology
Clinical Swallowing Specialist
Rusk Rehabilitation
NYU Langone Medical Center
New York, New York
Chapter 7

Abbey L. Berg, PhD
Professor, Communication Sciences & Disorders Program
Department of Health Studies
College of Health Professions
Co-Director, The Faculty Center for Innovative Teaching and
    Professional Development
Pace University
New York, New York
Chapter 6

Tanya Budilovskaya, MS, CCC-SLP
Speech-Language Pathologist
Woodhaven, New York
Chapter 1

Linda S. Carozza, PhD, CCC-SLP
Associate Professor and Program Director for Communication
    Sciences and Disorders
Department of Health Studies
College of Health Professions
Pace University
New York, New York
Chapters 2, 4, 5, 8, and Afterword

Elizabeth Hartowicz, MEd
Director, CARE Program of Lenox Hill Neighborhood House
New York, New York
Chapter 10

Joanne V. Loewy, DA, LCAT, MT-BC
Director, The Louis Armstrong Center for Music and
    Medicine
Associate Professor, Icahn School of Medicine at Mount Sinai
Mount Sinai Beth Israel
New York, New York
Chapter 12

Naoko Mizutani, MT-BC, CCLS
International Research Scholar
The Louis Armstrong Center for Music and Medicine
New York, New York
Chapter 12

Tricia Olea Santos, PhD, CCC-SLP
Adjunct Assistant Professor
Callier Center for Communication Disorders
School of Behavioral and Brain Sciences
University of Texas at Dallas
Dallas, Texas
Chapter 3

Yula C. Serpanos, PhD, CCC-A
Professor
Department of Communication Sciences and Disorders
Adelphi University
Garden City, New York
Chapter 6

Noel Shafi, MS
Freelance Writer
Bronx, New York
Chapters 2 and 8

Raquel Chapin Stephenson, PhD, ATR-BC, LCAT
Program Coordinator, Art Therapy
Assistant Professor
Expressive Therapies Division
Lesley University
Cambridge, Massachusetts
Chapter 11

Lauren Volkmer, LMSW
Manager, Early Stage Services
Alzheimer's Association
New York City Chapter
New York, New York
Chapter 9

This book is dedicated to the memory of my parents, Elmo Lawson and Patricia Burnett, who inspired my education and respect for humanity and life challenges. I am forever indebted to them for their unending devotion to faith and family. Their triumph of lives lived valiantly is an example I hope to give to my children and loved ones.

PART I

CHAPTER 1

Introduction

Tanya Budilovskaya

The inspiration for Communication and Aging: Creative Approaches to Improving Quality of Life comes from many sources, not the least of which is the love and appreciation of the lifespan and the rewards and challenges of each stage. Through years of working with individuals living with conditions such as aphasia and dementia, I learned firsthand that triumphs are possible even in the face of these issues, so long as there is human creativity and support for one another. I hope that the book will introduce some of the processes associated with aging, as well as the supports that various methodologies can provide.

—Linda S. Carozza

PART I

All stages of life, beginning at birth and continuing through the lifespan, encompass a series of changes in the physical being. These include both visible and underlying changes within our biological and physiological structures and functions. Our bodies and brains are significantly affected by both environment and personal experience, and as such the trajectory often varies considerably among individuals. Factors such as environmental hazards, life stressors, and genetics all play a large and important part in our cognitive functioning as we age. However, there is a series of biological changes that is experienced by most, particularly as we age. In this book we will examine the effects of aging on the speech and language of adults, both with and without speech-language impairments.

In the *Introduction*, an overview of communication development birth through adulthood will be provided. This will include important developmental milestones that are achieved at every stage of life. This section will also include an overview of the various communication demands and stressors that are incurred at each stage. The following section, *Communication and Aging*, looks more closely at the older population and explores some of the common myths and misconceptions about aging. Several theoretical perspectives on the effects of the aging process will also be examined in order to provide a framework on which to base the content of this book. Finally, the last section of this book will provide an in-depth analysis of the specific brain systems which are commonly affected during the aging process, including cognition, speech production, auditory/language comprehension, voice and swallowing, and social language. Comprehensive information about the appropriate diagnosis and treatment of each impairment will be provided and principles of evidence-based practice will be strongly incorporated and upheld throughout this book.

The demographic of the United States is currently undergoing dramatic changes and the face of America is changing. The following are some surprising facts and trends from recently compiled census data:

■ *The number of individuals reaching ages 65+ has nearly tripled over the last century.* In 1900, only 4.1% of the population was composed of older adults as compared to 13.3% in 2011 (U.S. Census Bureau, 2014).

■ *The number of individuals ages 65+ is expected to double in size within the next 25 years.* By 2030, one out of every five Americans (approximately 72 million people) will be 65 years or older as compared to one out of every eight in 2010 (U.S. Census Bureau, 2014).

■ *Females are outliving males, both with higher life expectancies and demographically.* Females outnumber males at 23.0 million to 17.5 million, but both groups have an additional 18.8 years of average life expectancy (20.0 years for females and 17.3 years for males).

■ Approximately 80% of centenarians are female (U.S. Census Bureau, 2014).

■ *The aging population is increasing in racial/ethnic diversity just like the rest of the population.* Demographic trends predict a shift in the demographic, with decreases in the non-Hispanic white group and increases in minority groups (black, Hispanic, and Asian) by the year 2030 (U.S. Census Bureau, 2014).

■ *The East Coast has higher populations of older residents than the West Coast.* Specifically, Florida (17.6%), Pennsylvania (15.6%), and West Virginia (15.3%) are the "oldest states" in the nation (U.S. Census Bureau, 2014).

■ *While the health of older Americans is improving, many still suffer from chronic conditions.* Some type of disability (i.e., difficulty in hearing, vision, cognition, ambulation, self-care, or independent living) was reported by 37% of older persons in 2010, mostly linked to a high prevalence of chronic conditions such as heart disease or arthritis (U.S. Census Bureau, 2014).

■ *Individuals ages 65+ are staying in the workforce longer.* In 2009, 6.7 million (17.4 %) Americans age 65 and over were in the labor force (working or actively seeking work), including 3.7 million men (22.1%) and 3.0 million women (13.8%). They constituted 4.4% of the U.S. labor force (U.S. Census Bureau, 2014).

■ *The educational level of the older population is increasing.* Between 1970 and 2010, the percentage of older persons who had completed high school rose from 28% to 79.5%. (Administration on Aging, 2012).

■ *The use of technology by the older population is increasing more than ever before.* More than half of older adults (ages 65+) report being Internet users, and 77% report being cell phone users (Pew Research Center, 2012).

This demographic trend of increased longevity is a twofold issue. On the one hand, it is allowing people to lead longer, healthier, and more fulfilling lives with their loved ones. On the other hand, it also poses several challenges, particularly when it comes to health and health-related issues. The age of retirement is something that most people spend many years saving and planning for—a time to enjoy the fruits of one's many years of labor and to indulge in recreational pastimes that have long been put on the back burner, as well as to spend precious time with friends and loved ones. However, there are also a number of disorders which are associated with age-related changes in cognition and memory, including Alzheimer's disease, Parkinson's disease, dementia, aphasia, apraxia, and so forth.

There are several theories related to the causes of age-related changes in cognition in older adults. Some propose that these changes are caused by a decrease in the speed at which mental operations can be performed (*slowing hypothesis*), a decline in the ability to perform basic processing operations and store/retrieve information adequately (*working memory hypothesis*), and a decrease in inhibitory functions, thereby making it more difficult to sift between meaningful and irrelevant information in context (*inhibition deficit hypothesis*) (Morrow & Shake, 2009, *Handbook of Neuroscience of Aging*). Most theories agree that these changes are brought about as a result of "two competing forces—a decline in mental mechanics as well as neural plasticity" (Stine-Morrow & Shake, 2009).

By the year 2050, it is expected that the number of individuals with dementia and Alzheimer's will rise to 11.3 to 16 million, making this group the fastest growing clinical population in the field of speech-language pathology (ASHA, 2005). The American Speech-Language Hearing Association (ASHA) clearly outlines the responsibilities of clinicians working with these populations and their families, which includes but is not limited to appropriate identification/assessment, intervention, collaboration, case management, and education/advocacy.

Performing adequate therapy for older patients with neurologically based impairments is posing an even greater risk for speech-language pathologists and other service providers due to issues with reimbursement for treatment. One such example is that Medicare has placed a "cap" on outpatient rehabilitation therapy services ever since the Balanced Budget Act of 1997. Therapy caps restrict the amount that Medicare will cover for rehabilitation services in a given year. These cuts are especially significant due to the fact that Medicare currently covers 93% of individuals 65+ (Administration on Aging, 2012).

The 2013 therapy cap for the combination of speech-language pathology and physical therapy has been set at $1,900 (Edgar, 2013). The therapy caps apply to all outpatient therapy services except for those provided through a hospital. While there are exceptions on a case-by-case basis, all services rendered which surpass the set amount must be subjected to review and be deemed medically necessary in order for services to be reimbursed (Edgar, 2013).

This poses a specific challenge for speech-language pathologists working with individuals with neurologically based impairments. Therapists are faced with the task of implementing therapy in larger group settings and getting more creative with their approaches to therapy in order to maximize both time and resources.

PART II

As the aging population continues to steadily increase, the Medicare limitations continue to place restrictions on the timeline of therapy. This poses a new set of challenges for therapists working with this population. Therapists are now facing having to work within the confines of larger service delivery groups and increased pressure to demonstrate therapeutic gains in a shorter period of time. Most health care professionals would agree, however, that the ultimate goal is to add "life to years rather than just years to life." This means enriching clients' lives in meaningful ways by helping them regain a sense of self and belonging within their families and communities, being able to participate functionally in activities of daily living, and lead more fulfilling lives.

In keeping with this trend, over the past several years the focus in both the research and literature has shifted toward more non-traditional methods of treatment, known broadly as "creative therapies." Broadly defined, creative therapies encompass a new movement and direction in rehabilitative therapy that uses diverse forms of creative self-expression in a therapeutic setting in order to provide a more holistic approach to rehabilitation. This is particularly important for clients with dementia and other cognitive-related issues for whom progress using traditional means may sometimes be slower and more difficult to accurately quantify. Allowing these clients to engage in pleasurable and entertaining activities in a relaxed and naturalistic atmosphere will both increase their level of motivation and allow greater potential for gains to be made, due to a greater focus on individual self-expression rather than on simply "getting it right."

There are a number of different treatment programs, each modeled on a specific creative medium, including art, drama, and music. The philosophy behind the creative therapy movement is to allow clients to tap into their own creative potentials and to "engage their emotions in a direct and physical way; to develop an ability to generate creative energy as a healing force for mind, body, and spirit; and to develop a belief that the creative imagination can find its way throughout most perplexing and complex problems and conflicts" (McNiff, 2005).

Music therapy is a form of therapy in which "music is used within a therapeutic relationship to address physical, emotional, cognitive, and social needs of individuals" and may include various aspects of music including singing, creating music, and listening to music (American Music Therapy Association, 2013). In several case studies with both children and adults, music therapy has proven to have multifold benefits (Geist et al., 2008; Gross, Linden, & Ostermann, 2010; Lagasse, 2012).

One study found the effects of music therapy to have benefits for a group of clients with Parkinson's disease, including significant improvements in singing quality and voice range. No significant changes were found for speaking quality or depressive symptom outcomes; however, there was an absence of decline on speaking quality outcomes over the intervention period (Elefant, Baker, Lotan, Lagesen, & Skeie, 2012). Additional benefits of music therapy include providing a platform for communicating for individuals who have difficulty doing so, providing increasing motivation for treatment, providing emotional support for clients and families, as well as providing an outlet for expression of feelings (American Music Therapy Association, 2013; Center for Spirituality and Healing, 2013).

Art therapy has been shown to be linked to significant gains on the outcomes of children and adults as well, particularly when used in conjunction with speech and/or occupational therapy in order to facilitate greater carryover. Art therapy focuses more on guiding the client on a journey of self-awareness and understanding and can be very helpful in improving self-esteem as well as unearthing repressed feelings and emotions (Center for Spirituality and Healing, 2013). Art therapy may take on different forms and is highly individualized. In one study conducted by Herzog-Rodriguez (2006), the therapy revolved around the construction of a series of projects, including a computer-generated story, a log house, a puppet show, and a movie about the construction of the Statue of Liberty.

Drama therapy incorporates storytelling, projective play, purposeful improvisation, and performance as a means by which to "rehearse desired behaviors, practice being in relationship, expand and find flexibility between life roles, and perform the change they wish to be and see in the world" (North American Drama Therapy Association, 2013). Drama therapy may be particularly helpful for individuals whose confidence and self-esteem has suffered as a result of their issues and who need help reintegrating into society and their communities. Drama therapy may also provide them with an outlet in which to explore their own feelings and perceptions of self, as well as changes in roles and family dynamics.

CONCLUSION

In sum, the communication challenges in the aging process can present many opportunities for creative programming. The goal of this book to provide current insights into the changes seen in the areas of cognition, language, hearing, and related functions that accompany healthy aging and neurogenic conditions;

and the strategies and methodologies of current models that can bring enhanced quality of life to individuals in this vital segment of our population.

REFERENCES

Administration on Aging. (2012). *A profile of older Americans: 2011.* Retrieved from http://www.aoa.gov/Aging_Statistics/Profile/2011/docs/2011profile.pdf

American Music Therapy Association. (2013). *What is music therapy?* Retrieved from http://www.musictherapy.org/about/musictherapy/

ASHA. (2005). *The roles of speech-language pathologists working with individuals with dementia-based communication disorders* [Position statement]. Retrieved from http://www.asha.org/policy/PS2005-00118/

Center for Spirituality and Healing. (2013). *Creative therapies.* Retrieved from http://www.takingcharge.csh.umn.edu/explore-healing-practices/creative-therapies

Edgar, C. (2013, October 14). *Medicare cap changes for 2013.* Retrieved from http://physical-therapy.advanceweb.com/Features/Articles/Medicare-Cap-Changes-for-2013.aspx

Elefant, C., Baker, F. A., Lotan, M., Lagesen, S. K., & Skeie, G. O. (2012). The effect of music therapy on mood, speech, and singing in individuals with Parkinson's disease: A feasibility study. *Journal of Music Therapy, 49*(3), 278–302.

Geist, K., McCarthy, J., Rodgers-Smith, A., & Porter, J. (2008). Integrating music therapy services and speech-language therapy services for children with severe communication impairments: A co-treatment model. *Journal of Instructional Psychology, 35*(4), 311–316.

Gross, W., Linden, U., & Ostermann, T. (2010). Effects of music therapy in the treatment of children with delayed speech development—results of a pilot study. *BMC Complementary and Alternative Medicine, 10,* 39.

Herzog-Rodriguez, T. (2006). Art therapy and speech/language therapy: An interdisciplinary approach. *Art Therapy, 23*(4).

LaGasse, A. B. (2012). Evaluation of modified melodic intonation therapy for developmental apraxia of speech. *Music Therapy Perspectives, 30*(1), 49–55.

McNiff, S. (2005). Foreword. In C. Malchiodi (Ed.), *Expressive Therapies.* New York, NY: Guilford Press.

North American Drama Therapy Association. (2013). Retrieved from http://www.nadta.org/

Pew Research Center. (2012). *Older adults and technology use.* Retrieved from http://www.pewinternet.org/2014/04/03/older-adults-and-technology-use/

Stine-Morrow, E. A. L., & Shake, M. C. (2009). Language in aged persons. In L. Squire (Ed.), *New encyclopedia of neuroscience* (pp. 337–342). New York, NY: Elsevier.

U.S. Census Bureau. (2014). *65+ in the United States: 2010.* Retrieved from http://www.census.gov/content/dam/Census/library/publications/2014/demo/p23-212.pdf

CHAPTER 2

Perspectives on Communication and Aging

Noel Shafi and Linda S. Carozza

One of the most salient characteristics of the human process of aging is the change in communication style. This may be in the form of communicative challenges, or simply in the form of topic choice and audience. The study of communication throughout the lifespan is a window of opportunity for the learner to examine cognitive, biological, and social-cultural changes that accompany aging and sets the stage for individualistic attention to enhancing quality of life approaches.

—Linda S. Carozza

THE DEFINITION OF AGING

Communicative disorder is an important medical issue that adversely impacts quality of life in the elderly. To understand the changes in communicative function in later stages of life, one should have a basic understanding of the aging process. Aging is defined broadly as "time-dependent functional decline"

(Lopez-Otin, Blasco, Partridge, Serrano, & Kromer, 2013). Several theories of aging as it relates to language processing have been proposed, and will be briefly considered in this chapter. In the forthcoming chapters, as we consider the impact of various communication disorders on older adults, let us keep in mind that language function may decline in cases of healthy and pathological aging. Health care professionals should be careful not to disregard the effect of such a decline on quality of life, regardless of the type of communication disorder in question.

PATTERNS OF AGE-RELATED DECLINE IN LANGUAGE FUNCTION

The relationship between aging and language function has long been a concern for speech-language pathologists. The focus on age-related health issues has gained increasing attention in the profession of speech-language pathology due in part to the increase in the average lifespan and in the percentage of elderly in the general population. According to the Centers for Disease Control and Prevention (2012), the average life span (of all male and female Americans) is about 78.7 years old. In 2000, people 65 years and older represented 12.4% of the population (Administration on Aging, http://www.aoa.gov). This number has risen over the years to 14.1% (Administration on Aging). These trends lead researchers to predict that people aged 65 and older will make up 19% of the population by 2030 (Administration on Aging). Given these significant demographic trends, which indicate a staggering increase in the aging population, there is a clear justification for specializing in communicative disorders in the elderly.

PATTERNS OF LANGUAGE DECLINE IN THE AGING—AN INTRODUCTION

According to the The Gerontological Society of America (2012) or GSA, the elderly may present with deficits in both language comprehension and production. The Society presents several explanations as to why language comprehension is affected by aging, including working memory impairment, reduced information processing speed, and long-term memory retrieval. The aforementioned cognitive functions are important factors in conversational discourse across the lifespan. In addition, age-related hearing loss impairs the ability to discriminate sounds in speech, due to high-frequency hearing loss specifically. Age-related visual deficits, in like manner, impair the ability to read, recognize communicative partners or environmental objects, and socially interact, depending on the nature and severity of vision loss. In combination, age-related declines in hearing, vision, speech production, and auditory comprehension significantly impact the quality of communication, as well as the overall quality of life. The GSA provides some key recommendations for communicating with older adults (Table 2–1).

The study by Yorkston, Bourgeois, and Baylor (2010) references several previous studies that looked at age-related changes in communication:

> A person's age can be predicted with fair accuracy by speech characteristics including voice tremor, pitch, speaking rate, loudness, and fluency. Some language skills remain intact, whereas others tend to decline. For example, vocabulary, grammatical judgment, and repetition ability are relatively stable with age; comprehension of complex utterances and naming may decline. Although changes in communication skills such as voice may be subtle and gradual, they have clear life consequences such as avoidance of social situations. (p. 310)

Such changes however, are not uniform, and therefore, one must be careful not to make any assumptions about an elder's communicative profile. As noted by Yorkston and colleagues (2010), the quality of communication in an elderly person would depend on any preexisting communicative disorder or onset of a new communicative disorder in old age. The type and severity of disorder and comorbidities are also contributing factors. Even among the healthy aging population, one should expect considerable variability in communicative function.

Cognitive decline in aging is selective in that language production in the elderly tends to be compromised to some extent while comprehension is relatively more preserved. The areas of

Table 2–1. General Communication Tips to Improve Interactions with Older Adults

General Tips for Improving Interactions With Older Adults
Recognize the tendency to stereotype older adults, and then conduct your own assessment.
Avoid speech that might be seen as patronizing to an older person ("elderspeak").

General Tips for Improving Face-to-Face Communication With Older Adults
Monitor and control your nonverbal behavior.
Minimize background noise.
Face older adults when you speak with them, with your lips at the same level as theirs.
Pay close attention to sentence structure when conveying critical information.
Use visual aids such as pictures and diagrams to help clarify and reinforce comprehension of key points.
Ask open-ended questions and genuinely listen.

Tips for Optimizing Interactions Between Health Care Professionals and Older Patients
Express understanding and compassion to help older patients manage fear and uncertainty related to the aging process and chronic diseases.
Ask questions about an older adult's living situation and social contacts.
Include older adults in the conversation even if their companion is in the room.
Customize care by seeking information about older adults' cultural beliefs and values pertaining to illness and death.
Engage in shared decision making.
Strike an appropriate balance between respecting patients' autonomy and stimulating their active participation in health care.
Avoid ageist assumptions when providing information and recommendations about preventive care.

Table 2–1. *continued*

Providing information to patients is important, but how you give information to patients may be even more important.

Use direct, concrete, actionable language when talking to older adults.

Verify listener comprehension during a conversation.

Set specific goals for listener comprehension.

Incorporate both technical knowledge and emotional appeal when discussing treatment regimens with older patients.

To provide quality health care, focus on enhancing patient satisfaction.

Use humor and a direct communication style with caution when interacting with non-Western older patients.

Help Internet-savvy older adults with chronic diseases find reputable sources of online support.

If computers are used during face-to-face visits with older adults, consider switching to models that facilitate collaborative use.

Source: Adapted from The Gerontological Society of America (2012).

spoken and written language production are more susceptible to decline with aging. In particular, word-finding issues in the elderly have been extensively documented in the literature, with increased frequency of anomia with aging (Burke & Shafto, 2004). In addition, Burke and Shafto (2004) found that older adults exhibited retrieval difficulties in spelling, indicating impaired representation systems for word phonology and orthography. A study by Schmitter-Edgeconbe, Vesneski, and Jones (2000) demonstrated that in comparison with young adults, older adults produced more filled pauses, ambiguous references, and reformulations at the word level. Apparently, the language production network—in the areas of naming, word-retrieval, spelling, and writing—undergoes decline over time as part of the typical aging process.

The cognition chapter of the present book provides a comprehensive review of issues related to the language models and aging. The following will highlight some of the relevant issues, by way of introduction.

Thornton and Light (2006) conducted a literature review of past research on language comprehension and production in normal aging, highlighting age-related changes in lexical, sentence, and discourse processing. The authors cited many studies that addressed age-related changes in each of the aforementioned categories. Lexical processing deficits in the elderly are characterized by a decrease in word recognition, lexical retrieval, and asymmetries in processing, which is the foundation of the brief review of literature that follows.

Word recognition is impaired in the elderly due to age-related conditions such as presbycusis and reduced temporal processing of speech. Specifically, age-related changes in the auditory nervous system lead to high-frequency hearing loss and decreased ability to differentiate phonemes, such as voiced from voiceless consonants.

Lexical retrieval is impaired in the elderly due to a combination of factors, with two major theories brought forth in the literature. Declines in lexical retrieval are proposed to be related to factors of inhibition theory which predicts that multiple lexical activations may "interfere" with specific lexical selection during retrieval tasks. The second hypothesis is a theory of a transmission deficit. This model is based on delay or possibly premature decay of semantic activations due to weakened semantic network communication. The fact that proper names are more difficult to recall supports the possibility of selective activation in that common nouns have greater semantically related associations that may assist in the retrieval process. Thornton and Light (2006) describe many other examples from experimental research that examine and offer insight into the nature of lexical retrieval issues which in turn are critical for comprehension and production of more semantically and syntactically complex linguistic units.

The question arises as to how the lexical retrieval changes affect sentence processing in general. Cognitive slowing explanations may be insufficient to explain the asymmetries noted in understanding and production of sentence forms observed as people age. Older individuals tend to be able to detect differences in sentences, but are slower than younger individuals in expressive tasks. There is a qualitative difference in the nature of errors made by older individuals such that semantic cues are more salient than phonological cues; therefore, older individuals are slower in expressive tasks but not in a streamlined general pattern. Older individuals' slowing has different patterns and is therefore not just a generalized difference. Healthy elderly exhibit differences in performance when stimuli are accompanied by distracting factors. Older subjects also demonstrate reliance on semantic over phonologic information during processing that speaks to a differential processing system as opposed to generalized slowing.

Thornton and Light (2006) continue to provide extensive information on listening impairment and discourse comprehension. Discourse processing deficits in the elderly are characterized by hearing loss and decreased listening comprehension, discourse comprehension, discourse production, and off-target verbosity. In language processing, issues of phonological processing, concept formation, thought boundaries, storage capacity, and individual factors all have effects on quality of information processing. Multiple resources are recruited differentially to process smaller units and overall part-whole relationships in understanding the "gestalt" of an utterance. This rich area of research is under ongoing investigation as will be discussed in detail in the subsequent chapter.

The cognitive underpinnings of language change throughout the lifespan are complex and diverse. Lexical processing at the word, sentence, and discourse level suggests differential functioning as a person ages with differing characteristic and causation as well as a range of information value. The aging person may achieve communicative competence by recruiting multiple resources from differing strategies based on language store, and ability to access language and cognitive operations to manipulate language operations. The interpretation of these findings will continue as science attempts to clarify these operations with increasingly sophisticated experimental paradigms and using increasingly sophisticated technology such as computer-assisted reaction time programs. The interested reader is encouraged to review Thornton and Light (2006) for a concise review of a wide range of highly pertinent information.

A final thought is the notion of public interaction with older individuals and the tendency to inappropriately use a communication style that may appear patronizing in tone and expression. This is a quality of life issue that is at the heart of communication competence across the lifespan and is essential as a "right" of all participants in a communication dyad, regardless of age or disability.

The following sections will address approaches to communication methodology and philosophy that will be emphasized throughout the book in terms of dignity and appropriateness of care and interaction in communication with healthy elderly as well as communication-disabled adults.

OTHER CONSIDERATIONS

According to Semsei (2000), in the article "On the Nature of Aging," a universal push to explain how people age has appeared in the research literature for many years, but with greatly increased attention recently. Since human beings show a generally similar pattern of age-related decline, aging was presumed to be the result of a single cause. Further thinking proposed several distinct theories, one being that the body is preprogrammed to deteriorate (program theory) and the other that multiple errors of metabolic patterns result in biologic disregulation; and that this is the primary mechanism for aging (error theory). More recently, emphasis has been placed on differential patterns of aging, and the attempt to account for this has led to a theory of multifactorial variations in the aging process. In this sense, aging is the result of the sum effect of internal as well as external factors, rather than one general cause. These factors can influence the aging process and in fact, affect systems such as the body's immune system or neuroendocrine regulating functions, leading to changes in regulation of the body. Aging in this case is seen as a "fluid" process that can be impacted. An example from the author is that it "seems that the role of common stress is still not widely realized as a substantial factor in decreasing the maximal life span." If it is the case that exogenous factors can affect the molecular basis of aging and accumulated cellular damage, then there is a strong foundation upon which to base some potential interventions; in addition to the diet and exercise advice given by physicians, there are important roles for social intervention that may impact quality of life. Understanding the underlying mechanisms that contribute to healthy aging is important for all members of society, both the well elderly, as well as aged individuals who may suffer neurologic impairment. This book will attempt to use the literature on aging to inform "best practices" regarding quality of life interventions and wellness for these populations.

Functional imaging studies have been in the forefront of examining age-related neural atrophy over time, including deterioration of gray matter in later stages of adulthood, and changes in functional activation. Consequently, language behaviors also change, and this is also reflected in the neural network underlying communication. A recent neuroimaging study showed that the neural basis of language function also demonstrates a shift toward a more extensive and bilateral language network (Tyler et al., 2010). This imaging study supports the notion that syntactic processing involves expanded left hemisphere activity, in addition to recruitment of frontotemporal regions of the right hemisphere. In pathological models of language functioning, bilateral and expanded neural networks may serve as a possible compensation mechanism for left-hemisphere atrophy.

Of equal importance is current information regarding the psychological aspects of aging. Morgan (2004) describes the two main parameters that have been examined on psychometric evaluations. Speed of processing (or reaction times) has been evaluated along with general intellectual performance (cognitive assessment). Understanding how these may change in aging can contribute to constructive interventions. As an example, stress can increase reaction time and this factor is seen in the biological study reported by Morgan (2004). In the evaluation of performances, the cognitive underpinning mechanisms include the ability to attend, the transmission of sensory information, and overall central processing. These processes allow for the activation of an individual to demonstrate his or her knowledge on performance tests. Morgan (2004) clarifies that some knowledge is the result of lifelong learning and exposure, and some is the result of the individual's own unique capacity to intuit relationships. Accumulated knowledge can be referred to as acquired knowledge and innate knowledge is more related to individual aptitude. Psychological tests are designed to compare these abilities. Morgan (2004) contends that performance can be modulated and that enriched life experiences are neuroprotective in the sense that they may mitigate decline.

The ability to shift between languages in multilingual adults is also a phenomenon under investigation. It appears that task set shifting in particular becomes deficient in older bilingual adults, indicating a functional decline in bilingual language processing in later stages of life. The Hernandez and Kohnert (1999) study revealed that bilingual adults showed slower response time and made more errors than their college-aged counterparts when asked to continually name a set of pictured objects in English or Spanish presented in alternating or randomized order. In summary, the inability to shift between languages in older adults demonstrates reduced efficiency in language processing and executive functioning as a consequence of aging.

Of special concern to the present readership is the finding that increased education, occupational mental workload, linguistic skills, and regular stimulation can be healthy for all individuals and may potentially have a sustained positive effect on function. These findings underscore the importance of meaningful providing social programming for all aging individuals in a highly targeted manner. The use of meaningful activities in the clinic can impact the "functional decline" that externally characterizes aging and can provide a quality-of-life intervention that defines well elderly. We may therefore discard the myths and misconceptions about aging and use this information to guide our understanding of healthy aging for all populations.

CONCLUSION

In summary, the hallmarks of aging take place on many levels—physiological, environmental, and interactive. As science moves closer to understanding these mechanisms, pharmaceutical agents may be developed to enhance language and performance memory and other disorders related to pathological aging patterns. The present state of understanding aging consists of multifactoral models that relate to automatic preprogrammed deterioration of the biological system as well as triggers of system breakdown that can occur separately. It appears as if the sum total of these results in overall aging.

The following chapters will provide readers with overviews of cognition, communication, physiological and psychological factors related to aging and conditions associated with aging. This chapter serves as a background to the description of wellness programs and models of interventions for individuals who may suffer neurogenic conditions and require specialized adaptations for sustained and meaningful interventions.

REFERENCES

Administration on Aging. *Aging Statistics*. Retrieved from http://www .aoa.gov/Aging_Statistics/

Burke, D. M., & Shafto, M. A. (2004). Aging and language production. *Current Directions in Psychological Science, 13*(1), 21–24.

Centers for Disease Control and Prevention. (2012). Deaths: Preliminary data for 2011. *National Vital Statistics Reports, 61*(6), 1–52.

The Gerontological Society of America. (2012). Communicating with older adults: An evidence-based review of what really works. *McNeil Consumer Healthcare*, 1–40.

Hernandez, A. E., & Kohnert, K. J. (1999). Aging and language switching in bilinguals. *Aging, Neuropsychology, and Cognition, 6*(2), 69–83.

Lopez-Otin, C., Blasco, M. A., Partridge, L., Serrano, M., & Kromer, G. (2013). The hallmarks of aging. *Cell, 153*, 1194–1217.

Morgan, K. (2004). Psychological aspects of ageing. *Psychiatry, 3*(12), 8–10.

Semsei, I. (2000). On the nature of aging. *Mechanisms of Aging and Development, 117*, 93–108.

Schmitter-Edgecombe, M., Vesneski, M., & Jones, D. W. R. (2000). Aging and word-finding: A comparison of spontaneous and constrained naming tests. *Archives of Clinical Neuropsychology, 15*(6), 479–493.

Thornton, R., & Light, L. L. (2006). Language comprehension and production in normal aging. *Handbook of the psychology of aging, 6*, 261–287.

Tyler, L. K., Shafto, M. A., Randall, B., Wright, P., Marslen-Wilson, W. D., & Stamatakis, E. A. (2010). Preserving syntactic processing across the adult life span: The modulation of the frontotemporal language system in the context of age-related atrophy. *Cerebral Cortex, 20*(2), 352–364.

Yorkston, K. M., Bourgeois, M. S., & Baylor, C. R. (2010). Communication and aging. *Physical medicine and rehabilitation clinics of North America, 21*(2), 309–319.

CHAPTER 3

Cognitive Changes in Aging: Implications for Discourse Processing

Tricia Olea Santos

*The study of the cognitive underpinnings of the
individual as he or she moves through the lifespan
is central to gathering information about healthy
aging as well as those associated with neurogenic
conditions. The interaction of the environment and
individual cognition is a universal question and
essential topic in considering the human process. This
chapter covers the important area of cognition and
aging and sets the stage for subsequent chapters about
cognitive related skills such as speech and language
communication in the later stages of the lifespan.*

—Linda S. Carozza

Cicero referred to aging as the *autumn of life*. As with the seasons, human life goes through gradual changes, be it in the physical, emotional, or cognitive domains. Cognitive changes become more apparent as a person ages: the individual may initially show occasional forgetfulness and later notice difficulties learning new information. Often these changes result in reduced participation in activities of daily living (Salthouse, 2005; Salthouse Atkinson & Berish, 2003). There is an inherent need to study cognitive-linguistic changes in aging; understanding the changes gives us a better appreciation of how these influence day-to-day interactions with the elderly.

This chapter focuses on the nonlanguage cognitive operations in aging. It is written in the context of discourse, otherwise referred to as connected language beyond the sentence level. Discourse is ecologically salient since it typifies daily communicative behavior. It can either be in the form of telling stories, giving procedures, engaging in conversation, or deliberating on topics with great detail. This chapter discusses the impact of older adults' cognitive skills in communication. It examines the cognitive gains and losses in language performance in healthy aging. In addition, this chapter briefly describes discourse patterns in mild cognitive impairment and Alzheimer's disease.

AGE-RELATED DECREMENTS: ACCOUNTING FOR THE LOSSES

Age-related decrements are guided by three basic hypotheses: (1) the cognitive slowing discourse hypothesis (Cohen, 1988); (2) the working memory discourse hypothesis (Stine & Wingfield, 1990); and (3) the inhibitory efficiency discourse hypothesis (Hasher & Zacks, 1988). In addition to this, neuropsychologists have explained age-related declines in the context of cortical changes in the brain via the frontal lobe hypothesis (West, 1996). Each of these hypotheses is interdependent and accounts for explanations behind most of the age-related declines in language performance.

The Cognitive Slowing Hypothesis

Cognitive psychologists suggest that performance on cognitive tasks is strongly determined by the speed-of-processing (Verhaeghen & Cerella, 2002; Verhaeghen & Salthouse, 1997). As one ages, general slowing of processes is more acutely experienced.

Discourse processing is a cognitive task that occurs rapidly (Kintsch & van Dijk, 1978); as such, it is identified as a primary area in which older adults show declines in language performance (Connor, 2001; Salthouse, 1985).

Declines in speed of processing affect other domains relevant to discourse processing, such as: working memory span, reasoning, naming and memory of past events (Bryan & Luszcz, 1996; Connor, 2001; Salthouse, 1985, 1990, 1992, 2000; Salthouse & Babcock, 1991; Verhaeghen & Salthouse, 1997). Recall among older adults is greatly impaired when information is rapidly presented (Gordon-Salant & Fitzgibbons, 1997; Stine & Wingfield, 1987; Tun, Wingfield, Stine, & Mecsas, 1992; Wingfield, 1996; Wingfield, Tun, Koh, & Rosen, 1999). Fast presentation of information also affects older adults' performance when generating inference, or deriving logical conclusions from a text. (Cohen, 1979). On the contrary, comparable performance between younger and older adults is apparent when the speed of information is reduced in free recall tasks (Bryan & Luszcz, 1996) and recall of text details (Lindenberger, Mayr, & Kliegl, 1993).

Studies analyzing reading times (Stine & Hindman, 1994; Stine & Wingfield, 1987) and auditory comprehension suggest that older adults require more time to organize thoughts when presented with complicated sentences. For texts requiring easy and difficult levels of inference, older adults show difficulties when information is presented at a standard speaking rate. However, difficulties are reduced when pacing is provided in a slower, controlled rate (Hasher & Zacks, 1988).

> Studies suggest that cognitive slowing is inherent in older adults and affects how discourse is processed. However, when tasks do not impose time constraints, older and younger adults demonstrate relatively comparable performance.

The Working Memory Discourse Hypothesis

Working memory is defined as the "brain system that provides temporary storage and manipulation of the information necessary for complex cognitive tasks, such as language comprehension, learning, and reasoning" (Baddeley, 1992, p. 556). The working memory discourse hypothesis (Stine & Wingfield, 1990) proposes that declines in language performance are a result of age-related changes in working memory storage and/or processing. Older adults have less storage capacity in working memory, which puts them at a disadvantage, especially when managing large amounts of information (Carpenter, Miyake, & Just, 1994; Salthouse, 1990, 1992; Salthouse & Babcock, 1991; Zacks, Hasher, & Li, 2000), remembering events, or using episodic memory (Kane & Engle, 2000; McCabe & Smith, 2002; McCabe, Smith, & Parks, 2007; Park et al., 1996; Park et al., 2002), inhibiting irrelevant information (Hasher & Zacks, 1988), and reasoning (Barrouillet, & Lecas, 1999; Kyllonen & Christal, 1990).

Age-related changes in memory interfere with recall of discourse. Older adults with smaller memory spans exhibit difficulties with sentence comprehension and remembering details in text (Norman, Kemper, Kynette, Cheung, & Anagnopoulos, 1991; Tun et al., 1992). Compared to younger adults, older adults have pronounced difficulties remembering individual words and syntactically complex sentences (Spilich & Voss, 1982; Stine & Wingfield, 1990; Stine-Morrow, Ryan, & Leonard, 2000). Those with decreased working memory capacity tend to process text details more slowly than older people with higher working memory span scores (Stine & Hindman, 1994).

When compared to younger adults, a number of studies proposed that older adults recall fewer details after reading or listening to texts (Adams, Smith, Pasupathi, & Vitolo, 2002; Hasher & Zacks, 1988; Hultsch & Dixon, 1984; Meyer & Rice, 1989; Spilich, 1983; Ulatowska, Cannito, Hayashi, & Fleming, 1985). A study by Fitzpatrick, Obler, Au, Nicholas, and Albert (1993) tasked participants with reading a story, copying, and then recalling it (immediate and delayed recall). Older adults recalled fewer information units than the younger participants in both immediate and delayed recall tasks. Although no age-related differences were observed with the main ideas in the story, older adults recalled fewer minor details. A related study by Juncos-Rabadán, Pereiro, and Rodríguez (2005) compared retelling a recently heard narrative among young and older adults. Older adults tended to give shorter, less relevant information as compared to young adults. Similar results were seen in studies by Ulatowska and colleagues

(Cannito, Hayashi, & Ulatowska, 1988; North & Ulatowska, 1981; North, Ulatowska, Macaluso-Haynes, & Bell, 1986; Ulatowska & Chapman, 1994; Ulatowska et al., 1985) that suggested how the older-old adults produce less overall information and less accurate information in narratives. Furthermore, these individuals indicated less relevant information when presented with complex sentence structures.

In a comparison of how older and younger women provided procedural discourse task, or chronological steps to a task, older women gave less information when describing essential steps in a task (North et al., 1986). A different study that compared recall of expository text of varying complexity and length in old and young adults (Stine & Wingfield, 1990) further indicated that older adults recalled less information, especially when passages were more complex. These studies underscored how limited working memory capacity of older adults can result in forgetting detailed information in text (Kwong See & Ryan, 1995). Stine-Morrow and colleagues (2002) explained how age-related decrements may be related to differences in reading strategies and cognitive resources for age groups: whereas younger adults recall detailed information from the text, older adults recall information by processing information globally, or from a bigger picture. Older adults may not pay enough attention to details since these may not be perceived as having much value to the overall meaning of the text (Castel, 2007).

In addition to recall of information, working memory capacity affects pronoun usage among older adults. Several studies (Light, Capps, Singh, & Albertson Owens, 1994; Marini, Boewe, Caltagirone, & Carlomagno, 2005; Morrow, Leirer, & Altieri, 1992; North et al., 1986) suggest that older adults tend to produce significantly fewer understandable stories than young adults due to ambiguous pronouns and shifts in events. Older adults tend to be less accurate than younger ones when referring to minor characters in a story (Morrow et al., 1992). Disruptions are more pronounced among older-old adults when the complexity of the task is increased (Cannito et al., 1988; North et al., 1986; Obler, 1980; Ulatowska & Chapman, 1991).

Limitations in working memory also affect inhibition, or the ability to minimize distracting information. Reduced working memory capacity and attention have been correlated with simultaneously tracking and coordinating multiple characters in a story (Noh & Stine-Morrow, 2009). Older adults tend to have difficulties remembering the initial character once a new character is introduced. They also have difficulties adding a new character while including other background characters in the story (Noh & Stine-Morrow, 2009).

> As a result of reduced working memory capacity in aging, older adults tend to recall less detailed information from text. Difficulties are more pronounced when stimuli are syntactically complex.

The Inhibitory Efficiency Discourse Hypothesis

The inhibitory mechanism is primarily responsible for preventing irrelevant thoughts from entering one's working memory when processing information (Gernsbacher, 1990; Kintsch, 1988). Inhibition downplays concepts that are no longer relevant in working memory, especially when a change occurs in the goals of a text (Gernsbacher, 1990; Hasher & Zacks, 1988).

The inhibitory efficiency discourse hypothesis suggests that language performance is affected by one's ability to inhibit irrelevant thoughts and stimuli as one ages (Hasher & Zacks, 1988). Decrements in inhibition seriously affect discourse comprehension in that the person includes and retains irrelevant information. These result in difficulties retrieving essential information from memory, as well as difficulties forming understandable text representations (Gerard, Zacks, Hasher, & Radvansky, 1991; Hasher & Zacks, 1988; Healey, Campbell & Hasher, 2008; Stevens, Hasher, Chiew, & Grady, 2008).

It is suggested that older adults are more vulnerable than younger ones with regard to inhibiting information. They demonstrate more difficulties than younger adults in identifying inappropriate responses and distinguishing relevant from irrelevant information (Barr & Giambra, 1990; Connelly, Hasher, Zacks, 1991; Hasher, Lustig, & Zacks, 2007; Hasher & Zacks, 1988; Hasher, Zacks, & May, 1999; Healey et al., 2008; Lustig, Hasher, & Tonev, 2006; Stevens et al., 2008; Tipper, 1991). A study by Connelly and colleagues (1991) tasked participants with reading short stories containing relevant and irrelevant text. In stories without distracting information, older adults had slightly slower reading speeds than younger adults. When presented with distracting words and phrases (text related but different in font size); however, older adults had significantly slower reading speeds. This suggested that older people were more likely to decode the meaning of irrelevant information. Another study (Lustig et al., 2006) indicated that older adults were slower than younger ones when presented with cluttered stimuli. However, comparable performance was observed when tasks had less distractions or interference (Lustig, May, & Hasher, 2001; May, Hasher, & Kane, 1999).

Distracting information is disruptive for older adults even in familiar, well-learned tasks (Healey et al., 2008). Older adults are less adept at inhibiting irrelevant environmental distractors during problem-solving and reading comprehension tasks (Connelly et al., 1991; Dywan & Murphy, 1996; Healey et al., 2008). They demonstrate difficulties inhibiting non-goal path thoughts during conversations (Obler, 1980) and tend to temporarily forget essential information. This is attributed in part to reduced inhibitory function or greater attention to non-goal information (Hasher & Zacks, 1988). Additionally, older adults are vulnerable to complex problem-solving tasks that require switching mental sets (Jong, 2001; Kray & Lindenberger, 2000; McDowd & Craik, 1988; Meiran & Gother, 2001; Park, Smith, Dudley, & Lafronza, 1989; Salthouse, Rogan, & Prill, 1984; Tsang & Shaner, 1998). Although they can generate new and correct inferences, they continue to maintain older, and occasionally contradictory, inference that may no longer be relevant (Eakin & Hertzog, 2006; Hamm & Hasher, 1992; Hasher & Zacks, 1988; Ikier & Hasher, 2006; Winocur & Moscovitch, 1983).

> Older adults demonstrate difficulties inhibiting information or modifying their understanding of a situation once they have established a mental representation of an event. However, comparable performance between younger and older adults is exhibited in tasks that have less distractions or interference.

Aging and Changes in Brain Structure: Frontal Aging Hypothesis

With the advances in technology, age-related cognitive declines have been explained in terms of changes in brain structure. The frontal aging hypothesis (Dempster, 1992) suggests that cognitive declines in aging are accompanied by changes in the frontal lobe. Following Dempster's work, West (1996) has specifically identified the prefrontal cortex as the primary area responsible for marked declines in executive function among healthy elderly. This is supported by several neuroimaging studies that document a greater decrease in brain volume of the frontal cortex as opposed to other brain areas (Albert & Kaplan, 1980; Andres & van der Linden, 2001; Crawford, Bryan, Luszcz, Obonsawin, & Stewart, 2000; Daigneault, Braun, & Whitaker, 1992; Dempster, 1992; Haug & Eggers, 1991; Kimberg, Esposito, & Farah, 1997; Mittenberg, Seidenberg, O'Leary, & DiGiulio, 1989; Parkin, 1997; Perfect, 1997; Raz, 2000, 2004; Raz, Gunning-Dixon, Head, Dupuis, & Acker, 1998; Raz & Rodriguez, 2006; Raz et al., 2003; Tisserand & Jolles, 2003). These neuroimaging studies suggest that the prefrontal cortex is sensitive to aging and demonstrates earlier age-related declines in cognitive function as compared to cognitive abilities supported by other areas of the brain.

Given the close link between the frontal lobes and executive function, neuropsychologists and cognitive psychologists have taken an interest in the role of executive function in aging. Broadly defined, executive functioning (EF) involves cognitive processes responsible for planning, making decisions, coordinating, sequencing, and monitoring or updating cognitive operations essential to activities of daily living (Salthouse et al., 2003). According to Malloy, Cohen, and Jenkins (1998), specific abilities encompass executive functions: "(1) Formulating goals with regard for long-term consequences; (2) Generating multiple response alternatives; (3) Choosing and initiating goal-directed behaviors; (4) Self-monitoring the adequacy and correctness of the behavior; (5) Correcting and modifying behaviors when conditions change; (6) Persisting in the face of distraction" (p. 574).

Executive function plays a central role in goal-directed behavior and updating demands of a task, inhibiting responses, shifting mental sets, or solutions to a problem, and adapting to new or complex situations which may deviate from the routine (Albinet, Tomprowski, Beasman, 2006; Banich, 2009; Bryan & Luszcz, 1999; Fuster, 1997; Jurado & Rosselli, 2007; Lezak, 1995; McCabe, Roediger, McDaniel, Balota, & Hambrinck, 2010; Salthouse et al., 2003). Some executive functions, such as updating information, are strongly associated with general cognitive functioning (Friedman, Miyake, Corley, Young, DeFries, & Hewitt, 2006; Kolb & Whishaw, 1990; Woodruff-Pak, 1997). In addition to this, there is a connection between EF and memory: remembering relies on strategically elaborating on information and systematically retrieving information from memory (Buckner, 2004).

In comparing frontal and nonfrontal tasks, studies have indicated poorer performance of older adults on executive functions linked to frontal lobe tasks (Phillips & Henry, 2005; Whelihan & Lesher, 1985). Healthy older adults are likely to have decreased performance on EF tasks such as inhibition of information (Lowe & Rabbitt, 1997; Rabbitt, Lowe, & Shilling, 2001), mental flexibility (Salthouse, Firstoe, McGuthry, & Hambrick, 1998; Verhaeghen & Cerella, 2002) and planning skills (Gilhooly, Phillips, Wynn, Logie, & Della Salla, 1999; Robbins et al., 1999). Research also suggests how declines in EF partly account for age-related decrements in memory (Clarys, Bugaiska, Tapia, & Baudouin, 2009; Head, Rodrigue, Kennedy, & Raz, 2008; Parkin, 1997), particularly strategic memory for activities of daily living (Vaughan & Giovanello, 2010).

In addition, declines in EF have been connected to difficulties with source memory (remembering the source of information) and temporal memory (chronological order of past experiences) (Buckner, 2004; Dempster, 1992; Johnson, Hashtroudi, & Linday, 1993; Parkin, 1997; Perfect, 1997; Schacter, Kaszniak, Kihlstrom, & Valdiserri, 1991; Troyer, Graves, & Cullum, 1994; West, 1996). Studies of older adults (Bunce, 2003; Parkin & Walter, 1992) document how declines in EF show difficulties with adequately encoding episodic details and recollecting events. In comparing older adults and patients with frontal lesions, studies document how both groups demonstrate impaired performance on similar tests, such as free recall (Craik & McDowd, 1987), control of interference or distractors (Dempster, 1992), remembering the source of information (Glisky, Rubin, & Davidson, 2001), and remembering the order in which information was presented

(Parkin, Walter, & Hunkin, 1995; Trott, Friedman, Fabiani, Ritter, & Snodgrass, 1999).

Researchers in cognitive aging have debated as to whether EF is a result of a unitary process, as opposed to several diverse processes (Duncan, Johnson, Swales, & Freer, 1997; Miyake, Friedman, Rettinger, Shah, & Hegarty, 2000; Stuss & Alexander, 2000; Teuber, 1972). More recent studies suggest that executive functions consist of both unitary and diverse processes (Banich, 2009; Friedman, Miyake, Young, DeFries, Coreley, & Hewitt, 2008; Garon, Bryson, & Smith, 2008; McCabe et al., 2010).

> Neuropsychologists suggest how declines in executive function are attributed to the deterioration of prefrontal cortex. Declines in executive function are particularly noted when remembering events, inhibiting distracting/irrelevant information, and problem solving.

In summary, studies have attributed older adults' declines in discourse processing to slower processing speeds, difficulties with inhibitory efficiency, smaller working memory capacity, and declines in executive function. Despite attempts to isolate these processes, it is suggested that these processes are not mutually exclusive (Albinet et al., 2006; Baudouin, Clarys, Vanneste, & Isingrini, 2009; Bugg, Zook, DeLosh, Davalos, & Davis, 2006; Lee et al., 2012; Parkin & Java, 2000; Piccinin & Rabbitt, 1999; Salthouse 1992; Schretlen, Pealrson, Aylward, Augustine, Davis, & Barta, 2000). This is explained in part by studies that indcate how all of these processes become less dissociable as a person ages (Albinet et al., 2006; Salthouse, 1992; Salthouse et al., 2003; Vaughan & Giovannello, 2010).

Decrements in language performance are particularly noted under the following conditions: (a) when the information to be processed is too dense and/or unfamiliar to them, (b) when information is presented in a distracting environment, (c) when information does not relate well to their expertise or prior knowledge, and/or (d) when information is less redundant or disorganized (Dixon & Gould, 1996; Hultsch & Dixon, 1984; Hultsch, Hertzog, & Dixon, 1990; Olson, 1987; Rabbitt, 1965; Salthouse, 1990; Shadden, 1997; Zelinski & Hyde, 1996). Such tasks challenge the individual's ability to allocate sufficient resources to process and integrate discourse (Hartley, 1993; Kahn & Cordon, 1993). Controlling for speed in particular is suggested to strongly reduce age differences in memory (Bryan & Luszcz, 1996; Clarys, Isingrini, & Gana, 2002), general intelligence and reasoning (Hertzog & Bleckley, 2001; Zimprich & Martin, 2002), as well as spatial abilities (Finkel, McArdle, Reynolds, & Pedersen, 2007; Verhaeghen & Salthouse, 1997).

PRESERVED SKILLS IN OLD AGE: THE BIGGER PICTURE

In recent years, there has been a growing interest in more comprehensive studies of language changes across the lifespan. Scholars have stressed the importance of generalizing findings to ordinary, day-to-day functioning of older adults (Hess & Pullen, 1996; Marini et al., 2005; West & Sinnott, 1992). This section discusses the preserved skills in aging that are relevant to discourse processing and further examines the neuropsychologists' take on brain plasticity and compensation despite age-related changes.

Several cognitive operations account for comparable performance of older adults to younger ones. Older adults demonstrate commensurate and sometimes superior performance in tests involving semantic memory, or recollected facts gathered throughout a lifetime, and decision making (Kim & Hasher, 2005; Mather, 2006). Higher levels of education or vocabulary skills in older adults (Craik, Morris, Morris, & Loewen, 1990; Hasher & Zacks, 1988; Meyer & Rice, 1981, 1983, 1989; Nyberg, Backman, Erngrund, Olofsson, & Nilsson, 1996; Park et al., 2002; Schaie, 1996; Verhaeghen, 2003), deeper processing of information (Till & Walsh, 1980), and/or increased cognitive control are some skills that offset declines in language performance. Furthermore, older-old adults are documented to produce in-depth evaluations of personally meaningful experiences (Ulatowska, Garst Walsh, Olea Santos, & Reyes, 2014).

Minimal age differences are observed when older individuals are provided greater contextual support, minimal distraction, and more time to process information (Light et al., 1994). In addition to this, older adults use external memory strategies, such as lists, to remember information (Bouazzaoui et al., 2010). They may identify the linguistic context to recognize words (Pichora-Fuller, Schneider, & Daneman, 1995; Wingfield, Aberdeen & Stine, 1991) or rely on speech intonation patterns to help identify the main ideas in syntactically complex sentences (Kjelgaard, Titone, & Wingfield, 1999). Other preserved skills relevant to discourse processing that are discussed in this chapter include: crystallized intelligence, gist-based processing, and situation modeling.

Crystallized Intelligence

Fluid intelligence is described as active manipulation of information (Radvansky& Dijkstra, 2007). It requires working memory capacity and the integration of information within a short time frame (Labouvie-Vief, 1985). Crystallized intelligence is background knowledge collected over a lifetime, such as vocabulary or world knowledge acquired from formal education and life experiences (Cattel, 1963; Horn & Cattel, 1966; Radvansky & Dijkstra, 2007). It encompasses familiar scripts, such as daily routines (Arbuckle, Vanderleck, Harsany, & Lapidus, 1990; Hess, 2005), and is necessary in forming a global inference, or deriving a logical conclusion, from the text (Cattell, 1963; Horn & Cattell, 1966).

Crystallized intelligence is preserved in old age (Baltes, 1993; Schaie, 1990; Stine-Morrow, Soederberg Miller, Gagne, & Hertzog, 2008). Older readers effectively use previous reading experiences and schemas (common representation of concepts) to facilitate text comprehension (Radvansky & Dijkstra, 2007; Stine-Morrow, Shake, Miles, & Noh, 2006). Cross-sectional and longitudinal studies indicate how older readers form inferences comparable to those of younger adults via crystallized intelligence (Andrews, Clark, & Luszcz, 2002; Newson & Kemps, 2005; Radvansky & Dijkstra, 2007; Stine-Morrow et al., 2006). Background knowledge and expertise reinforce how older readers generate an inference (Hess, 2005; Miller, Stine-Morrow, Kirkorian, & Conroy, 2004; Soederberg Miller, 2009).

In addition to improving text comprehension, crystallized intelligence reinforces memory for text (Arbuckle et al., 1990; Chiesi, Spilich & Voss; 1979; Kintsch, 1998; Olea Santos, 2013; Santos & Ulatowska, 2014; Soederberg Miller, 2009; Soederberg Miller, Cohen, & Wingfield, 2006; Spilich, Vesonder, Voss, Chiesi, & Voss, 1979; Voss, Vesonder, & Spilich, 1980). Older readers with more background knowledge on a topic tend to draw more meaningful inferences and are better able to integrate the text than younger adult readers (Miller, Cohen, & Wingfield, 2006; Miller et al., 2004; Stine-Morrow et al., 2008). Studies (Castel, 2007; Poon, 1985) further suggest that older adults are better at performing ecologically salient tasks, or tasks used in daily interactions, than those not used in day-to-day function. Although a decrease in performance on neuropsychological tests is observed over time, older adults maintain competence in performing tasks in specific, familiar environments (Schludermann, Schludermann, Merryman, & Brown, 1983). For example, they tend to remember regularly priced items but demonstrate difficulties remembering uncommon or overpriced grocery items (Castel, 2007).

Background knowledge aids in reducing processing time for text (Stine-Morrow et al., 2008; Radvansky & Dijkstra, 2007; Miller & Stine-Morrow, 1998). Older readers, for example, spend less time processing final words of sentences once they draw on the basic knowledge indicated in the text (Sharkey & Sharkey, 1987). Faster processing time is also demonstrated when the concepts in the text and the reader's knowledge base overlap (Miller & Stine-Morrow, 1998; Sharkey & Sharkey, 1987). However, when text and knowledge base do not overlap (i.e., text contains contradictory or new information), text processing time is increased (Miller, 2003). Researchers further postulate that older adults make greater use of knowledge from personal experiences and values that are easily accessible from memory when interpreting information (Labouvie-Vief & Blanchard-Fields, 1982; Olea Santos, 2013; Santos & Ulatowska, 2014) or making decisions (Hasher & Zacks, 1988).

> Crystallized intelligence, or background knowledge collected over a lifetime, is preserved in aging. It is used to facilitate comprehension of and memory for information.

Gist-Based Processing

Gist-based processing involves identifying the main theme in a text, or the most important information, while ignoring less important details (Adams, Labouvie-Vief, Hobart, & Dorosz, 1990; Ulatowska & Chapman, 1994). This is another preserved skill in elderly adults, especially in simple texts that do not require speed-of-processing demands (Chapman, Anand, Sparks, & Cullum, 2006; Ulatowska, Allard, & Donnell, 1998; Ulatowska, Chapman, & Johnson, 1999).

Despite difficulties remembering details, older adults maintain gist-based processing (Adams, Labouvie-Vief, Hobart, & Dorosz, 1990; Adams, Smith, Nyquist, & Perlmutter,1997; Baltes, 1993; Chapman, Anand, Sparks, & Cullum, 2006; Chapman & Johnson, 1999; Hasher & Zacks, 1988; Labouvie-Vief, 1985; North et al., 1986; Olness, 2000; Marini et al., 2005; Meyer & Rice, 1981; Ulatowska, Chapman, Highley, & Prince, 1998; Ulatowska et al., 1985; Zelinski & Gilewski,1988). Even under conditions of noise, older and younger adults show comparable performance on identifying the main point of the story (Schneider, Daneman, Murphy, & See, 2000). Older adults also maintain their ability to integrate and interpret meanings of text; this is attributed to the wide range of experiences of older readers (Adams, Smith, Nyquist, & Perlmutter, 1997; Adams et al., 1990).

Several reasons point to why older adults tend to resort to gist-based processing. First, gist-based is strongly linked to world knowledge (Hess, 1990; Schanck & Abelson, 1977, 1995); second, it is integrated with information already stored in memory (Till & Walsh, 1980); and third, it is more accessible as a means of retrieving conceptual information from memory (Hess, 2005).

> Despite difficulties remembering text details, older adults' ability to remember the main point of a text remains intact.

Situation Modeling

Situation modeling pertains to comprehension of and memory for situation-specific information (Johnson-Laird, 1983; van Dijk & Kintsch, 1983). It differs from gist-based processing in that situation modeling uses both the schemas and functional relations between objects or persons in an event (Radvansky & Dijkstra,

2007). The person pays attention to how objects/persons in a specific situation interact in a meaningful way.

Older adults are documented to perform better than younger adults with situation modeling tasks (Noh & Stine-Morrow, 2009; Radvansky, Copeland, & Zwaan 2003; Radvansky & Dijkstra, 2007; Radvansky, Gerard, Zacks, & Hasher, 1990; Radvansky, Zwaan, Curiel, & Copeland, 2001; Stine-Morrow, Morrow, & Leno, 2002).When comparing strategies to effectively memorize text, older individuals use situation modeling strategies as opposed to younger adults who spend more time memorizing details in text (Stine-Morrow, Loveless, & Soederberg, 1996). Although processing of text details is necessary to initially comprehend information, situation modeling provides the person with simulations of experiences (Radvansky & Dijkstra, 2007).

When presented with stories, older adults are able to understand situations, detect temporal and spatial shifts, track information across shifts, and update character goals or emotional states (Morrow, Leirer, Altieri, & Fitzsimmons, 1994; Radvansky & Dijkstra, 2007; Stine-Morrow et al., 2002). Although age differences are noted with retaining information on minor characters, minimal differences are noted with recalling information on protagonists or the protagonist's environment (Morrow et al., 1992, 1994; Stine-Morrow, Morrow, & Leno, 2002).

Situation modeling affects processing time (Radvansky & Dijkstra, 2007). When a shift in situation occurs (Radvansky, Zwaan, Curiel, & Copeland, 2001) or when a new character is introduced in a story goal (Miller & Stine-Morrow, 1998; Stine-Morrow, Loveless, & Soederberg, 1996), older adults show slower reading times. It is suggested that during these periods, individuals update their situation models to accommodate for changes. Despite slower processing times, however, only minor differences in situation modeling are observed between younger and older adults. It is suggested that the older adult remembers details or shifts in a story since the person is more active in recreating the scene and developing rich mental representations of situations (Radvansky & Dijkstra, 2007).

In the context of medical education of the elderly, several studies have compared recall of medical information in narrative as opposed to expository form. These studies suggest that adults from at-risk groups retain more medical information when it is presented in the context of a story (Dillard, Fagerlin, Dal Cin, Zikmund-Fisher, & Ubel, 2010; Kreuter et al., 2010; Olea Santos, 2013; Santos & Ulatowska, 2014; Wise, Han, Shaw, McTavish, & Gustafon, 2008). These studies further highlight the importance of situation modeling in facilitating recall of information.

> Situation modeling is another strategy employed by older adults to offset declines in processing text. Since the older adult is more active in recreating a scene, this allows the individual to remember details pertaining to the protagonist in the story.

Aging and Changes in Brain Structure: Neural Recruitment

Neuroimaging techniques have been used to explain how cognitive-linguistic skills remain intact despite neurobiological changes associated with aging. When healthy young and older adults are compared, imaging studies indicate differences in neural activation between both groups when performing the same task. Young adults show focal activation of the brain, in contrast to the more widespread patterns of neural activation in older adults (Cabeza 2002; Logan, Sanders, Snyder, Morris, & Buckner, 2002). This is described as neural recruitment and is documented in tasks involving encoding pictures (Gutchess et al., 2005) and episodic memory, or memory for autobiographical events (Cabeza, 2001).

The concept of neural recruitment is explained by two hypotheses, namely the *dedifferentiation hypothesis* and the *compensation hypothesis* (Wingfield & Grossman, 2006). The *dedifferentiation hypothesis* proposes that widespread activation in older adults is a result of declines in neural efficiency; thus, the need to activate additional brain areas (Park et al., 2003; Wingfield & Grossman, 2006). The *compensation hypothesis* suggests that widespread neural activation of older adults is a result of strategically recruiting additional cortical areas of the brain to maintain high levels of performance in cognitive tasks

(Wingfield & Grossman, 2006). When performing sensory tasks that require executive function, older adults exhibit recruitment of the frontal cortex while younger adults do not (Cabeza et al., 2004). Cabeza and colleagues (2004) suggest that recruitment of the frontal cortex may be the older adults' attempts to use executive function skills to compensate for sensory declines.

> Young adults show focal activation of the brain, in contrast to the more widespread patterns of neural activation in older adults. This suggests that older adults recruit other brain areas to maintain high language performance.

In summary, healthy older adults use cognitive strategies, such as crystallized intelligence, gist-based processing, and situation modeling, to augment age-related declines in language performance. With the advances in technology, neuroimaging studies have further shown the adaptive nature of the brain to optimize its language processing system.

COGNITIVE-LINGUISTIC CHANGES IN MILD COGNITIVE IMPAIRMENT AND ALZHEIMER'S DISEASE

In recent years, there has been a growing interest in distinguishing communicative patterns of healthy aging, mild cognitive impairment (MCI), and mild dementia (early stages of Alzheimer's disease/AD). Although some changes may be determined via language tasks, subtle changes may remain undetected with current assessment measures (Obler & Pekkala, 2008). This section briefly outlines changes in discourse in mild cognitive impairment and Alzheimer's disease. For a more in-depth discussion on these areas, the reader is encouraged to read related sources cited in the reference section of this chapter.

Mild cognitive impairment (MCI) is defined as a "transitional state between normal aging and dementia . . . with heterogeneous symptoms" (Nordlund et al., 2005, p. 1485). According to the International Working Group on Mild Cognitive Impairment (Winblad et al., 2004), the general criteria for MCI include the following: the individual neither presents with normal cognition nor fulfills the diagnostic criteria for dementia, cognitive declines are self-reported or reflected in an objective cognitive task, and minimal-to-no impairments are demonstrated with complex cognitive function and activities of daily living. Gauthier and colleagues (2006) suggest that 50% of individuals with MCI progress to Alzheimer's dementia within 5 years, whereas others either remain stable or return to their prior level of functioning.

Persons with MCI often notice and self-report memory difficulties (Fleming, 2013). Comprehension of casual conversation is relatively preserved in MCI (Fleming & Harris, 2008; Obler & Pekkala, 2008). However, difficulties with executive function and learning are exhibited among these individuals (Fleming, 2013; Fleming & Harris, 2008; Obler & Pekkala, 2008). Difficulties are also demonstrated in comprehension tasks (i.e., performance on the Token Test) and naming tasks (i.e., performance on the Boston Naming Test) (Nordlund et al., 2005). Breakdowns are also exhibited with syntactically complex sentence structures (Nordlund et al., 2005) or in comprehension tasks requiring additional knowledge on the part of the listener (Obler & Pekkala, 2008). Tasks requiring inference generation, such as providing the gist of a story, may also be very difficult for those with MCI (Chapman et al., 2002).

Persons with MCI demonstrate difficulties evaluating object knowledge, suggesting a deficit in semantic memory (Adlam, Bozeat, Arnold, Watson, & Hodges, 2006; Duong, Whitehead, Hanratty, & Chertkow, 2006). Spontaneous speech is typically characterized by word retrieval difficulties (Fleming & Harris, 2008; Obler & Pekkala, 2008). Additionally, there is a lack of thematic completeness at the discourse level when compared to healthy adults (Fleming, 2013; Fleming & Harris, 2008).

Alzheimer's disease is the most common form of dementia caused by the degeneration of the frontal and medial temporal lobes. Early stage dementia is characterized by linguistic and behavioral changes, declines in memory, and difficulties learning or applying knowledge (Bayles, Kaszniak, & Tomoeda, 1987; Obler & Pekkala, 2008; Ulatowska & Chapman, 1991). Language changes are initial salient features; memory deficits are more pronounced features as the condition progresses (Bowles, Olber & Albert, 1987; Obler & Albert, 1984; Obler & Pekkala, 2008). Similar to individuals with MCI, persons with early stage AD do not have difficulties comprehending everyday language (Obler & Pekkala, 2008). However, discourse comprehension declines steadily over time. Individuals exhibit difficulties with abstract language (i.e., humor or sarcasm) (Ripich & Ziol, 1998). They tend to omit main ideas, and demonstrate breakdowns in organizing and sequencing information (Chenery & Murdoch, 1994). Similar to MCI, persons with dementia demonstrate difficulties producing the summary/gist of a story (Chapman et al., 2002, 2006). These breakdowns reflect failures in retrieving information and limitations in working memory. As the condition progresses, declines in standardized comprehension tests become more apparent (Obler & Pekkala, 2008). These declines in comprehension are attributed to deficits in executive function, particularly semantic memory, working memory and episodic memory (Dijkstra, Bourgeois, Allen, & Burgio, 2004; Mahendra & Apple, 2007; Obler & Pekkala, 2008; Orange & Purves, 1996).

Simple conversation is relatively preserved in the early stages of AD (Chapman et al., 2002; Chenery & Murdoch, 1994; Obler & Pekkala, 2008). Ulatowska and colleagues (Ulatowska, Garst Walsh, Santos, & Reyes, 2014; Ulatowska, Garst, Reyes, Olea Santos, & Kim, 2013) have documented the use of general, nonspecific evaluations in stories of persons with dementia of mild-to-moderate severity levels. Difficulties in discourse are more apparent when tasks become less redundant or require high levels of inference (Chapman et al., 2002; Chenery & Murdoch, 1994; Obler & Pekkala, 2008). Persons with dementia exhibit word finding difficulties, produce less language (fewer information units), and use simple syntactic structures (Azuma & Bayles, 1997; Bayles & Tomoeda, 2007; Causino-Lamar, Obler, Knoefel, & Albert, 1994; Dijkstra et al., 2004; Forbes-McKay & Venneri, 2005; Obler & Pekkala, 2008; Ulatowska et al., 2013, 2014). In addition to this, they may redundantly repeat information, resort to nonspecific language (i.e., "thing," "stuff," or "do"), or use pronouns inappropriately (Bayles & Tomoeda, 1991; Bowles, Obler, & Albert, 1987; Kempler, 1991; Nicholas, Obler, Albert, & Helm-Estabrooks, 1985; Obler & Pekkala, 2008; Ripich & Terrell, 1988; Tomoeda & Bayles, 1993; Ulatowska et al., 1998; Ulatowska et al.,

2013; Ulatowska et al., 2014). These suggest impairments in monitoring one's discourse, hence, making conversations difficult for the listener to understand. Individuals may also exhibit difficulties independently initiating conversation, maintaining a topic, or following through the conversation (Bayles, 1985; Dijkstra, Bourgeois, Allen, & Burgio, 2004; Obler & Pekkala, 2008). Toward the end-stage of the condition, persons with AD demonstrate minimal or no production or comprehension (Causino-Lamar, Obler, Knoefel, & Albert, 1994; Obler & Pekkala, 2008).

Undoubtedly, there is a need to individualize communication strategies of persons with dementia. Studies (Petryk & Hopper, 2009; Small & Perry, 2005) suggest directing conversation and using a combination of open- and closed-ended questions as means to facilitate responses. Simplifying syntax and paraphrasing complex sentences are other strategies to facilitate communication in dementia (Ripich, 1994; Small, Gutman, Makela, & Hillhouse, 2003; Small, Kemper, & Lyons, 1997). One needs to take into account several factors that contribute to differences in discourse patterns among persons with dementia, such as personal speaking style, education, and different communication environments. Cohen-Mansfield and colleagues (Camp, Cohen-Mansfield, & Capezuti, 2002; Cohen-Mansfield, Golander, & Arnheim, 2000; Cohen-Mansfield & Mintzer, 2005) emphasize the importance of determining the general and individuals needs of persons with dementia to better address greater levels of well-being.

CONCLUSION

Age differences in cognitive performance reveal a distinct developmental trajectory, evidenced by gains and losses. Certain language components are more vulnerable to these changes than others. Cognitive slowing, difficulties with interference, limited working memory capacity, and declines in executive function are intertwined factors that account for age-related decrements. Despite these declines, recent studies have emphasized cognitive strategies used by older adults to compensate for these changes. Crystallized intelligence, gist-based processing, and situation modeling are among preserved skills that maintain language performance in old age.

In considering the cognitive aspects of healthy aging as it relates to discourse, three basic tenets to facilitating successful communication environments for the elderly are proposed:

a. First, it is essential to recognize the person as a successful communicator.

b. Second, it is important to highlight cognitive skills preserved in aging, such as the person's world knowledge or specific expertise. Recognizing the older adult's ability to view things from a bigger picture, as opposed to details, is also essential. In addition, packaging information in the context of a narrative may be beneficial for some older adults.

c. Third, there is a need to control external factors, such as distractions or time constraints, that may impede comprehension or production of discourse.

As regards MCI and dementia, much work has yet to be done on differentially diagnosing these conditions from healthy aging. Perhaps language tasks may be a means through which early diagnosis can be achieved (Fleming, 2013; Obler & Pekkala, 2008). Further research is needed to address questions pertaining to the cognitive-linguistic treatment for these individuals. Reminiscence therapy, group therapy, music, and photography have been suggested as potential avenues to facilitate communication with these individuals. There is a continual need for studies to explore how to best address the general and individual communication needs of persons with MCI and dementia.

CODA

Among some peoples old age is esteemed and valued, while among others this is much less the case, due to a mentality which gives priority to immediate human usefulness and productivity. Such an attitude frequently leads to contempt for the later years of life . . . older people themselves are led to wonder whether their lives are still worthwhile. . . . There is an urgent need to recover a correct perspective on life as a whole . . .

Elderly people help us to see human affairs with greater wisdom, because life's vicissitudes have brought them knowledge and maturity. They are the guardians of our collective memory, and thus the privileged interpreters of that body of ideals and common values which support and guide life in society. To exclude the elderly is in a sense to deny the past, in which the present is firmly rooted.

—Karol Wojtyla, October 1999

REFERENCES

Adams, C., Labouvie-Vief, G., Hobart, C. J., & Dorosz, M. (1990). Adult age group differences in story recall style. *Journal of Gerontology, 45*(1), 17–27.

Adams, C., Smith, M. C., Nyquist, L., & Perlmutter, M. (1997). Adult age-group differences in recall for the literal and interpretive meanings of narrative text. *The Journals of Gerontology Series B: Psychological Sciences and Social Sciences, 52*(4), 187–195.

Adams, C., Smith, M. C., Pasupathi, M., & Vitolo, L. (2002). Social context effects on story recall in older and younger women does the listener make a difference? *The Journals of Gerontology Series B: Psychological Sciences and Social Sciences, 57*(1), 28–40.

Adlam, A. L. R., Bozeat, S., Arnold, R., Watson, P., & Hodges, J. R. (2006). Semantic knowledge in mild cognitive impairment and mild Alzheimer's disease. *Cortex, 42*(5), 675–684.

Albert, M. S., & Kaplan, E. (1980). Organic implications of neuropsychological deficits in the elderly. In L. W. Poon, J. L. Fozard, L. S. Cermak, D. Arenberg, & L. W. Thompson (Eds.), *New directions in memory and aging: Proceedings of the George A. Talland Memorial Conference* (pp. 403–432). Hillsdale, NJ: Erlbaum.

Albinet, C., Tomporowski, P. D., & Beasman, K. (2006). Aging and concurrent task performance: Cognitive demand and motor control. *Educational Gerontology, 32*(9), 689–706.

Andres, P., & van der Linden, M. (2001). Age-related differences in supervisory attentional system functions. *Journal of Gerontology: Psychological Science, 55B*, 373–380.

Andrews, G., Clark, M., & Luszcz, M. (2002). Successful aging in the Australian longitudinal study of aging: Applying the Macarthur model cross-nationally. *Journal of Social Issues, 58*(4), 749–765.

Arbuckle, T. Y., Vanderleck, V. F., Harsany, M., & Lapidus, S. (1990). Adult age differences in memory in relation to availability and accessibility of knowledge-based schemas. *Journal of Experimental Psychology: Learning, Memory, and Cognition, 16*(2), 305–315.

Azuma, T., & Bayles, K. A. (1997). Memory impairments underlying language difficulties in dementia. *Topics in Language Disorders, 18*(1), 58–71.

Baddeley, A. D. (1992). Working memory. *Science, 255*, 556–559.

Baltes, P. B. (1993). The aging mind: Potential and limits. *The Gerontologist, 33*(5), 580–594.

Banich, M. T. (2009). Executive function the search for an integrated account. *Current Directions in Psychological Science, 18*(2), 89–94.

Barr, R. A., & Giambra, L. M. (1990). Age-related decrement in auditory selective attention. *Psychology and Aging, 5*(4), 597–599.

Barrouillet, P., & Lecas, J. F. (1999). Mental models in conditional reasoning and working memory. *Thinking & Reasoning, 5*(4), 289–302.

Baudouin, A., Clarys, D., Vanneste, S., & Isingrini, M. (2009). Executive functioning and processing speed in age-related differences in memory: Contribution of a coding task. *Brain and Cognition, 71*(3), 240–245.

Bayles, K. A. (1985). Communication in dementia. In H. Ulatowska (Ed.), *The aging brain: Communication in the elderly*. Boston, MA: College-Hill Press.

Bayles, K. A., Kaszniak, A. W., & Tomoeda, C. K. (1987). *Communication and cognition in normal aging and dementia*. Boston, MA: College-Hill Press/Little, Brown & Co.

Bayles, K. A., & Tomoeda, C. K. (1991). Caregiver report of prevalence and appearance order of linguistic symptoms in Alzheimer's patients. *The Gerontologist, 31*(2), 210–216.

Bayles, K., & Tomoeda, C. (2007). *Cognitive-communication disorders of dementia*. San Diego, CA: Plural.

Bouazzaoui, B., Isingrini, M., Fay, S., Angel, L., Vanneste, S., Clarys, D., & Taconnat, L. (2010). Aging and self-reported internal and external memory strategy uses: The role of executive functioning. *Acta Psychologica, 135*(1), 59–66.

Bowles, N. L., Obler, L. K., & Albert, M. L. (1987). Naming errors in healthy aging and dementia of the Alzheimer type. *Cortex, 23*(3), 519–524.

Bryan, J., & Luszcz, M. A. (1996). Speed of information processing as a mediator between age and free-recall performance. *Psychology and Aging, 11*(1), 3–9.

Bryan, J., Luszcz, M. A., & Pointer, S. (1999). Executive function and processing resources as predictors of adult age differences in the implementation of encoding strategies. *Aging, Neuropsychology, and Cognition, 6*, 273–287.

Buckner, R. L. (2004). Memory and executive function in aging and AD: Multiple factors that cause decline and reserve factors that compensate. *Neuron, 44*(1), 195–208.

Bugg, J. M., Zook, N. A., DeLosh, E. L., Davalos, D. B., & Davis, H. P. (2006). Age differences in fluid intelligence: Contributions of general slowing and frontal decline. *Brain and Cognition, 62*(1), 9–16.

Bunce, D. (2003). Cognitive support at encoding attenuates age differences in recollective experience among adults of lower frontal lobe function. *Neuropsychology, 17*(3), 353–361.

Cabeza, R. (2001). Functional neuroimaging of cognitive aging. In R. Cabeza & A. Kingstone (Eds.), *Handbook of functional neuroimaging of cognition* (pp. 331–378). Cambridge, MA: MIT Press.

Cabeza, R. (2002). Hemispheric asymmetry reduction in older adults: The HAROLD model. *Psychology and Aging, 17*(1), 85–100.

Cabeza, R., Daselaar, S. M., Dolcos, F., Prince, S. E., Budde, M., & Nyberg, L. (2004). Task-independent and task-specific age effects on brain activity during working memory, visual attention and episodic retrieval. *Cerebral Cortex, 14*(4), 364–375.

Camp, C. J., Cohen-Mansfield, J., & Capezuti, E. A. (2002). *Psychiatric Services, 53*(11), 1397–1401.

Cannito, M. P., Hayashi, M. M., & Ulatowska, H. K. (1988). Discourse in normal and pathologic aging: Background and assessment strategies. *Seminars in Speech and Language, 9*(2), 117–134.

Carpenter, P. A., Miyake, A., & Just, M. A. (1994). Working memory constraints in comprehension: Evidence from individual differences, aphasia, and aging. *Handbook of psycholinguistics*, 1075–1122.

Castel, A. D. (2007). The adaptive and strategic use of memory by older adults: Evaluative processing and value-directed remembering. *Psychology of Learning and Motivation, 48*, 225–270.

Cattell, R. B. (1963). Theory of fluid and crystallized intelligence: A critical experiment. *Journal of Educational Psychology, 54*(1), 1–22.

Causino-Lamar, M. A., Obler, L. K., Knoefel, J. E., & Albert, M. L. (1994). Communication patterns in end-stage Alzheimer's disease: Pragmatic analyses. In R. L. Bloom, L. K. Obler, S. De Santi, & J. S. Ehrlich (Eds.), *Discourse analysis and applications: Studies in adult clinical populations* (pp. 217–235). Hillsdale, NJ: Lawrence Erlbaum Associates.

Chapman, S. B., Anand, R., Sparks, G. & Cullum, C. M. (2006) Gist distinctions in healthy cognitive aging versus mild Alzheimer's disease. *Brain Impairment, 7*(3), 223–233.

Chapman, S. B., Zientz, J., Weiner, M., Rosenberg, R., Frawley, W., & Burns, M. H. (2002). Discourse changes in early Alzheimer disease, mild cognitive impairment, and normal aging. *Alzheimer Disease & Associated Disorders, 16*(3), 177–186.

Chenery, H. J., & Murdoch, B. E. (1994). The production of narrative discourse in response to animations in persons with dementia of the Alzheimer's type: Preliminary findings. *Aphasiology, 8*(2), 159–171.

Chiesi, H. L., Spilich, G. J., & Voss, J. F. (1979). Acquisition of domain-related information in relation to high and low domain knowledge. *Journal of Verbal Learning and Verbal Behavior, 18*(3), 257–273.

Clarys, D., Bugaiska, A., Tapia, G., & Baudouin, A. (2009). Ageing, remembering, and executive function. *Memory, 17*(2), 158–168.

Clarys, D., Isingrini, M., & Gana, K. (2002). Mediators of age-related differences in recollective experience in recognition memory. *Acta Psychologica, 109*(3), 315–329.

Cohen, G. (1979). Language comprehension in old age. *Cognitive Psychology, 11*(4), 412–429.

Cohen, G. (1988). Age differences in memory for texts: Production deficiency or processing limitations? In L. Light & D. Burke (Eds.), *Language, memory and aging* (pp. 171–190). New York, NY: Cambridge University Press.

Cohen-Mansfield, J., Golander, H., & Arnheim, G. (2000). Self-identity in older persons suffering from dementia: Preliminary results. *Social Science and Medicine, 51*, 381–394.

Cohen-Mansfield, J., & Mintzer, J. E. (2005). Time for change: The role of nonpharmacological interventions in treating behavior problems in nursing home residents with dementia. *Alzheimer's Disease and Associated Disorders, 19*(1), 37–40.

Connelly, S. L., Hasher, L., & Zacks, R. T. (1991). Age and reading: The impact of distraction. *Psychology and Aging, 6*(4), 533–541.

Connor, L. (2001). Memory in old age: Patterns of decline and preservation. *Seminars in Speech and Language, 22*(2), 117–125.

Craik, F. I., & McDowd, J. M. (1987). Age differences in recall and recognition. *Journal of Experimental Psychology: Learning, Memory, and Cognition, 13*(3), 474–479.

Craik, F. I., Morris, L. W., Morris, R. G., & Loewen, E. R. (1990). Relations between source amnesia and frontal lobe functioning in older adults. *Psychology and Aging, 5*(1), 148–151.

Crawford, J. R., Bryan, J., Luszcz, M. A., Obonsawin, M. C., & Stewart, L. (2000). The executive decline hypothesis of cognitive aging: Do executive deficits qualify as differential deficits and do they mediate age-related memory decline? *Aging, Neuropsychology, and Cognition, 7*, 9–31.

Daigneault, S., Braun, C. M. J., & Whitaker, H. A. (1992). Early effects of normal aging in perseverative and non-perseverative prefrontal measures. *Developmental Neuropsychology, 8*, 99–114.

Dempster, F. N. (1992). The rise and fall of the inhibitory mechanism. Toward a unified theory of cognitive development and aging. *Developmental Review, 12*, 45–75.

Dijkstra, K., Bourgeois, M. S., Allen, R. S., & Burgio, L. D. (2004). Conversational coherence: Discourse analysis of older adults with and without dementia. *Journal of Neurolinguistics, 17*(4), 263–283.

Dillard, A., Fagerlin, A., Dal Cin, S., Zikmund-Fisher, B. & Ubel, P. (2010). Narratives that address affective forecasting errors reduce perceived barriers to colorectal cancer screening. *Social Science & Medicine, 71*, 45–52.

Dixon, R. A. & Gould, O. N. (1996). Adults telling and retelling stories collaboratively. In P. Baltes & U. Staudinger (Eds.), *Interactive minds: Life-span perspectives on the social foundation of cognition* (pp. 221–241). New York, NY: New York University Press.

Duncan, R., Johnson, M., Swales, C., & Freer, J. (1997). Frontal lobe deficits after head injury: Unity and diversity of function. *Cognitive Neuropsychology, 14*(5), 713–741.

Duong, A., Whitehead, V., Hanratty, K., & Chertkow, H. (2006). The nature of lexico-semantic processing deficits in mild cognitive impairment. *Neuropsychologia, 44*(10), 1928–1935.

Dywan, J., & Murphy, W. E. (1996). Aging and inhibitory control in text comprehension. *Psychology and Aging, 11*(2), 199–206.

Eakin, D. K., & Hertzog, C. (2006). Release from implicit interference in memory and metamemory: Older adults know that they can't let go. *The Journals of Gerontology Series B: Psychological Sciences and Social Sciences, 61*(6), 340–347.

Finkel, D., Reynolds, C. A., McArdle, J. J., & Pedersen, N. L. (2007). Age changes in processing speed as a leading indicator of cognitive aging. *Psychology and Aging, 22*(3), 558–568.

Fitzpatrick, P. M., Obler, L. K., Au, R., Nicholas, M. L., & Albert, M. L. (1993). Story recall in normal aging. In J. E. Alatis (Ed.), *Georgetown University round table on language and linguistics*. Washington, DC: Georgetown University Press.

Fleming, V. B. (2013). Normal cognitive aging and mild cognitive impairment: Drawing the fine line. *SIG 2 Perspectives on Neurophysiology and Neurogenic Speech and Language Disorders, 23*(1), 1–9.

Fleming, V. B., & Harris, J. L. (2008). Complex discourse production in mild cognitive impairment: Detecting subtle changes. *Aphasiology, 22*(7–8), 729–740.

Forbes-McKay, K., & Venneri, A. (2005). Detecting subtle spontaneous language decline in early Alzheimer's disease with a picture description task. *Neurological Sciences, 36*, 243–254.

Friedman, N. P., Miyake, A., Corley, R. P., Young, S. E., DeFries, J. C., & Hewitt, J. K. (2006). Not all executive functions are related to intelligence. *Psychological Science, 17*(2), 172–179.

Friedman, N. P., Miyake, A., Young, S. E., DeFries, J. C., Corley, R. P., & Hewitt, J. K. (2008). Individual differences in executive functions are almost entirely genetic in origin. *Journal of Experimental Psychology: General, 137*(2), 201–225.

Fuster, J. M. (1997). *The prefrontal cortex* (3rd ed). Philadelphia, PA: Lippincott-Raven.

Garon, N., Bryson, S. E., & Smith, I. M. (2008). Executive function in preschoolers: A review using an integrative framework. *Psychological Bulletin, 134*(1), 31–60.

Gauthier, S., Reisberg, B., Zaudig, M., Petersen, R. C., Ritchie, K., & Broich, K., . . . International Psychogeriatric Association Expert Conference on Mild Cognitive Impairment. (2006). Mild cognitive impairment. *The Lancet, 367,* 1262–1270.

Gerard, L., Zacks, R. T., Hasher, L., & Radvansky, G. A. (1991). Age deficits in retrieval: The fan effect. *Journal of Gerontology, 46*(4), 131–136.

Gernsbacher, M. A. (1990). *Language comprehension as structure building.* Hillsdale, NJ: Erlbaum.

Gilhooly, K. J., Phillips, L. H., Wynn, V., Logie, R. H., & Della Sala, S. (1999). Planning processes and age in the five-disc Tower of London task. *Thinking and Reasoning, 5,* 339–361.

Glisky, E. L., Rubin, S. R., & Davidson, P. S. (2001). Source memory in older adults: An encoding or retrieval problem? *Journal of Experimental Psychology: Learning, Memory, and Cognition, 27*(5), 1131–1146.

Gordon-Salant, S., & Fitzgibbons, P. J. (1997). Selected cognitive factors and speech recognition performance among young and elderly listeners. *Journal of Speech, Language, and Hearing Research, 40*(2), 423–431.

Gutchess, A., Welsh, R., Hedden, T., Bangert, A., Minear, M., Liu, L., & Park, D. (2005). Aging and the neural correlates of successful picture encoding: Frontal activations compensate for decreased medial-temporal activity. *Journal of Cognitive Neuroscience, 17*(1), 84–96.

Hamm, V. P., & Hasher, L. (1992). Age and the availability of inferences. *Psychology and Aging, 7*(1), 56–64.

Hartley, J. T. (1993). Aging and prose memory: Tests of the resource-deficit hypothesis. *Psychology and Aging, 8*(4), 538–551.

Hasher, L., Lustig, C., & Zacks, R. T. (2007). Inhibitory mechanisms and the control of attention. In A. Conway, C. Jarrold, M. Kane, A, Miyake,

& J. Towse (Eds.), *Variation in working memory* (pp. 227–249). New York, NY: Oxford University Press.

Hasher, L., & Zacks, R. T. (1988). Working memory, comprehension, and aging: A review and a new view. *Psychology of Learning and Motivation, 22*, 193–225.

Hasher, L., Zacks, R. T., & May, C. P. (1999). Inhibitory control, circadian arousal, and age. In: D. Gopher & A. Koriat (Eds), *Attention and performance XVII: Cognitive regulation of performance: Interaction of theory and application* (pp. 653–675). Cambridge, MA: MIT Press.

Haug, H., & Eggers, R. (1991). Morphometry of the human cortex cerebri and corpus striatum during aging. *Neurobiology of Aging, 12*(4), 336–338.

Head, D., Rodrigue, K. M., Kennedy, K. M., & Raz, N. (2008). Neuroanatomical and cognitive mediators of age-related differences in episodic memory. *Neuropsychology, 22*(4), 491–507.

Healey, M. K., Campbell, K. L., & Hasher, L. (2008). Cognitive aging and increased distractibility: Costs and potential benefits. In W. Sossin, J. C. Lacaille, V. F. Castellucci, & S. Bellebillie (Eds.), *Progress in brain research* (pp. 353–363). Amsterdam, The Netherlands: Elsevier.

Hertzog, C., & Bleckley, M. K. (2001). Age differences in the structure of intelligence: Influences of information processing speed. *Intelligence, 29*(3), 191–217.

Hess, T. M. (1990). Aging and schematic influences on memory. In T. Hess (Ed.), *Aging and cognition: Knowledge organization and utilization* (pp. 93–160). Amsterdam, The Netherlands: North-Holland.

Hess, T. M. (2005). Memory and aging in context. *Psychological Bulletin, 131*(3), 383–406.

Hess, T. M., & Pullen, S. M. (1996). Memory in context. In F. Blanchard-Fields & T. M. Hess (Eds.), *Perspectives on cognitive change in adulthood and aging* (pp. 387–427). Burr Ridge, IL: McGraw-Hill.

Horn, J. L., & Cattell, R. B. (1966). Refinement and test of the theory of fluid and crystallized general intelligences. *Journal of Educational Psychology, 57*(5), 253–270.

Hultsch, D. F., & Dixon, R. A. (1984). Memory for text materials in adulthood. In P. Baltes & O. Brim, Jr. (Eds.), *Life-span development and behavior* (Vol. 6, pp. 77–108). New York, NY: Academic Press.

Hultsch, D. F., Hertzog, C., & Dixon, R. A. (1990). Ability correlates of memory performance in adulthood and aging. *Psychology and Aging, 5*(3), 356–368.

Ikier, S., & Hasher, L. (2006). Age differences in implicit interference. *The Journals of Gerontology Series B: Psychological Sciences and Social Sciences, 61*(5), 278–284.

Johnson, M. K., Hashtroudi, S., & Linday, D. S. (1993). Source monitoring. *Psychological Bulletin, 114,* 3–28.

Johnson-Laird, P. (1983). *Mental models: Towards a cognitive science of language, inference and consciousness.* Cambridge, UK: Cambridge University Press.

Jong, R. D. (2001). Adult age differences in goal activation and goal maintenance. *European Journal of Cognitive Psychology, 13*(1–2), 71–89.

Juncos-Rabadán, O., Pereiro, A. X., & Rodríguez, M. S. (2005). Narrative speech in aging: Quantity, information content, and cohesion. *Brain and Language, 95*(3), 423–434.

Jurado, M. B., & Rosselli, M. (2007). The elusive nature of executive functions: A review of our current understanding. *Neuropsychology Review, 17*(3), 213–233.

Kahn, H. J., & Cordon, D. (1993). Qualitative differences in working memory and discourse comprehension in normal aging. In H. H. Brownell & Y. Joanette (Eds.), *Narrative discourse in neurologically impaired and normal aging adults* (pp. 103–114). San Diego, CA: Singular.

Kane, M. J., & Engle, R. W. (2000). Working-memory capacity, proactive interference, and divided attention: Limits on long-term memory retrieval. *Journal of Experimental Psychology: Learning, Memory, and Cognition, 26*(2), 336–358.

Kempler, D. (1991). Language changes in dementia of the Alzheimer type. In R. Lubinski, J. B. Orange, D. Henderson, & N. Stecker (Eds.), *Dementia and Communication* (pp. 98–114). Philadelphia, PA: B. C. Decker.

Kim, S., & Hasher, L. (2005). The attraction effect in decision making: Superior performance by older adults. *The Quarterly Journal of Experimental Psychology Section A, 58*(1), 120–133.

Kimberg, D. Y., D'Esposito, M., & Farah, M. J. (1997). Cognitive functions in the prefrontal cortex: Working memory and executive control. *Current Directions in Psychological Science, 6,* 185–192.

Kintsch, W. (1998). *Comprehension: A paradigm for cognition.* New York, NY: Cambridge University Press.

Kintsch, W., & Van Dijk, T. A. (1978). Toward a model of text comprehension and production. *Psychological Review, 85*(5), 363–394.

Kjelgaard, M. K., Titone, D., & Wingfield, A. (1999). The influence of prosodic structure on the interpretation of temporary syntactic ambiguity by young and elderly listeners. *Experimental Aging Research, 25*(3), 187–207.

Kolb, B., & Whishaw, I. Q. (1996). *Fundamentals of human neuropsychology* (4th ed). New York, NY: Freeman.

Kray, J., & Lindenberger, U. (2000). Adult age differences in task switching. *Psychology and Aging, 15*(1), 126–147.

Kreuter, M., Holmes, K., Alcaraz, K., Kalesan, B., Rath, S., Richert, M., . . . Clark, E. (2010). Comparing narrative and informational videos to increase mammography in low-income African American women. *Patient Education and Counseling, 81,* S6–S14.

Kwong See, S. T., & Ryan, E. B. (1995). Cognitive mediation of adult age differences in language performance. *Psychology and Aging, 10*(3), 458–468.

Kyllonen, P. C., & Christal, R. E. (1990). Reasoning ability is (little more than) working-memory capacity. *Intelligence, 14*(4), 389–433.

Labouvie-Vief, G. (1985). Intelligence and cognition. In J. Birren & W. Schaie (Eds), *Handbook of the psychology of aging* (2nd ed., pp. 500–530). New York, NY: Van Nostrand Reinhold.

Labouvie-Vief, G., & Blanchard-Fields, F. (1982). Cognitive ageing and psychological growth. *Ageing and Society, 2*(2), 183–209.

Lee, T., Crawford, J. D., Henry, J. D., Trollor, J. N., Kochan, N. A., Wright, M. J., . . . Sachdev, P. S. (2012). Mediating effects of processing speed and executive functions in age-related differences in episodic memory performance: A cross-validation study. *Neuropsychology, 26*(6), 776–784.

Lezak, M. (1995). *Neuropsychological assessment* (3rd ed.). New York, NY: Oxford University Press.

Light, L. L., Capps, J. L., Singh, A., & Albertson Owens, S. A. (1994). Comprehension and use of anaphoric devices in young and older adults. *Discourse Processes, 18*(1), 77–103.

Lindenberger, U., Mayr, U., & Kliegl, R. (1993). Speed and intelligence in old age. *Psychology and Aging, 8*(2), 207–220.

Logan, J. M., Sanders, A. L., Snyder, A. Z., Morris, J. C., & Buckner, R. L. (2002). Under-recruitment and nonselective recruitment: dissociable neural mechanisms associated with aging. *Neuron, 33*(5), 827–840.

Lowe, C., & Rabbitt, P. (1997). Cognitive models of ageing and frontal lobe deficits. In P. Rabbitt (Ed.), *Methodology of frontal and executive function* (pp. 39–60). Hove, UK: Psychology Press.

Lustig, C., Hasher, L., & Tonev, S. T. (2006). Distraction as a determinant of processing speed. *Psychonomic Bulletin & Review, 13*(4), 619–625.

Lustig, C., May, C. P., & Hasher, L. (2001). Working memory span and the role of proactive interference. *Journal of Experimental Psychology: General, 130*(2), 199–207.

Mahendra, N., & Apple, A. (2007). Human memory systems: A framework for understanding dementia. *The ASHA Leader, 12*(16), 8–11.

Malloy, P. F., Cohen, R. A., & Jenkins, M. A. (1998). Frontal lobe function and dysfunction. In P. J. Snyder & P. D. Nussbaum (Eds.), *Clinical neuropsychology: A pocket handbook for assessment* (pp. 573–590). Washington, DC: American Psychological Association.

Marini, A., Boewe, A., Caltagirone, C., & Carlomagno, S. (2005). Age-related differences in the production of textual descriptions. *Journal of Psycholinguistic Research, 34*(5), 439–463.

Mather, M. (2006). A review of decision-making processes: Weighing the risks and benefits of aging. In L. Carstensen & C. Hartel (Eds.), *When I'm 64* (pp.145–173). Washington, DC: National Academies Press.

May, C. P., Hasher, L., & Kane, M. J. (1999). The role of interference in memory span. *Memory & Cognition, 27*(5), 759–767.

McCabe, D. P., & Smith, A. D. (2002). The effect of warnings on false memories in young and older adults. *Memory & Cognition, 30*(7), 1065–1077.

McCabe, D. P., Roediger III, H. L., McDaniel, M. A., Balota, D. A., & Hambrick, D. Z. (2010). The relationship between working memory capacity and executive functioning: Evidence for a common executive attention construct. *Neuropsychology, 24*(2), 222–243.

McCabe, D. P., Smith, A. D., & Parks, C. M. (2007). Inadvertent plagiarism in young and older adults: The role of working memory capacity in reducing memory errors. *Memory & Cognition, 35*(2), 231–241.

McDowd, J. M., & Craik, F. I. (1988). Effects of aging and task difficulty on divided attention performance. *Journal of Experimental Psychology: Human Perception and Performance, 14*(2), 267–280.

Meiran, N., & Gotler, A. (2001). Modelling cognitive control in task switching and ageing. *European Journal of Cognitive Psychology, 13*(1–2), 165–186.

Meyer, B. J., & Rice, G. E. (1981). Information recalled from prose by young, middle, and old adult readers. *Experimental Aging Research, 7*(3), 253–268.

Meyer, B. J., & Rice, G. E. (1983). Learning and memory from text across the adult life span. In J. Fine & R. Freedle (Eds.), *Developmental studies in discourse* (pp. 291–306). Norwood, NJ: Ablex.

Meyer, B. J., & Rice, G. E. (1989). Prose processing in adulthood: The text, the reader and the task. In L. Poon, D. Rubin, B. Wilson (Eds.), *Everyday cognition in adulthood and late life* (pp. 157–194). Cambridge, UK: Cambridge University Press.

Miller, L. M. S. (2003). The effects of age and domain knowledge on text processing. *The Journals of Gerontology Series B: Psychological Sciences and Social Sciences, 58*(4), 217–223.

Miller, L. M. S., Cohen, J. A., & Wingfield, A. (2006). Contextual knowledge reduces demands on working memory during reading. *Memory & Cognition, 34*(6), 1355–1367.

Miller, L. M. S., & Stine-Morrow, E. A. (1998). Aging and the effects of knowledge on on-line reading strategies. *The Journals of Gerontology Series B: Psychological Sciences and Social Sciences, 53*(4), 223–233.

Miller, L. M. S., Stine-Morrow, E. A., Kirkorian, H. L., & Conroy, M. L. (2004). Adult age differences in knowledge-driven reading. *Journal of Educational Psychology, 96*(4), 811–821.

Mittenberg, W., Seidenberg, M., O'Leary, D. S., & DiGiulio, D. V. (1989). Changes in cerebral functioning associated with normal aging. *Journal of Clinical and Experimental Neuropsychology, 11*, 918–932.

Miyake, A., Friedman, N. P., Emerson, M. J., Witzki, A. H., Howerter, A., & Wager, T. D. (2000). The unity and diversity of executive functions and their contributions to complex "frontal lobe" tasks: A latent variable analysis. *Cognitive Psychology, 41*(1), 49–100.

Morrow, D. G., Leirer, V. O., & Altieri, P. A. (1992). Aging, expertise, and narrative processing. *Psychology and Aging, 7*(3), 376–388.

Morrow, D. G., Leirer, V., Altiteri, P., & Fitzsimmons, C. (1994). When expertise reduces age differences in performance. *Psychology and Aging, 9*(1), 134–148.

Newson, R. S., & Kemps, E. B. (2005). General lifestyle activities as a predictor of current cognition and cognitive change in older adults: A cross-sectional and longitudinal examination. *The Journals of Gerontology Series B: Psychological Sciences and Social Sciences, 60*(3), 113–120.

Nicholas, M., Obler, L. K., Albert, M. L., & Helm-Estabrooks, N. (1985). Empty speech in Alzheimer's disease and fluent aphasia. *Journal of Speech, Language, and Hearing Research, 28*(3), 405–410.

Noh, S. R., & Stine-Morrow, E. (2009). Age differences in tracking characters during narrative comprehension. *Memory & Cognition, 37*(6), 769–778.

Nordlund, A., Rolstad, S., Hellström, P., Sjögren, M., Hansen, S., & Wallin, A. (2005). The Goteborg MCI study: Mild cognitive impairment is a heterogeneous condition. *Journal of Neurology, Neurosurgery & Psychiatry, 76*(11), 1485–1490.

Norman, S., Kemper, S., Kynette, D., Cheung, H., & Anagnopoulos, C. (1991). Syntactic complexity and adults' running memory span. *Journal of Gerontology, 46*(6), 346–351.

North, A., & Ulatowska, H. (1981). Competence in independently living olderadults: Assessment and correlates. *Journal of Gerontology, 36*(5), 576–582.

North, A., Ulatowska, H. K., Macaluso-Haynes, S., & Bell, H. (1986). Discourse performance in older adults. *The International Journal of Aging and Human Development, 23*(4), 267–283.

Nyberg, L., Bäckman, L., Erngrund, K., Olofsson, U., & Nilsson, L. G. (1996). Age differences in episodic memory, semantic memory, and priming: Relationships to demographic, intellectual, and biological factors. *The Journals of Gerontology Series B: Psychological Sciences and Social Sciences, 51*(4), 234–240.

Obler, L. K. (1980). Narrative discourse style in the elderly. In L. Obler & M. Albert (Eds.), *Language and communication in the elderly* (pp. 75–90). Lexington, MA: Heath.

Obler, L. K., & Albert, M. L. (1984). Language in aging. In M. L. Albert (Ed.), *Clinical neurology of aging* (pp. 245–253). New York, NY: Oxford University Press.

Obler, L. K., & Pekkala, S. (2008). Language and communication in aging. In B. Stemmer & H. Whitaker (Eds.), *Handbook of neurolinguistics* (pp. 351–359). Oxford, UK: Elsevier Press.

Olea Santos, T. (2013). *Comprehension of medical information in narrative and expository discourse: Implications for health literacy among the Filipino American elderly* (Unpublished doctoral dissertation). University of Texas at Dallas, Richardson, TX.

Olness, G. (2000). *Expression of narrative main-point inferences in adults: A developmental perspective* (Unpublished doctoral dissertation). University of Texas at Dallas, Richardson, TX.

Olson, C. B. (1987). A review of why and how we age: A defense of multifactorial aging. *Mechanisms of Ageing and Development, 41*(1), 1–28.

Orange, J. B., & Purves, B. (1996). Conversational discourse and cognitive impairment: Implications for Alzheimer's disease. *Journal of Speech-Language and Audiology, 20,* 139–153.

Park, D. C., Lautenschlager, G., Hedden, T., Davidson, N. S., Smith, A. D., & Smith, P. K. (2002). Models of visuospatial and verbal memory across the adult life span. *Psychology and Aging, 17*(2), 299–320.

Park, D. C., Smith, A. D., Dudley, W. N., & Lafronza, V. N. (1989). Effects of age and a divided attention task presented during encoding and retrieval on memory. *Journal of Experimental Psychology: Learning, Memory, and Cognition, 15*(6), 1185–1191.

Park, D. C., Smith, A. D., Lautenschlager, G., Earles, J. L., Frieske, D., Zwahr, M., & Gaines, C. L. (1996). Mediators of long-term memory performance across the life span. *Psychology and Aging, 11*(4), 621–637.

Park, D. C., Welsh, R., Marshuetz, C., Gutchess, A., Mikels, J., Polk, T., . . . Taylor, S. (2003). Working memory for complex scenes: age differences in frontal and hippocampal activations. *Journal of Cognitive Neuroscience, 15*(8), 1122–1134.

Parkin, A. J. (1997). Normal age-related memory loss and its relation to frontal lobe dysfunction. In P. Rabbitt (Ed.), *Methodology of frontal and executive function* (pp. 177–190). Hove, UK: Psychology Press.

Parkin, A. J., & Java, R. I. (2000). Determinants of age-related memory loss. In T. J. Perfect, E. A. Maylor (Eds.), *Models of cognitive aging* (pp. 188–203). Oxford, UK: Oxford University Press.

Parkin, A. J., & Walter, B. M. (1992). Recollective experience, normal aging, and frontal dysfunction. *Psychology and Aging, 7,* 290–298.

Parkin, A. J., Walter, B. M., & Hunkin, N. M. (1995). Relationships between normal aging, frontal lobe functioning, and memory for temporal and spatial information. *Neuropsychology, 9,* 304–312.

Perfect, T. (1997). Memory aging as frontal lobe dysfunction. In M. A. Conway (Ed.), *Cognitive models of memory* (pp. 315–339). Cambridge, MA: MIT Press.

Petryk, M., & Hopper, T. (2009). The effects of question type on conversational discourse in Alzheimer's disease. *SIG 2 Perspectives on Neurophysiology and Neurogenic Speech and Language Disorders, 19*(4), 126–134.

Phillips, L. H., & Henry, J. D. (2005). An evaluation of the frontal lobe theory of cognitive aging. In: J. Duncan, L. H. Phillips, P. McLeod (Eds.), *Measuring the mind: Speed, control and age* (pp. 191–216). Oxford, UK: Oxford University Press.

Piccinin, A. M., & Rabbitt, P. M. A. (1999). Contribution of cognitive abilities to performance and improvement on a substitution coding task. *Psychology and Aging, 14*(4), 539–551.

Pichora-Fuller, M. K., Schneider, B. A., & Daneman, M. (1995). How young and old adults listen to and remember speech in noise. *The Journal of the Acoustical Society of America, 97*(1), 593–608.

Poon, L. W. (1985). Differences in human memory with aging: Nature, causes, and clinical implications. In J. E. Birren & K. W. Schaie (Eds.), *Handbook of the psychology of aging* (2nd ed., pp. 427–462). New York, NY: Van Nostrand Reinhold.

Rabbitt, P. (1965). An age-decrement in the ability to ignore irrelevant information. *Journal of Gerontology, 20*(2), 233–238.

Rabbitt, P., Lowe, C., & Shilling, V. (2001). Frontal tests and models for cognitive ageing. *European Journal of Cognitive Psychology, 13*(1–2), 5–28.

Radvansky, G. A., Copeland, D. E., & Zwaan, R. A. (2003). Brief report: Aging and functional spatial relations in comprehension and memory. *Psychology and Aging, 18*(1), 161–165.

Radvansky, G. A., & Dijkstra, K. (2007). Aging and situation model processing. *Psychonomic Bulletin & Review, 14*(6), 1027–1042.

Radvansky, G. A., Gerard, L. D., Zacks, R. T., & Hasher, L. (1990). Younger and older adults' use of mental models as representations for text materials. *Psychology and Aging, 5*(2), 209–214.

Radvansky, G. A., Zwaan, R. A., Curiel, J. M., & Copeland, D. E. (2001). Situation models and aging. *Psychology and Aging, 16*(1), 145–160.

Raz, N. (2000). Aging of the brain and its impact on cognitive performance: Integration of structural and functional findings. In F. I. M. Craik & T. A. Salthouse (Eds.), *The handbook of aging and cognition* (2nd ed., pp. 1–90). Mahwah, NJ: Erlbaum.

Raz, N. (2004). The aging brain observed *in vivo:* differential changes and their modifiers. In R. Cabeza, L. Nyberg, D. Parks (Eds.), *Cognitive neuroscience of aging: linking cognitive and cerebral aging* (pp. 17–55). New York, NY: Oxford University Press.

Raz, N., Gunning-Dixon, F. M., Head, D., Dupuis, J. H., & Acker, J. D. (1998). Neuroanatomical correlates of cognitive aging: Evidence from structural magnetic resonance imaging. *Neuropsychology, 12,* 1–20.

Raz, N., & Rodrigue, K. M. (2006). Differential aging of the brain: Patterns, cognitive correlates and modifiers. *Neuroscience & Biobehavioral Reviews, 30*(6), 730–748.

Raz, N., Rodrigue, K. M., Kennedy, K. M., Head, D., Gunning-Dixon, F., & Acker, J. D. (2003). Differential aging of the human striatum: Longitudinal evidence. *American Journal of Neuroradiology, 24*(9), 1849–1856.

Ripich, D. N. (1994). Functional communication with AD patients: A caregiver training program. *Alzheimer Disease & Associated Disorders, 8*(Suppl. 3), 95–109.

Ripich, D. N., & Terrell, B. Y. (1988). Patterns of discourse cohesion and coherence in Alzheimer's disease. *Journal of Speech and Hearing Disorders, 53,* 8–15.

Ripich, D. N., & Ziol, E. (1998). Dementia: A review for the speech-language pathologist. *Medical speech-language pathology: A practitioner's guide,* 467–494.

Robbins, T. W., James, M., Owen, A. M., Sahakian, B. J., Lawrence, L. D., McInnes, L., . . . Janowsky, J. S. (1999). Prefrontal gray and white matter volumes in healthy aging and Alzheimer disease. *Archives of Neurology, 56*(3), 338–344.

Salthouse, T. (1990). Working memory as a processing resource in cognitive aging. *Developmental Review, 10*(1), 101–124.

Salthouse, T. A. (1985). Speed of behavior and its implications for cognition. In J. Birren & K. Schaie (Eds.), *Handbook of the psychology of aging* (pp. 400–426). New York, NY: Van Nostrand Reinhold.

Salthouse, T. A. (1992). What do adult age differences in the digit symbol substitution test reflect? *The Journals of Gerontology, 47*(3), 121–128.

Salthouse, T. A. (2000). Aging and measures of processing speed. *Biological Psychology, 54*(1), 35–54.

Salthouse, T. A. (2005). Relations between cognitive abilities and measures of executive functioning. *Neuropsychology, 19*(4), 532–545.

Salthouse, T. A., Atkinson, T. M., & Berish, D. E. (2003). Executive functioning as a potential mediator of age-related cognitive decline in normal adults. *Journal of Experimental Psychology: General, 132*(4), 566–594.

Salthouse, T. A., & Babcock, R. L. (1991). Decomposing adult age differences in working memory. *Developmental Psychology, 27*(5), 763–776.

Salthouse, T. A., Fristoe, N., McGuthry, K. E., & Hambrick, D. Z. (1998). Relation of task switching to speed, age, and fluid intelligence. *Psychology and Aging, 13*(3), 445.

Salthouse, T. A., Rogan, J. D., & Prill, K. A. (1984). Division of attention: Age differences on a visually presented memory task. *Memory & Cognition, 12*(6), 613–620.

Santos, T. O., & Ulatowska, H. K. (2014, October). *Stroke education for the at-risk elderly: Do words really matter?* Proceedings for the 2014 Academy of Aphasia, Miami, FL.

Schacter, D. L., Kaszniak, A. W., Kihlstrom, J. F., & Valdiserri, M. (1991). The relation between source memory and aging. *Psychology of Aging, 6,* 559–568.

Schaie, K. W. (1990). Intellectual development in adulthood. In J. Birren & K. W. Schaie (Eds.), *Handbook of the psychology of aging* (2nd ed., pp. 291–310). San Diego, CA: Academic Press.

Schaie, K. W. (1996). *Intellectual development in adulthood: The Seattle Longitudinal Study.* Cambridge, UK: Cambridge University Press.

Schank, R., & Abelson, R. (1977). *Scripts, plans, goals and understanding: An inquiry into human knowledge structures.* Hillsdale, NJ: Lawrence Erlbaum.

Schank, R., & Abelson, R. (1995). Knowledge and memory: The real story. In R. Wyer Jr. (Ed.), *The automaticity of everyday life: Advances in social cognition* (Vol. 8, pp. 1–85). Hillsdale, NJ: Erlbaum.

Schludermann, E., Schludermann, S., Merryman, P., & Brown, B. (1983). Halstead's studies in the neuropsychology of aging. *Archives of Gerontology and Geriatrics, 2,* 49–72.

Schneider, B. A., Daneman, M., Murphy, D. R., & See, S. K. (2000). Listening to discourse in distracting settings: The effects of aging. *Psychology and Aging, 15*(1), 110–125.

Schretlen, D., Pearlson, G. D., Anthony, J. C., Aylward, E. H., Augustine, A. M., Davis, A., & Barta, P. (2000). Elucidating the contributions of processing speed, executive ability, and frontal lobe volume to normal age-related differences in fluid intelligence. *Journal of the International Neuropsychological Society, 6*(1), 52–61.

Shadden, B. B. (1997). Discourse behaviors in older adults. *Seminars in Speech and Language, 18*(2), 143–157.

Sharkey, N. E., & Sharkey, A. J. (1987). What is the point of integration? The loci of knowledge-based facilitation in sentence processing. *Journal of Memory and Language, 26*(3), 255–276.

Small, J. A., Gutman, G., Makela, S., & Hillhouse, B. (2003). Effectiveness of communication strategies used by caregivers of persons with Alzheimer's disease during activities of daily living. *Journal of Speech, Language, and Hearing Research, 46*(2), 353–367.

Small, J. A., Kemper, S., & Lyons, K. (1997). Sentence comprehension in Alzheimer's disease: Effects of grammatical complexity, speech rate, and repetition. *Psychology and Aging, 12*(1), 3–11.

Small, J. A., & Perry, J. (2005). Do you remember? How caregivers question their spouses who have Alzheimer's disease and the impact on communication. *Journal of Speech, Language, and Hearing Research, 48*(1), 125–136.

Soederberg Miller, L. M. (2009). Age differences in the effects of domain knowledge on reading efficiency. *Psychology and Aging, 24*(1), 63–84.

Soederberg Miller, L. M. S., Cohen, J. A., & Wingfield, A. (2006). Contextual knowledge reduces demands on working memory during reading. *Memory & Cognition, 34*(6), 1355–1367.

Spilich, G. J. (1983). Life-span components of text processing: Structural and procedural differences. *Journal of Verbal Learning and Verbal Behavior, 22*(2), 231–244.

Spilich, G. J., Vesonder, G. T., Chiesi, H. L., & Voss, J. F. (1979). Text processing of domain-related information for individuals with high and low domain knowledge. *Journal of Verbal Learning and Verbal Behavior, 18*(3), 275–290.

Spilich, G. J., & Voss, J. F. (1982). Contextual effects upon text memory for young, aged-normal, and aged memory-impaired individuals. *Experimental Aging Research, 8*(3), 147–151.

Stevens, W. D., Hasher, L., Chiew, K. S., & Grady, C. L. (2008). A neural mechanism underlying memory failure in older adults. *The Journal of Neuroscience, 28*(48), 12820–12824.

Stine, E. A., & Hindman, J. (1994). Age differences in reading time allocation for propositionally dense sentences. *Aging and Cognition, 1*(1), 2–16.

Stine, E. A., & Wingfield, A. (1987). Process and strategy in memory for speech among younger and older adults. *Psychology and Aging, 2*(3), 272–279.

Stine, E. A., & Wingfield, A. (1990). How much do working memory deficits contribute to age differences in discourse memory?. *European Journal of Cognitive Psychology, 2*(3), 289–304.

Stine-Morrow, E. A., Loveless, M. K., & Soederberg, L. M. (1996). Resource allocation in on-line reading by younger and older adults. *Psychology and Aging, 11*(3), 475–486.

Stine-Morrow, E. A., Morrow, D. G., & Leno, R. (2002). Aging and the representation of spatial situations in narrative understanding. *The Journals of Gerontology Series B: Psychological Sciences and Social Sciences, 57*(4), 291–297.

Stine-Morrow, E. A., Ryan, S., & Leonard, S. (2000). Age differences in on-line syntactic processing. *Experimental Aging Research, 26*(4), 315–322.

Stine-Morrow, E. A., Shake, M. C., Miles, J. R., & Noh, S. R. (2006). Adult age differences in the effects of goals on self-regulated sentence processing. *Psychology and Aging, 21*(4), 790–813.

Stine-Morrow, E. A., Soederberg Miller, L. M., Gagne, D. D., & Hertzog, C. (2008). Self-regulated reading in adulthood. *Psychology and Aging, 23*(1), 131–163.

Stuss, D. T., & Alexander, M. P. (2000). Executive functions and the frontal lobes: A conceptual view. *Psychological Research, 63*(3–4), 289–298.

Teuber, H. L. (1972). Unity and diversity of frontal lobe functions. *Acta Neurobiologiae Experimentalis, 32,* 615–656.

Till, R. E., & Walsh, D. A. (1980). Encoding and retrieval factors in adult memory for implicational sentences. *Journal of Verbal Learning and Verbal Behavior, 19*(1), 1–16.

Tipper, S. P. (1991). Less attentional selectivity as a result of declining inhibition in older adults. *Bulletin of the Psychonomic Society, 29*(1), 45–47.

Tisserand, D. J., & Jolles, J. (2003). On the involvement of prefrontal networks in cognitive ageing. *Cortex, 39*(4), 1107–1128.

Tomoeda, C. K., & Bayles, K. A. (1993). Longitudinal effects of Alzheimer disease on discourse production. *Alzheimer Disease and Associated Disorders, 4*(7), 223–36.

Trott, C. T., Friedman, D., Ritter, W., Fabiani, M., & Snodgrass, J. G. (1999). Episodic priming and memory for temporal source: Event-related potentials reveal age-related differences in prefrontal functioning. *Psychology and Aging, 14*(3), 390–413.

Troyer, A. K., Graves, R. E., & Cullum, C. M. (1994). Executive functioning as a mediator of the relationship between age and episodic memory in healthy aging. *Aging and Cognition, 1,* 45–53.

Tsang, P. S., & Shaner, T. L. (1998). Age, attention, expertise, and time-sharing performance. *Psychology and Aging, 13,* 323–347.

Tun, P. A., Wingfield, A., Stine, E. A., & Mecsas, C. (1992). Rapid speech processing and divided attention: Processing rate versus processing resources as an explanation of age effects. *Psychology and Aging,* *7*(4), 546–550.

Ulatowska, H. K., Allard, L., & Donnell, A. (1988). Discourse performance in subjects with dementia of the Alzheimer type. In H. Whitaker (Ed.), *Neuropsychological studies of nonfocal brain damage* (pp. 108–131). New York, NY: Springer.

Ulatowska, H. K., Cannito, M., Hayashi, M., & Fleming, S. (1985). Language in the elderly. In H. Ulatowska (Ed.), *The aging brain: Communication in the elderly* (pp. 125–140). San Diego, CA: College-Hill Press.

Ulatowska, H. K., & Chapman, S. (1994). Discourse macrostructure in aphasia. In R. Bloom, L. Obler, S. De Santi & J. Ehrlich (Eds.), *Discourse analysis and applications: Studies in adult clinical populations* (pp. 29–46). Hillsdale, NJ: Lawrence Erlbaum.

Ulatowska, H. K., & Chapman, S. B. (1991). Discourse studies. In R. Lubinski (Ed.), *Dementia and Communication* (pp. 115–132). Philadelphia, PA: B. C. Decker.

Ulatowska, H. K., Chapman, S. B., Highley, A. P., & Prince, J. (1998). Discourse in healthy old-elderly adults: A longitudinal study. *Aphasiology, 12*(7–8), 619–633.

Ulatowska, H. K., Chapman, S., & Johnson, J. (1999). Inferences in processing of text in elderly populations. In H. Hamilton (Ed.), *Language and communication in old age: Multidisciplinary perspectives* (pp. 91–114). New York, NY: Garland.

Ulatowska, H. K., Garst, D., Reyes, B. A., Olea Santos, T., & Kim, Y. C. (2013). *Forms and function of reminiscence: Elderly veterans with and without dementia.* Poster presented at the 2013 ASHA Convention, Chicago, IL.

Ulatowska, H. K., & Garst Walsh, D., Olea Santos, T., & Reyes, B. (2014). *Life review of American veterans of the Second World War: remember and reflecting on "the good war."* Poster presented at the American Society of Gerontology, Washington, DC.

Van Dijk, T., & Kintsch, W. (1983). *Strategies of discourse comprehension.* New York, NY: Academic Press.

Vaughan, L., & Giovanello, K. (2010). Executive function in daily life: Age-related influences of executive processes on instrumental activities of daily living. *Psychology and Aging, 25*(2), 343–355.

Verhaeghen, P. (2003). Aging and vocabulary score: A meta-analysis. *Psychology and Aging, 18*(2), 332–339.

Verhaeghen, P., & Cerella, J. (2002). Aging, executive function and attention: A review of meta-analysis. *Neuroscience and Biobehavioral Reviews, 26*, 849–857.

Verhaeghen, P., & Salthouse, T. A. (1997). Meta-analyses of age–cognition relations in adulthood: Estimates of linear and nonlinear age effects and structural models. *Psychological Bulletin, 122*(3), 231–249.

Voss, J. F., Vesonder, G. T., & Spilich, G. J. (1980). Text generation and recall by high-knowledge and low-knowledge individuals. *Journal of Verbal Learning and Verbal Behavior, 19*(6), 651–667.

West, R. L. (1996). An application of prefrontal cortex function theory to cognitive aging. *Psychological Bulletin, 120*(2), 272–292.

West, R. L., & Sinnott, J. D. (1992). *Everyday memory and aging: Current research and methodology.* New York, NY: Springer-Verlag.

Whelihan, W. M., & Lesher, E. L. (1985). Neuropsychological changes in frontal function with aging. *Developmental Neuropsychology, 1,* 371–380.

Winblad, B., Palmer, K., Kivipelto, M., Jelic, V., Fratiglioni, L., Wahlund, L., . . . Petersen, R. C. (2004). Mild cognitive impairment: Beyond controversies, towards a consensus—Report of the international working group on mild cognitive impairment. *Journal of Internal Medicine, 256*(3), 240–246.

Wingfield, A. (1996). Cognitive factors in auditory performance: Context, speed of processing, and constraints of memory. *Journal of the American Academy of Audiology, 7*(3), 175–182.

Wingfield, A., Aberdeen, J. S., & Stine, E. A. (1991). Word onset gating and linguistic context in spoken word recognition by young and elderly adults. *Journal of Gerontology, 46*(3), 127–129.

Wingfield, A., & Grossman, M. (2006). Language and the aging brain: Patterns of neural compensation revealed by functional brain imaging. *Journal of Neurophysiology, 96*(6), 2830–2839.

Wingfield, A., Tun, P. A., Koh, C. K., & Rosen, M. J. (1999). Regaining lost time: Adult aging and the effect of time restoration on recall of time-compressed speech. *Psychology and Aging, 14*(3), 380–389.

Winocur, G., & Moscovitch, M. (1983). Paired-associate learning in institutionalized and noninstitutionalized old people: An analysis of interference and context effects. *Journal of Gerontology, 38*(4), 455–464.

Wise, M., Han, J., Shaw, B., McTavish, F., & Gustafson, D. (2008). Effects of using online narrative and didactic information on healthcare participation for breast cancer patients. *Patient Education and Counseling, 70*(3), 348–356.

Wojtyla, K. (1999). *Encyclical letter to the elderly.* Retrieved January 11, 2014, from http://w2.vatican.va/content/john-paul-ii/en/letters/1999/documents/hf_jp-ii_let_01101999_elderly.html

Woodruff-Pak, D. S. (1997). *The neuropsychology of aging.* Malden, MA: Blackwell.

Zacks, R., Hasher, L., & Li, K. (2000). Human memory. In F. Craik & T. Salthouse (Eds.), *The handbook of aging and cognition* (2nd ed., pp. 293–357). Mahwah, NJ: Lawrence Erlbaum Associates.

Zelinski, E. M., & Gilewski, M. (1988). Memory for prose and aging: A meta-analysis. In M. Howe & C. Brainerd (Eds.), *Cognitive development in adulthood: Progress in adult development research* (pp. 133–158). New York, NY: Springer Verlag.

Zelinski, E. M., & Hyde, J. C. (1996). Old words, new meanings: Aging and sense creation. *Journal of Memory and Language, 35*(5), 689–707.

Zimprich, D., & Martin, M. (2002). Can longitudinal changes in processing speed explain longitudinal age changes in fluid intelligence? *Psychology and Aging, 17*(4), 690–695.

CHAPTER 4

The Effect of Aging and Neurogenic Conditions on Speech Production: Recent Advances

Linda S. Carozza

This chapter describes the motor speech related components of human communication as it pertains to physical characteristics such as speech timing and other factors. The aging speech pattern is a rich area of research in the area of both changes associated with healthy aging as well as those associated with neurogenic communication disorders. This understanding is important in seeking to understand methodologies that may maintain speech quality and life participation via creative performance approaches contained in the second portion of the book.

—Linda S. Carozza

OVERVIEW

This chapter will summarize the changes in speech articulation that take place during the aging process. Since speech is produced via a multisystem coordination effort and depends on a functional power source (i.e., the voice), an initial discussion of the voice will be included here as well.

INTRODUCTION: THE IMPORTANCE OF RESEARCH ABOUT HEALTHY ELDERLY SPEAKERS

Clinicians recognize that the aging demographic will be increasing in the caseloads of speech-language pathologists in the years to come. Older adults are the fastest growing segment of the population, with adults over age 85 requiring skilled diagnostic and intervention services (Hooper & Cralidis, 2009). These facts reflect the general increase in the number of older adults worldwide and, as such, have prompted the use of the term, "graying of the planet" (Sowers & Rowe, 2007).

Speech and aging is a growing area of research in the field of communication sciences, with laboratory-based analyses of speech patterns being most prevalent. Temporal characteristics of speech are especially revealing and have been analyzed in both healthy aging and other populations, using computer-assisted displays of speech patterns. Studies that measure timing characteristics have been among the richest in quantifying and qualifying healthy aging patterns as distinct from other populations, and as such form a benchmark to understanding speech rate declines in healthy aging (Hooper & Cralidis, 2009).

The goal of much of the recent motor speech research has been to add further data to a model of speech dissolution with the goal of eventually shedding light on the neural substrates of speech decline. With assessment of minute timing differences via computer assisted analysis, speech changes that are not yet discernible in standard off-line examinations can be detected and tracked earlier in speech progression. This may be accomplished via evaluation of temporal speech characteristics using a standard syllable set as stimuli, as was done in several of the studies cited above. These stimuli were developed to capture changes in vowel length duration and other salient characteristics. Determining the onset of the earliest motor speech impairment has been an area of interest for international scientists. These studies are important because findings of this nature can lead to earlier disease detection and can help to unravel the complex system of motor speech integration in general.

As an example, Satt et al. (2013) have reported a protocol and system for status tracking of early dementia progression from speech and voice recordings. The authors compiled recordings of 80 diagnosed subjects. Statistical properties of the voice yielded information regarding slower brain processing and neuromuscular properties of the speech production system, with research continuing in this direction for purposes of early detection. This line of study has potential to lead to newer treatments, earlier detection, and hence improved quality of life for patients.

Speech Production

Normal speech depends on the complex integration of approximately 100 different muscles producing sounds at a rate of as high as 15 sounds per second. These movements rely on precise respiratory, laryngeal, and oral adjustments. Normal speech depends on the rapid and precise integration of respiration, phonation and articulation. These systems must be structurally and functionally intact, separately as well as together, to form the rapid aerodynamic and muscular adjustments that comprise the normal speech stream. Rate of speech and breath support are two of the most salient characteristics underlying normal voice and articulation. Speech function is considered normal when it meets the various demands of daily living activities for personal and social independence.

Changes in speech production co-occur with biological, psychological, and physiological changes in adults as they age. Changes in speech production occur throughout the lifespan as a result of specific changes throughout the speech and language processing system, including changes in the anatomy, physiology, sensory feedback, motor control, and central processing of speech (Kahane, 1981). Kent and Burkard (1981) refer to the fact that, in understanding changes that occur in the aging process and diseases that most commonly impact aged persons, it is appropriate to consider measures that focus on finer aspects of speech motor control. It is difficult to separate the distinct causes that can potentially lead to changes in speech production performance as a result of normal aging.

Regardless, it is necessary to monitor whether these changes occur because they can serve as a template upon which to compare healthy elderly individuals with those who have been diagnosed with neurological disorders. This is particularly challenging given the simultaneous interaction of respiration, phonation, articulation, and prosody that mark the production of voice and speech during normal function.

Changes in speech production may fall into one of two broad categories: "functional" or "organic." An organic disorder indicates there is a physical cause for a disorder whereas a functional disorder is not caused by any anatomic or physiological impairment (Owens, 2011, pp. 192 & 239). These broad terms are used to distinguish changes that are due to misuse or overuse of an otherwise intact mechanism versus those that are related to specific anatomic or physiological differences. Both of these etiologies warrant the attention of professionals if the deviation significantly detracts from the quality of life of an individual in various interpersonal settings. For example, an older person with a weakening voice may have difficulty being heard or understood in a professional setting. This can be related to organic changes that occur as people age. The case of this vocal insufficiency can be evaluated by a team of professionals via perceptual and objective assessment to determine whether the etiology is functional, organic, or mixed. The results may then determine an appropriate course of intervention.

Deviations in vocal pitch, vocal loudness, and vocal quality are the three primary properties that are used to determine whether an individual is suffering from a voice disorder. Pitch refers to "the perceptual correlate of fundamental frequency" (Owens, 2011). Aspects of pitch such as monopitch (a voice lacking "normal inflectional variation"), inappropriate pitch (a voice considered to be "outside the normal range of pitch for age and/or sex") and pitch breaks ("sudden uncontrolled upward or downward changes in pitch") are aspects that are seen as potential indicators of a vocal pitch disorder (Owens, 2011). Loudness, a characteristic by which dysarthria can be differentiated, is defined as "the perceptual correlate of vocal intensity" (Owens, 2011). Both monoloudness, a voice that does not vary in intensity at expected points in speech, and loudness variations are aspects of vocal loudness that may suggest a voice disorder. Lastly, perceptual characteristics of vocal quality include hoarseness/roughness, breathiness, vocal tremor, and strain and struggle (Owens, 2011).

Speech Rate

Speech timing, or rate of speech, is described by Bell-Berti and Chevrie-Muller in terms of "fluent speech" (1991), synonymous with undisturbed ongoing rate of speech from a motoric standpoint. The authors state that fluent speech is the listener's perception of the rhythm of speech production. The modalities underlying fluent rate of speech, however, may have multiple neurological roots. Two levels of control are hypothesized: a motor planning level and a motor execution level. Bell-Berti and Chevrie-Muller state that "timing patterns resulting from planning are thought to reflect linguistic intent, whereas those resulting from the execution reflect the biomechanical properties of the system" (1991). Their study was specifically designed to test whether different breakdowns could be found in cerebellar ataxic dysarthric patients, as opposed to global slowing.

The authors were able to isolate patterns of speech that derived from the planning stage and differing aspects that derived from the execution stage. The different patterns of speech observed in the ataxic patients versus the healthy controls suggest that the cerebellum is responsible for "fluent" speech and influences speech rate. The nature of this study is unique in that it provides information about the underpinnings of neurological control of speech in vivo. Carryover extensions of this research appear in the studies of Carozza et al. (2014) that examine dementia and speech timing; one of those studies is described below.

The study of the temporal structure of speech in individuals with early neurogenic disease has been revealing in regard to drawing implications for the speech and voice changes in healthy elderly. Reductions in speech rate have been reported to be a characteristic of many motor speech disorders (Darley, Aronson, & Brown, 1975). Motor speech declines suggested by decreased speech rate may be associated with neurological degradation to the areas responsible for speech (Carozza, Quinn, Nack, & Bell-Berti, 2011a, 2011b). In several comparison sets of studies (Heffinger, Damico, Carozza, Bell-Berti, & Krieger, 2014), a subject demonstrates rates of declines at 6 month intervals using measurements of spectral analyses including spectrogram findings of phrase boundaries, compensatory shortening, and voice onset times. Differences in speech rate comparing healthy elderly and demented subjects were also found. This decline in the rate of speech observed for speakers with dementia differs in characteristics from the expecting slowing of speech rate in speech reported for normally aging individuals (Hooper & Cralidis, 2009).

THE AGING VOICE

Characteristics of the aging voice have been studied extensively. Stathopoulos, Huber, and Sussman (2011) reported that the voice changes throughout our lifespan, although not always in the same fashion for everyone, and with gender differences as well. Variability in voice is closely related to changes that take place in structure. In women, the vocal folds become heavier due to calcification and frequency decreases. Therefore, as women age their voices become deeper. In men, quite the opposite occurs, whereby the vocal folds decrease in weight and as a result, aging men speak at a higher frequency. In addition, in the way in which aging anatomical systems function, there is also a change in quality of integration and motor control. Presbyphonia is the term used to describe the generic "aging voice."

Perhaps one of the most "visible" signs of aging is the change in speech characteristics and quality that mark a speaker as "elderly." Since this is apparent in all face-to-face communication and telephone usage, there can be a tendency to alienate the speaker and disregard what he or she has to say. Voice and speech hygiene in the form of supported voice techniques, indirect voice enhancement via controlled exercise, and even singing can help to maintain a typically smoothly working voice and speech system. The use of an effective daily voice program, including appropriate levels of hydration and voice conservation measures (such as learning how to speak with less strain in noisy environments), are among many strategies that can be employed.

A consultation with an otolaryngologist for medical evaluation and services of a qualified speech-language pathologist are necessary with any changes of a sudden or concerning nature to the individual or family member. Individuals with voice-related changes due to neurogenic or traumatic conditions require skilled medical assessment. Changes in voice quality may indicate serious conditions such as the onset of progressive neurological disease and warrant immediate attention as voice issues may indicate undetected etiologies not yet suspected by the patient or family. A full description of the physiological changes that occur to the speech mechanism and related swallowing (dysphagia) and voice complications can be found in a subsequent chapter by Matina Balou.

Data: Comparing Healthy Elderly Individuals with Those Diagnosed with Neurological Disorders

In summation, both age and cognitive decline have an effect on speech rate (Kail & Salthouse, 1994; Schneider, Daneman, & Murphy, 2005; Small, Kemper, & Lyons, 1997; Vaughan & Letowski, 1997). However, other contributory factors have been suggested. While healthy elderly speakers are reported to speak at a slower rate than their younger counterparts, it has also been noted that elderly patients with a general cognitive decline speak more slowly than their healthy elderly peers (Hooper & Cralidis, 2009). The typical speech and language loss of individuals with dementia may provide a comparison to assess patterns of speech/language deterioration. As an example, patients diagnosed with dementia may start out exhibiting minor symptoms such as general language reduction that then leads to deficits that eventually segue into generalized tangential speech, then to only rote speech, and ultimately to mutism and loss of even the vegetative function of the articulators (Carozza et al., 2011a, 2011b). This gradual loss of speech suggests a continuum of decline from the highest level skills to the most basic functions. The eventual total loss of language in dementia may indeed have its origin in the initial motor speech breakdown described in these studies.

MOTOR SPEECH DISORDERS

When speech function declines differentially as compared to expectations, a motor speech disorder may be suspected. Overall, according to the classic definition by Darley, Aronson, and Brown (1969a, 1969b), motor speech disorders are a group of speech disorders resulting from disturbances in muscular control: weakness, slowness, or incoordination of the speech mechanism due to damage to the central or peripheral nervous system or both. The term encompasses coexisting neurogenic disorders of several or all of the basic processes of speech: respiration, phonation, resonance, articulation, and prosody. Salient characteristics of dysarthric conditions include localization of injury, perceptual analysis of multisystem speech/voice affects, cluster classifications, and neuroanatomical correlates. These aspects are referred to in subsequent detail to follow.

APRAXIA OF SPEECH

What Is Apraxia of Speech?

Apraxia of speech, an example of a motor speech disorder, is included in this section because it occurs in connection with stroke and other acquired disorders that may happen in aging. It is characterized by difficulty in motor planning and organization of speech units to form ongoing word streams. The difficulty becomes more apparent with longer and more complex speech patterns. Characteristically, a person with apraxia of speech may exhibit off-target approximations, leading to an appearance of "groping" for speech production. There are additional hallmarks of this pattern including the fact that nonvolitional postures of the articulators may not be affected. This distinguishes apraxia of speech from dysarthria which is a motor dysfunction affecting both vegetative and nonvegetative uses of the articulators. In disease states as well as stroke-related communication impairment, it is not uncommon to see the presence of apraxia of speech, dysarthria, and aphasia all in the same patient. Careful evaluation should reveal the differential patterns of impairment, and the ongoing course of the disease may cause a change in the relative severity of each of these components (Table 4–1).

Causes and Classifications of Apraxia of Speech

Apraxia of speech acquired in adulthood generally arises from a neurologic or traumatic condition affecting brain areas responsible for the smooth coordination of ongoing speech. Speech apraxia is differentiated from limb and oral apraxia by the incoordination of motor planning for speech units. The specifics of these contributions will relate to how a person is able to produce speech and possibly other fine motor tasks. Intelligibility of a person with severe apraxia of speech can be markedly reduced. It can affect individuals with a brain-based acquired speech communication disorder and frequently coexists with other speech symptoms, which may make differential diagnosis difficult. One of the primary diagnostic categories that may be associated with apraxia of speech is stroke-related aphasia, which will be discussed separately as a language disorder as opposed to a primary motor speech impairment.

Treatment of Apraxia of Speech

The following section provides a brief overview of various treatments that have been applied to apraxia of speech. The examination of treatment of apraxia of speech is particularly relevant because it provides additional examples of how an adult motor speech disorder that directly impacts an individual's ability to participate in the world is addressed. However, apraxia of speech is a complex disorder and extended information beyond the

Table 4–1. Characteristics of Apraxia of Speech

Localization	Speech Characteristics	
	Articulation Process	*Prosody Process*
• Apraxia results from a unilateral, left hemisphere lesion involving the third frontal convolution, Broca's area. There is a possibility of apraxia following more posterior, probably parietal lesions.	• One common characteristic is the patient's groping to find the correct articulatory postures and sequences.	• Durational relationships of vowels and consonants are distorted
	• Facial grimaces, moments of silence, and phonated movements of articulators are common occurrences.	• Rate of production is slow
	• Consonant phonemes are involved more often than vowel phonemes	• Alterations of the intonation occur.
	• Articulation errors are inconsistent and highly variable, not referable to specific muscle dysfunction	
	• Articulatory errors are primarily substitutions, additions, repetitions, and prolongations— essentially complications of the act of articulation.	

Source: Adapted from Duffy (2013); Owens (2011).

description of treatment plans fall outside the scope of this work. One treatment strategy for adult apraxia of speech that has growing supportive evidence is a program called PROMPT (Prompts for Restructuring Oral Muscular Phonetic Targets), which is designed to restructure oral motor targets, and is a special certification course that is offered to practicing speech clinicians. Although the primary target population has been children, there is research that reports success with adult apraxia (PROMPT Institute). According to the PROMPT Institute website,

During the 1980s, the first empirical studies of PROMPT's treatment efficacy were done. These studies led to the development of the first manual describing the technique of PROMPTing. In 1985, the first publication describing PROMPT appeared (Square, Chumpelik, Morningstar, & Adams, 1985). It described the technique and use of "surface" tactile PROMPTs. They provide input about place of articulation, the amount and type of muscular contraction, movement transition and timing needed to produce speech sounds. At the same time, the issue of how a three-dimensional "intraoral" target movement system might affect coarticulatory reality began to be explored. This exploration focused on how phonatory, mandibular, labial-facial and lingual movements worked interactively in speech production and on how these subsystems could be rebalanced using tactile input to develop clear speech (http://www.promptinstitute.com/).

Modification of this and related oral motor techniques has been used for patients with severe apraxia of speech as a component to speech remediation from the standpoint of "reprogramming" articulatory patterns.

Other traditional approaches include phonetic derivation of words, which can be likened to the shaping of speech sounds based on nonspeech postures, and progressive approximations, which is the gradually shaping speech segments from other speech segments. In addition, the phonetic placement approach focuses on the articulators' position during speech production. Key word approach, another traditional approach, uses words commonly produced by an individual to present new words with similar components. Phonetic contrasts, the imitation of minimally contrasted words, and Melodic Intonation Therapy (MIT), therapy with an emphasis on speech rate and rhythm, are also examples of traditional approaches (Brendel & Ziegler, 2008, p. 2). These programs are all based on principles of motor learning described by Maas and colleagues (2008).

A program called VAST (video assisted speech technology treatment) is aimed at simultaneous speech production rather than speech production after a target stimulus. SpeakinMotion. com describes the mobile application that prompts patients to speak along with a video animation:

> VAST is an innovative application of video technology to facilitate and improve communication abilities for speech-impaired individuals. Following close-up video of mouth movements allows these individuals to speak full sentences. The simultaneous combination of visual, auditory, and, in some cases, written cues, allows these individuals to readily produce speech. VAST facilitates live communication and individualized, mobile speech practice. (http://www.speak inmotion.com).

The target population for this application includes individuals with apraxia of speech as well as aphasia. This mobile application uses principles of motor learning to produce a resource that individuals use on their own and that encourages the practice of these motor skills as the model is presented. The goal is to increase patients' understanding of the "special dimensions" involved in producing single speech sounds, syllables, and words. Individuals can work towards modifying their production of sounds with the visual aid providing them a model that those individuals can imitate (Brendel & Ziegler, 2008, p. 2).

Norton, Zipse, Marchina, and Schaug (2008) describe the general principles and versatility of melodic intonation therapy.

The main principles involved in this approach include: intonation patterns, left-handed tapping, inner rehearsal, and auditory-motor feedback training. The program was primarily designed for individuals with aphasia; however, it has been reportedly to have been successfully applied to apraxia of speech (Norton et al., 2008). According to the authors, research is still underway to determine the exact neural processes that are stimulated via this approach.

Another option for the treatment of apraxia of speech comes in the form of the Motor Reconnect Apraxia Program (MRAP), founded by Bill Connors, that treats apraxia of speech as a "movement disorder" (Aphasia Toolbox, 2011). The goal of the program is to take "advantage of neural plasticity to maximize recovery from aphasia and related disorders" (Minnesota Speech Language Hearing Association, 2012), and to "help the brain reorganize itself with renewed and new neural connections" (Connors, 2014). MRAP uses therapy and practice principles with a focus on motor skills to achieve this goal. One primary principle of the program is the concept that "if you can plan it, you can say it" (Connors, 2014). MRAP focuses on the "internal mental processes," the ability of a patient to preplan for speech, and uses many strategies to aid people with aphasia and related disorders to translate and bridge those internal processes to the motoric aspects of speech.

DYSARTHRIA

What Is Dysarthria?

A major class of speech dysfunction is dysarthria. Dysarthria is defined as a speech disorder due to lesions in the nervous system affecting how structures function during speech production, and is considered to be the most common of acquired speech disorders in speech-language pathology. Yorkston, Miller, and Strand (1995) are major contributors to our understanding of this phenomenon. In adult-acquired dysarthria, there are many challenges to the patient including basic feeding and use of the oral motor system, as well as difficulty with clear and precise articulation and voice stream. Dysarthria is frequently described as a system-wide complex because it affects respiration, phonation, resonance, and articulation. These systems function together to produce vocal effort, modify the voice stream, and ultimately the articulation postures that we recognize as speech. Since this is a highly complex area of motor planning, execution, and feedback, dysarthric involvement can cause highly unintelligible speech. Chronic disorders like dysarthria have a number of differing consequences on speech and motor behaviors. These can range from the inhibition of daily functioning to the point of creating a disability/social handicap.

The term "motor speech disorder" is distinguished from dysarthria in that the term "dysarthria" generally does not include speech disorders of structural, psychological or motor planning origins. A wide range of types of dysarthric involvement is seen in individuals. In some cases, speech changes are hardly noticeable, while on the other end of the spectrum, a person can essentially be rendered without vocal speech. (In this latter case, the term *anarthria* is used, as opposed to *dysarthria*). According to Enderby (2000, p. 248), "dysarthria is present in approximately 33% of all patients with brain injuries; 8% of individuals with cerebral palsy patients; and varies from 19% to 100% in individuals with degenerative neurological diseases." In the latter example, the lowest incidence occurs in patients with multiple sclerosis. However, later stage Parkinson's patients and motor neuron disease patients tend to exhibit at least moderate to severe dysarthria.

The Causes and Classifications of Dysarthria

The causes of adult dysarthria are many (Table 4–2). The discussion here will focus on those that appear in adulthood after the acquisition of normal speech and language functions. One of the most devastating classes of adult dysarthria is that of progressive neurological disease. These may include: bulbar palsy, pseudobulbar palsy, amyotrophic lateral sclerosis ("Lou Gehrig's disease"), multiple sclerosis, myasthenia gravis, late onset Tay-Sach's disease, and many others, such as Parkinson's disease and

Table 4–2. Dysarthria Characteristics

Type of Dysarthria	Site of Lesion	Physical Concomitance	Voice & Speech Characteristics
Flaccid Dysarthria	• Peripheral nervous system • Lower motor neuron system	• Weakness • Lack of normal muscle tone	• Hypernasality • Imprecise consonant productions • Breathiness of voice
Spastic Dysarthria	• Pyramidal and extrapyramidal systems	• Muscular weakness • Greater than normal muscular tone	• Imprecise consonants • Harsh voice quality • Hypernasality • Strained-strangled voice quality
Ataxic Dysarthria	• Cerebellum	• Inaccuracy of movement • Slowness of movement	• Imprecise consonants • Irregular articulatory breakdowns • Prolonged phonemes • Prolonged intervals • Slow rate
Hypokinetic Dysarthria	• Subcortical structures involving basal ganglia	• Slow movements • Movements limited in extent (limited range of movement)	• Articulatory mechanism impaired due to reduced range of motion involving lips, tongue, and jaw. • Disturbance may range from mildly imprecise to total unintelligibility

continues

Table 4–2. *continued*

Hyperkinetic Dysarthria	• Subcortical structures involving basal ganglia	• Quick, unsustained, involuntary movements • Emission of grunts as a result of spontaneous contractions of the respiratory and phonatory muscles • Barking noises • Echolalia • Coprolalia (obscene language without provocation or reason)
Mixed Dysarthrias	• Progressive degeneration of the upper and lower neuron system. Most cases appear without a cause	• Amyotrophic Lateral Sclerosis: Impairs the function (weakness and paralysis) of all the muscles used in speech production • Slow rate • Shortness of phrase • Imprecision of consonants • Hypernasality • Harshness

Source: Adapted from Duffy (2013); Owens (2011).

stroke-related dysarthria. Recently, the presence of a motor speech disorder such as dysarthria has been recognized as contributing to the diagnosis of neurological disease even when a diagnosis has not yet otherwise been established (Aronson 1987; Duffy, 2008). In addition, the various forms of dementia produce a loss of speech control that ultimately affects processes involved in feeding such as swallowing (discussed extensively in the chapter by Balou in this text).

To review, classification of the dysarthrias by Duffy (2013) has been a milestone contribution in research on the motor speech area. The classification system is sometimes referred to as the "Mayo system" because the original thinking on this area took place there in the 1960's by Darley et al. (1969a, 1969b, 1975), and it rests on several major tenets, and is still used as the underlying principles in this area of research. These are:

1. That dysarthrias are recognized by how they sound (such that the different disorders affect speech systems differently leading to characteristic speech)

2. That dysarthria can be distinguished from non-neurological speech disorders

3. That not all affected speakers sound identical in severity and characteristics

4. That similar speech patterns reflect a common underlying neuropathology.

This paradigm and its extensions have helped clinicians understand dysarthria in a much more specific way than simply grouping all neurological speech disorders in the same broad category. Subtypes of dysarthrias caused by primary lesions to different locations in the central nervous system have led rise to further categorizations. Furthermore, motor speech is multidimensional and can be described in clusters of interrelated contributing factors of respiration, voice, phonation, and articulation (Duffy, 1986, 2005). The simultaneous integration of these factors that make up the speech signal impacts the production and perception of motor speech characteristics such as speech rate, prosody, loudness, and pitch. Overall, the integrated components of the speech system and which aspect of the dysarthria predominates, has been a monumental contribution to the field of acquired neurological speech disorders. Darley et al. (1969a, 1969b, 1975) discovered six perceptual characteristics by which dysarthrias could be distinguished, depending on their location of damage in the nervous system: (1) Pitch, (2) Loudness, (3) Vocal Quality, (4) Respiration, (5) Prosody, and (6) Articulation (see Table 4–2). While the terms pitch, loudness, and vocal quality were described in greater detail earlier in the chapter, it is important to define the following terms as well. Damage in the nervous system that impacts respiration is notable because respiration is the system that supports the ability to speak by producing the air pressure that vibrates the vocal folds (Owens, 2011, p. 42). Prosody refers to features of speech such as stress and intonation (Owens, 2011, p. 81). Lastly, articulation is the "coordinated movement of the tongue, teeth, lips and palate" that produce meaningful speech sounds (Owens, 2011, p. 383). In this sense, speech production is a dynamic system-wide integration of respiration, phonation, and articulation.

Treatment of Dysarthria

Dysarthria has received less attention than other clinical disorders because it is a complex multisystem disorder manifesting differently depending on underlying ideology. The purpose of speech treatment has justifiably shifted to functionality of communicative effectiveness and an approach that emphasizing strategies and techniques. Listener and speaker variables, such as breath control and maximizing contextual cues, are taken into account in this holistic view of management. There are many ways in which creative clinicians can maximize speech cues and promote effective environmental supports (such as controlling competing noise) to help promote intelligibility. Based on disease characteristics, outcome measurement varies according to client diagnosis and related expectations and needs. The input of a range of professionals, including occupational and physical therapists, can greatly assist in finding the best fit when deciding on a professional model to increase function in the daily environment.

A very significant contribution has been provided by Yorkston and her colleagues in "Perspectives on Dysarthria" (2013). This work describes the evolution of dysarthria assessment and treatment. Future technologies that will enhance speech intelligibility and overall quality of life—such as computer applications, portable speech devices, alternative and augmentative communication devices (AAC), and specific software—are in development These technologies will require the skills of a speech-language pathologist for best selection and patient training for optimal use.

WHAT IS PARKINSON'S DISEASE?

One of the more common degenerative diseases that may appear in speech-language pathologist caseloads is Parkinson's disease (PD), which is estimated to affect upwards of ten million people worldwide (National Parkinson Foundation, 2008). PD is an impairment in neurotransmission with certain characteristics that make Parkinsonism readily recognizable to the trained listener. Parkinson's disease is particularly highlighted in this chapter because it is a common etiology in adult caseloads and represents a form of dysarthria, hypokinetic dysarthria. Hypokinetic dysarthria is a prevalent symptom of Parkinson's disease, making the inclusion of Parkinson's disease particularly relevant to this chapter's examination of dysarthria. This symptom results in slow and limited muscular movements as well as a reduced range of motion in the lips, tongue, and jaw (Owens, 2011). As a result, loss of voice support and oral motor precision are hallmarks of the disease. Many patients seek therapeutic services to forestall worsening of these symptoms. In addition to the motoric impairments affecting gross motor control, Parkinson's patients lose control over speech rate, speech initiation, effortful speech, precision, and vocal volume, and therefore seek therapeutic services.

Treatment of PD

Successful treatment of motor speech disorders secondary to progressive disorders such as Parkinson's disease is especially challenging and, in fact, controversial because there is generally no reasonable expectation of recovery. According to Trail et al. (2005), of the 89% of PD patients who have speech disorders, only 3% to 4% will receive intervention. This is significant in that the nature of PD, as with most neurologically based systemic disorders, affects laryngeal, respiratory, and articulatory efforts in a progressive and highly debilitating manner.

Positive gains, however, have been made in studying interventions that address the underlying deficits of the PD speech disorder. Recently, evidence-based strategies such as the Lee Silverman Voice Technique (LSVT) (Fox, Morrison, Ramig, & Sapir, 2002) have received a great deal of attention, with certifications available for speech clinicians. This technique uses cues to signal louder speech volume, which triggers a series of processes that contribute to speech clarity such as open mouth posture increasing resource capacity of the phonatory system and stimulating many cortical areas supporting speech. This treatment, which has been the treatment of choice for many individuals due to its relative ease of access and training, has been well suited to many individuals, including those with PD-related cognitive deficits. The technique includes loudness training as a way to recruit subsystems of articulation, swallowing, and neural substrates. The tasks are relatively straightforward and contain an internal redundancy in instruction that makes the program easier to be maintained by patients. The functional goal of increased loudness helps patients with sensory awareness that in turn improves underlying functions as well. The program directly addresses the reduced neural drive to the speech system by amplification of vocal effort. In addition, the clear directions of increasing loudness help patients to self-generate and monitor greater effort (which are areas of concern with PD patients). The authors conclude that changes in voice effort may be related to a common neurological mechanism and that the LSVT program may address these central deficits. These include fronto-limbic systems and related basal ganglia regions—areas associated with PD pathology. The goal of the program and its carryover training modules is to continue to maintain improvement over time. Overall, current trends continue to support efficacy of this approach (Clair, Lyons & Hamburg, 2012) with PD and other related disorders.

A second approach is deep brain stimulation, which is an approach requiring medical eligibility and also reports gait improvement more than speech improvement. There are various forms of stimulation techniques that a medical practitioner may prescribe to a patient such as sites of stimulation. The final frontier is the ongoing development of technological software applications. In addition, there are many emerging programs that center on maximizing function through social engagement and mobility. These are two areas that contribute to quality of life after diagnosis.

Rudzicz (2013) recently reported on a software system by which dysarthric speech signals can be adjusted to be more intelligible. This software would be potentially groundbreaking in apraxia of speech treatment because the disorder comprises motor planning of increasing complex syllable length units. The system is based on modifying pronunciation patterns to correct repeated sound syllables, inserting sounds that are omitted in the person's speech pattern, and adjusting the speed of voice and the range of frequency. Marked improvements in speech recognition were reported, and the research is highly promising for the advancement in the assistive speech communication technology field.

THE IMPORTANCE OF CREATIVE APPROACHES

The overall goal of improving speech intelligibility is a functionally based approach. The aim of the speech-language pathologist is to develop goals that matter to the patient, taking into account skill level and daily communication needs. Patients in need of specific strategies are generally in treatment-driven services and one of the biggest hurdles is the maintenance and self-cueing of the patient. Simplicity of technique is very helpful to patients who may have coexisting neurogenic conditions. The simple ability to use the self-cue "Slow down" may assist many patients in enhancing intelligibility. A metronome or computer application of timing support is one of the most basic ways for patients to adhere to a speech improvement protocol after formal treatment is discontinued. Technology may assist patients in home practice as well, with adaptations of programs such as those developed for speech research via companies such as

Kay Pentax (http://www.kayelemetrics.com/). Biofeedback and visual stimuli will help a patients to "hear" themselves better and to take advantage of the portability of speech devices that are increasingly available such as "text to talk" programs in use for the general population.

In addition, certain patients may find that a reevaluation and return to treatment with newer methodologies may be appropriate. These newer, creative approaches are those that differ from the traditional speech correction models based on articulatory imitation drill and repetition practices that formed the foundation of the earlier interventions. A list of some of these newer approaches cited in current literature about speech improvement includes resources from the National Apraxia Association, oral-motor approaches, PROMPT therapy, Talk Tools programs, and rhythmic entrainment intervention, in addition to many websites of interest such as LearningLoud.com. As in all interventions, clinicians and families are urged to research levels of practice and outcomes with the approaches because each program has distinct training protocols and related, yet different, methodological considerations necessary to consider in determining programs of choice.

In my experience, the variations and informal modifications of the Lee Silverman Voice Technique (LSVT) have been useful across different patient settings. For example, in my current clinical practice, the use of the loudness cue, which is central to the program, has been anecdotally observed to support maximal phonation time and sound pressure levels post group-singing trials.

The test of efficacy of any long-term management of speech intelligibility training has yet to be accomplished, however. It bears mention that the American Speech-Language-Hearing Association is involved in many rigorous studies of the effects of various interventions and that the data overall is equivocal about the relationship between overt articulator training and carryover to speech articulation as an example. See McCauley, Strand, Lof, Schooling, and Frymak (2009) in *The American Journal of Speech-Language Pathology* for a complete discussion on this topic. Ongoing research and development in these areas can be obtained through both American Speech-Language-Hearing Association's Evidence-Based Practice website (http://

www.asha.org/members/ebp/) and evidence maps (http://ncep maps.org/). These resources provide clinical practice guidelines and are recommended resources for clinicians in this field. (See ASHA's "Special Interest Group 2, Neurophysiology and Neurogenic Speech and Language Disorders" at http://www.asha.org/ SIG/02/About-SIG-2/ and "The Academy of Neurologic Communications Disorders and Sciences" at http://www.ancds.org/ for additional resources.)

CONCLUSIONS

Speech production and intelligibility in all its forms remains at the forefront for practitioners who serve the elderly population. The prevalence of speech disorders in the aging population is directly related to the occurrence of disease processes that affect the central and peripheral nervous system. Acquired speech disorders in adulthood is a complex area of speech-language pathology practice, involving an understanding of the complex nature of the speech production process including the component systems of respiration, phonation, and articulation. Therefore, what we may perceive as a disorder of "pronunciation" may in fact be a combination of voice and speech control dynamic issues. Since intelligibility of communication is central to personhood, the detection and amelioration of speech disorders is of high priority in aging populations. Knowledge of the commonly occurring comorbidities, potential patterns, and remedial access is crucial to maintaining quality of life in affected individuals. Research is driving therapy toward increasingly more targeted and efficient methodologies for these patients who suffer from speech breakdowns due to neurogenic communication disorders. Some of these are mentioned within this chapter (e.g., PROMPT; Motor Reconnect Apraxia Program; Melodic Intonation Therapy). These efforts are greatly enhanced by computer and software technologies in the speech science arena that capture speech as a digital signal that can be converted into different formats for study of speech characteristics. The PCQuirer software, as an example, works with analysis of spectral data. This is an area of current research in many laboratories in institutions of graduate education in communication sciences and disorders that will undoubtedly lead to enhanced patient applications.

REFERENCES

Academy of Neurologic Communication Disorders and Sciences. (2014). http://www.ancds.org/

American Speech-Language Hearing Association. (n.d.). *Evidence-Based Practice (EBP)*. Retrieved from http://www.asha.org/members/ebp/

American Speech-Language Hearing Association. (n.d.). *Evidence maps*. Retrieved from http://ncepmaps.org/

Aphasia Toolbox. (May 24, 2011). *Motor reconnect apraxia program*. Retrieved from http://aphasiatoolbox.blogspot.com/2011/05/motor-reconnect-apraxia-program5242011.html

Aronson, T. A. (1987). Is panic disorder a distinct diagnostic entity? A critical review of the borders of a syndrome. *Journal of Nervous and Mental Disease, 175*(10), 584–594.

Bell-Berti, F., & Chevrie-Muller. (1991). Motor levels of speech timing: Evidence from studies of ataxia. *Haskins Laboratory Studies Report on Speech Research*, SR-107/108, 87–92.

Brendel, B., & Ziegler, W. (2008). Effectiveness of metrical pacing in treatment of apraxia. *Aphasiology, 22*, 77–102.

Carozza, L., Quinn, M., Nack, J., & Bell-Berti, F. (2011a). *Temporal structure in the speech of a person with dementia: A longitudinal study*. Presented at The Acoustical Society of America conference proceedings, Seattle, WA.

Carozza, L., Quinn, M., Nack, J., & Bell-Berti, F. (2011b). *A continuing study of the temporal structure of the speech of a person with dementia*. Presented at The Journal of the Acoustical Society of America conference proceedings, San Diego, CA.

Clair, A., Lyons, K., & Hamburg, J. (2012). A feasibility study of the effects of music and movement on physical function, quality of life, depression, and anxiety in patients with Parkinson's disease. *Music and Medicine, 4*(1), 49–55.

Connors, B. (2014, March 7–8). *Aphasia-apraxia therapy: Exploiting neuroplasticity*. Retrieved from http://www.ushaonline.net/Resources/Documents /SLP%20handout%20without%20apps-Connors.pdf

Darley, F., Aronson, A., & Brown, J. (1969a). Differential diagnostic patterns of dysarthria. *Journal of Speech and Hearing Research, 12*, 246–269.

Darley, F., Aronson, A., & Brown, J. (1969b). Clusters of deviant speech dimensions in the dysarthrias. *Journal of Speech and Hearing Research, 12*, 462–496.

Darley, F. L., Aronson, A. E., & Brown, J. R. (1975). *Motor speech disorders*. Philadelphia, PA: W. B. Saunders.

Duffy, J. R. (2005). *Motor speech disorders: Substrates, differential diagnosis, and management* (2nd ed.). St. Louis, MO: Elsevier Mosby.

Duffy, J. R. (2008). Motor speech disorders and the diagnosis of neurologic disease: Still a well-kept secret? *The ASHA Leader.* Retrieved from http://www.asha.org/Publications/leader/2008/081125/f081125a.htm

Duffy, J. R. (2013). *Motor speech disorders: Substrates, differential diagnosis, and management* (3rd ed.). St. Louis, MO: Elsevier Mosby.

Duffy, J. R., & Folger, N. W. (1986). *Dysarthria in unilateral central nervous system lesions*. Paper presented at the annual meeting of the American Speech-Language-Hearing Association, Detroit, MI.

Enderby, P. M. (2000). Assessment and treatment of functional communication in dysarthria. In L. E. Worrall & C. M. Frattali (Eds.), *Neurogenic communication disorders: A functional approach* (pp. 247–259). New York, NY: Thieme Medical.

Fox, C. M., Morrison, C. E., Ramig, L. O., & Sapir, S. (2002). Current perspectives on the Lee Silverman Voice Treatment (LSVT) for individuals with idiopathic Parkinson's disease. *American Journal of Speech Language Pathology, 11*(2), 111–123.

Heffinger, M., Damico, G., Carozza, L., Bell-Berti, F., & Krieger, P. C. (2014). Assessing the effects of cognitive decline on the speech rate of demented and healthy elderly speakers. *The Journal of the Acoustical Society of America, 135*(4), 2293.

Hooper, C. R., & Cralidis, A. (2009). Normal changes in the speech of older adults: You've still got what it takes; it just takes a little longer! *SIG 15 Perspectives on Gerontology, 14*(2), 47–56.

Kahane, J. C. (1981). Anatomic and physiologic changes in the aging peripheral speech mechanism. In D. S. Beasley & G. A. Davis (Eds.), *Aging: Communication processes and disorders* (pp. 47–62). New York, NY: Grune & Stratton.

Kail, R., & Salthouse, T. (1994). Processing speed as a mental capacity. *Acta Psychologica, 86*(2–3), 199–225.

Kay Pentax. Retrieved from http://www.kayelemetrics.com/

Kent. R. D., & Burkard, R. (1981). Changes in acoustic correlates of speech production. In D. Beasley & G. Davis (Eds.), *Aging: Communication processes and disorders* (pp. 47–62.) New York, NY: Grune & Strattorn.

Maas, E., Robin, D., Austermann, S., Wulf, G., Freedman S. E., Ballard, K., & Schmidt, R. A. (2008). Principles of motor learning in treatment of motor speech disorders. *American Journal of Speech-Language Pathology, 17*, 277–298.

McCauley, R. J., Strand, E., Lof, G. L., Schooling, T., & Frymark, T. (2009). Evidence-based systematic review: Effects of nonspeech oral motor exercises on speech. *American Journal of Speech-Language Pathology, 18*(4), 343.

Minnesota Speech-Language-Hearing Association (MSHA). Retrieved from http://www.msha.net/?page=conv_ 2012_descript

National Parkinson Foundation. (2008). *Parkinson disease: A global view.* Retrieved from http://www.parkinson.org/NationalParkinson Foundation/files/84/84233ed6-196b-4f80-85dd-77a5720c0f5a.pdf

Norton, A., Zipse, L., Marchina, S., & Schaug, G. (2008). Melodic intonation therapy: Shared insights in how it is done and why it might help. *Annals of the New York Academy of Sciences, 1169*, 431–436.

Owens, R. E. (2011) *Language development: An introduction* (8th ed.). London, UK: Pearson.

The Prompt Institute. (n.d.). Retrieved from http://www.promptinsti tute.com/

Rudzicz, F. (2013). Adjusting dysarthric speech signals to be more intelligible. *Computer Speech and Language, 27*(6), 1163–1177.

Satt, A., Sorin, A. M, Toledo-Ronen, O., Barkan, O., Kompatsiaris, I., Kokonozi, A., & Tsolaki, M. (2013). *Evaluation of speech-based protocol for detection of early-stage dementia.* Proceedings from Interspeech Conference, Lyon, France.

Schneider, B., Daneman, M., & Murphy, D. (2005). Speech comprehension difficulties in older adults: cognitive slowing or age-related changes in hearing? *Psychology and Aging, 20*(2), 261–271.

Small, J., Kemper, S., & Lyons, K. (1997). Sentence comprehension in Alzheimer's disease: Effects of grammatical complexity, speech rate, and repetition. *Psychology and Aging, 12*(1), 3–11.

Sowers, K. M., & Rowe, W. S. (2007). Global aging. In J. A. Blackburn, & C. N. Dulmus (Eds.), *Handbook of gerontology: Evidence-based practice approaches to theory, practice, and policy* (pp. 3–19). Hoboken, NJ: John Wiley & Sons.

Square, P. A., Chumpelik, D. A., Morningstar, D., & Adams, S. G. (1985). Efficacy of the PROMPT system of therapy for the treatment of acquired apraxia of speech. In R. H. Brookshire (Ed.), *Clinical aphasiology: Conference proceedings* (pp. 319–320). Minneapolis, MN: BRK.

Stathopoulos, E. T., Huber, J. E., & Sussman, J. E. (2011). Changes in acoustic characteristics of the voice across the life span: Measures from individuals 4–93 years of age. *Journal of Speech, Language, and Hearing Research, 54*(4), 1011–1021.

Trail, M., Fox, C., Ramig, L. O., Sapir, S., Howard, J., & Lai, E. C. (2005). Speech treatment for Parkinson's disease. *NeuroRehabilitation, 20,* 205–221.

VAST. *Speak in Motion: Watch, Listen, Speak, Anywhere.* Retrieved from http://www.speakinmotion.com/

Vaughan, N. E., & Letowski, T. (1997). Effects of age, speech rate, and type of test on temporal auditory processing. *Journal of Speech, Language, and Hearing Research, 40,* 1192–1200.

Yorkston, K. M., & Beukelman, D. R. (2013) Evidence supporting dysarthria intervention: An update of systematic reviews. *Perspectives on Neurophysiology and Neurogenic Speech and Language Disorders, 23*(3), 105–111.

Yorkston, K. M., Miller, R. M., & Strand, E. A. (1995). *Management of speech and swallowing in degenerative diseases.* Tucson, AZ: Communication Skill Builders.

CHAPTER 4 RECOMMENDED ADDITIONAL SOURCES

American Speech-Language-Hearing Association. (2014). http://www.asha.org

Bose, A., & Square, P. A. (2001). PROMPT treatment method and apraxia of speech. *SID2 Newsletter, 11*(4), 5–8.

Bose, A., Square, P. A., Schlosser, R., & van Lieshout, P. (2001). Effects of PROMPT therapy on speech motor function in a person with aphasia and apraxia of speech. *Aphasiology, 15*(8), 767–785.

Freed, D. B., Marshal, R. C., & Frazier, K. E. (1997). Long-term effectiveness of PROMPT treatment in a severely apraxic-aphasic speaker. *Aphasiology, 11*(4/5), 365–342.

Square, P. A., Chumpelik, D. A., Morningstar, D., & Adams, S. G. (1986). Efficacy of the PROMPT system of therapy for the treatment of apraxia of speech: A follow-up investigation. In R. H. Brookshire (Ed.), *Clinical aphasiology: Conference proceedings* (pp. 221–226). Minneapolis, MN: BRK.

Yorkston, K. M., Beukelman, D., & Bell, K. (1988). *Clinical management of dysarthric speakers.* Boston, MA: Little, Brown & Co.

CHAPTER 5

Language Comprehension and Production in Dementia and Aphasia

Linda S. Carozza

The hallmark of interpersonal communication is individual communication style. It marks our personhood and identity in many ways. Linguistic changes that accompany aging or communication disorders of a neurological origin are among the most challenging for individuals to cope with, but also provide rich opportunities for many various creative methodologies that do not depend solely on verbal communication strategies. This may include art therapies and similar important modes of creativity and self-expression.

—Linda S. Carozza

INTRODUCTION

This chapter focuses on one of the most important characteristics of human interpersonal relations: the capacity to communicate thoughts, feelings and words through language. We take for granted the ability to use language to communicate, because it is a process that generally develops seamlessly throughout the normal lifespan, and the changes that take place through healthy aging can be anticipated and accommodated. However, living with a condition that impairs the ability to talk or understand language can be life-altering. This chapter covers the phenomena of dementia, the general decline in mental abilities due to the death of brain cells, and aphasia, the loss of language due to neurogenic origin. The scope of these areas in terms of empirical research as well as clinical applications is huge in the field of communication sciences. Therefore, the chapter will discuss the most salient features that pertain to recovery and improving the quality of life for individuals suffering from these conditions. In addition to the motor-speech changes that were described previously, language-related changes associated with healthy aging include increases in latency in word finding and naming. Syntax reasoning, perception, and comprehension are unimpaired and in fact may improve with conceptual growth and "wisdom." Specific changes ascribed to healthy language and aging is reviewed by Capilouto, Wright, and Srinivasan (2009); Rogalski, Fleming, Bourgeois, Key-DeLyria, and Quintana (2013); and Stead, Donovan, and Hoffman (2011). These changes are not pathology, progressive and differ markedly from the signs and symptoms of neurogenic communication disease.

DEMENTIA

What Is Dementia?

According to the Alzheimer's Foundation of America (AFA), dementia is a general term that describes a group of symptoms such as loss of memory, judgment, language, complex motor skills and other intellectual function that are caused by the permanent damage or death of the brain's nerve cells (Alzheimer's Foundation of America, 2014). The specific signs and symptoms of dementia may vary along with the course of the disease, which can lead to a variety of presenting symptoms and behaviors (Table 5–1). Most types of dementia have a gradual course of onset, beginning with mild occasional symptoms and ultimately resulting in complete neurophysiological breakdown.

Each type of dementia is related to different physical and functional differences in the brain, such as the accumulation of neurofibrillary plaques and tangles in Alzheimer's disease, and the presence of Lewy bodies in Lewy body dementia. There are several neurological diseases which can result in a dementing condition, with Alzheimer's disease (AD) accounting for the preponderance of cases; approximately 60% according to statistics from the AFA (Alzheimer's Foundation of America, 2014). Other causes include vascular dementia or multi-infarct dementia (MID) (related to possible stroke or blockage of blood supply), Lewy body disease-related dementia (related to abnormal protein deposits in the brainstem), alcohol-induced dementia (where the brain cells are damaged due to prolonged alcohol use rather than mere aging), traumatic brain injury, and frontotemporal dementia, frequently referred to as primary progressive aphasia.

Dementia is diagnosed via a variety of measures, including neuropsychological and medical laboratory testing. The ultimate diagnosis of the type of dementia can be made following a brain autopsy to determine the neurological changes. Determining the stage of the disease is accomplished by measuring patient performance on tasks of processing speed, language, memory, attention and other related areas of cognition.

Alzheimer's Disease

According to Carozza (1995), Alzheimer's disease (AD) in its earliest stages is chiefly characterized by semantic memory impairment. This impairment is reflected in deficits in word finding, use, and understanding of semantic attributes and associations, and difficulty with categorization (Nebes, 1989). However, the

Table 5–1. Types of Dementia

Type of Dementia	Symptoms	Brain Changes
Alzheimer's Disease	• Difficulty remembering recent conversations, names, or events (early clinical symptom) • Apathy and depression (early symptoms) • Impaired communication • Poor judgment • Disorientation • Confusion • Behavior changes • Difficulty speaking, swallowing, and walking	• Deposits of the protein fragment beta-amyloid (plaques) • Twisted strands of the protein tau (tangles) • Nerve cell damage and death in the brain
Vascular Dementia	• Impaired judgment or ability to make decisions, plan, or organize	• Brain imaging can often detect blood vessel problems • Vascular brain charges often coexist with changes linked to other types of dementia
Dementia with Lewy bodies (DLB)	• Memory loss and thinking problems common in Alzheimer's • Sleep disturbances • Well-formed visual hallucinations • Muscle rigidity	• When Lewy bodies (abnormal aggregations of the protein alpha-synuclein) develop in the cortex, dementia can result
Mixed Dementia	• Abnormalities linked to more than one type of dementia occur simultaneously in the brain	• Characterized by the abnormalities of more than one type of dementia

Type of Dementia	Symptoms	Brain Changes
Parkinson's Disease	• Symptoms similar to dementia with Lewy bodies (if developed)	• Alpha-synuclein clumps begin in the substantia nigra and are thought to cause degeneration of the nerve cells that produce dopamine
Frontotemporal Dementia	• Changes in personality and behavior • Difficulty with language • Nerve cells in the front and side regions of the brain	• No distinguishing microscopic abnormality is linked to all cases • Generally symptoms develop at about age 60
Creutzfieldt-Jakob Disease	• Impairs memory and coordination • Causes behavior changes	• Misfolded prion protein causes a "domino effect" in which prion protein throughout the brain malfunctions
Normal pressure hydrocephalus	• Difficulty walking • Memory loss • Inability to control urination	• Caused by the buildup of fluid in the brain
Huntington's Disease	• Abnormal involuntary movements • Severe decline in thinking and reasoning skills • Irritability • Depression and other mood changes	• A progressive brain disorder caused by a single defective gene resulting in abnormalities in a brain protein
Wernicke-Korsakoff Syndrome	• Memory problems • Other thinking and social skills relatively unaffected	• Thiamine levels low resulting in brain cells unable to generate enough energy to function properly

Source: Adapted from The Alzheimer's Association (Retrieved from http://www.alz.org/dementia/types-of-dementia.asp).

underlying cause for this difficulty in semantic representation is still poorly understood. In addition, there are several disagreements in current research about the level at which the semantic disruption takes place. There are claims that suggest a diminished quality of mental representation and those that suggest impaired access to stored word meanings. Specific proposals include: that AD causes a loss of semantic information; that lexical information is preserved, but that retrieval is impaired; and, finally, that AD disrupts the organization of the internal lexicon (Kempler, 1991). It is also possible that AD causes simultaneous deficits in all these domains (Kempler, 1991). The fact that cognitive processes such as working memory, "the temporary storage and manipulation of information" (Baddeley, 2003) and attention interrelate with language function has posed a difficult challenge to psycholinguists seeking to clarify these models. (See Chapter 3 for a full discussion of cognitive changes in aging.)

An Overview: Additional Subtypes of Dementia

Multi-Infarct Dementia. Multi-infarct Dementia (MID), also known as vascular dementia, is considered to be the second most common cause of dementia. The progression of decline seen during MID is commonly referred to as step-wise, as opposed to the gradual onset of Alzheimer's disease and other dementias. Similar to the other subtypes of dementia, there is a wide array of symptomatology in the moderate to severe stages that overlap with the other dementias.

Frontotemporal Dementia. Frontotemporal Degeneration (FTD) is considered to have various subtypes characterized by the primary symptomatology. These include behavioral-variant frontotemporal degeneration, primary-progressive aphasia, and frontotemporal movement disorders (The Association for Frontotemporal Degeneration). There are some specific differences in FTD as compared to Alzheimer's disease. In general, these differences include age of onset and quality of memory loss, as well as differences in behavioral components. However, in the advanced stages of illness, the subtypes of dementia become less clear.

Subcortical Dementias. Unlike the other dementing conditions that are the result of cortical (outer) layer damage, the subcortical dementia pathology lies beneath the cortex. The symptoms of the subcortical dementias therefore are different than the cortical dementias. Whereas the cortical dementias present with primary language and memory deficits, the subcortical patients demonstrate difficulty with speed of thought and ability to initiate actions.

Treatment of Dementia

Treatments aimed at improving quality of life of dementia patients have called upon various areas of interdisciplinary work; this includes social communication, art programs, music programs, and person centered approaches. These specific methodologies are discussed in depth in part two of the book as well as in Chapter 8. One methodology, spaced retrieval, has been widely studied for efficacy assessment. Spaced retrieval is a technique used to enhance memory by having an individual with dementia repeat and recall information at increasingly longer time intervals (Camp & Stevens, 1990). Hopper et al. (2005) reviewed quantitative studies using the spaced retrieval method. Participants, between the ages of 52 to 96, were included in a total of 15 separate studies. In the area of cognitive-communication, overall review of the studies supports the use of spaced retrieval training for individuals with dementia. The best candidates, according to the authors, are individuals with declarative memory impairment and the ability to participate in structured training, along with sufficient visual and hearing acuity to participate. Training should be conducted on at least a weekly basis. Outcomes such as improvement in trained information as well as retention for several months post study can be expected with some capacity for generalization. However, there would be no anticipated change in overall diagnostic category of the patients. This methodology has been adapted to other communication disorders such as aphasia (Fridriksson, Holland, Beeson, & Morrow, 2005).

Conclusions

As outlined above, dementia impacts a person's memory, judgment, language, and motor skills as a result of damage to the brain's nerve cells. While different types of dementia have unique impacts on these cognitive functions, each greatly impacts an individual's ability to communicate thoughts, feelings, and words through language. One prominent treatment of dementia, also stated above, is the spaced retrieval method. This methodology as well as others have been used to treat other communication disorders as well, one being aphasia. Aphasia, also a neurogenic communication disorder, vastly impacts language comprehension and production used and will be described below.

APHASIA

What Is Aphasia?

Aphasia is the loss of language abilities, typically secondary to a focal neurological insult to the language centers of the brain. The critical areas for understanding the sequelae of aphasia include analyzing the type and degree of aphasia severity and the duration of time since onset. It is interesting to note that even though statistics indicate that approximately 1,000,000 Americans are living with some form of aphasia (National Aphasia Association, 2011), the majority of the general public has never heard of the disorder, adding to the anonymity that survivors may feel. It is estimated that in 2020 approximately two million American stroke or brain injury survivors will be living with aphasia according to the American Speech-Language-Hearing Association (ASHA).

As per the American Speech-Language-Hearing Association (ASHA), the following are critical markers in understanding aphasia. One of the main systems for categorizing aphasia is based on the primary presenting characteristics of the disease. Aphasia can affect all modalities of language to differing extents, including primary communication modalities of speaking and understanding as well as secondary modalities such as reading and writing. In addition, other symbolic systems such as the ability to use math and other subsystems that depend on storage and organization of stimuli may be impaired as well. For the purposes of this section, we will limit the discussion to the classical language symptoms.

In the majority of right-handed individuals, language dominance is controlled in specialized language areas in the brain located in the left temporoparietal regions. These areas connect and associate with other brain processing areas such as those in the right brain hemisphere. Consequently, individuals who suffer brain injury in the right hemisphere may also experience language problems, although the features may differ. It is also common for aphasics to have difficulties with additional functions specialized in related oral musculature regions. Therefore, an individual with aphasia may have also simultaneous dysarthria. This may occur in addition to apraxia and dysphagia, two additional conditions that will be described in additional sections.

Types and Symptoms of Aphasia

It is easiest to describe symptoms in terms of their outward characteristics. Two classical distinctions, based on the primary site of the lesion, have been made when describing aphasia. Broca's aphasia, also known as expressive or anterior aphasia, is characterized by halting or "telegraphic" speech and expressive language deficits in the face of relatively normal receptive/comprehension skills. When an individual's impairment is predominantly expressive, his or her language will be restricted in length and complexity. His or her output will tend to consist of smaller "content" words such as basic nouns, and grammatical forms will be highly limited. A person with Broca's aphasia may say, "Foam, foam, phone, damn, phone . . . not ude . . . phone not ude . . . use . . . ude . . . use . . . can't ude . . . no foam can ude" (Owens, 2011, p. 151). The individual may also have difficulty in word order usage in sentences and sound order in words (making sound substitutions that are described as phonemic transpositions). Depending on the exact site of damage (anterior or posterior in the language region), a person may have a differing profile of language.

Patients with posterior lesions tend to have more word output but frequently use them in incorrect contexts. This variant of aphasia, also known as Wernicke's aphasia, is generally associated with a more posterior foci of lesion. A person with Wernicke's aphasia may say, "I love to go for rides in the car. Cars are expensive these days. Everything is expensive these days. Even groceries. When I was a child you could spend five dollars and get a whole wagon full. I had a red wagon" (Owens, 2011, p. 149). The individual may have relatively more fluent speech output but restricted comprehension. These patients may be described as having a "press" of speech because their language is marked by confabulation and lack of comprehensibility.

If the individual with aphasia has these types of comprehension deficits (so-called "receptive" aphasia), he or she will experience difficulty in understanding rapid, normal speech strings. This is a challenge in speech and language treatment since the understanding of instructions must be carefully managed in order for the patient to benefit. Careful testing of the patient is necessary to determine areas of deficit and ability. Many specialists think that regardless of category, any type of aphasia affects both understanding and production of language in affected individuals, although to varying degrees.

Additional categories of aphasia include mixed aphasia and global aphasia, in which an individual has severe deficits in all language systems. Furthermore, a specific subclass of aphasia, primary progressive aphasia, is a rare but challenging diagnosis which is found when the aphasia is not due to a specific focal lesion but is rather the initial symptom of a dementing process. In some cases, aphasia evolves and patients are left with residual symptoms (i.e., word finding issues) after a period of time. In that case, these patients may be candidates for longer term management on how to adjust to living with the residual effects.

Right hemisphere damage (RHD) can result in a form of aphasia as well, with the use of language and integration of communication deficits most prominent. The deficits associated with RHD are categorized as extra-linguistic, linguistic, and nonlinguistic deficits. Some extra-linguistic deficits include impulsivity, difficultly comprehending nonliteral information (e.g., sarcasm, metaphors, etc.), and an inability to interpret body language and facial expressions. Difficulty writing, naming body parts and comprehending complex material are all symptoms associated with linguistic deficits of a person with RHD. Lastly, examples of symptoms of nonlinguistic deficits include disorientation to time and direction, anosognosia (a symptom whereby RHD patients will deny the existence of their deficits), and visuospatial deficits (trouble processing visual stimuli as a result of being unable to integrate information) (Myers 1994).

The relative presence of strength and weakness patterns contribute to the classification of the aphasia. In the case of milder aphasia's, the person may be functional in many social-level conversational settings, but demonstrate more restrictions as language becomes longer in length or more abstract in concept. In contrast, a moderate to severe case would mean that the individual might have little verbal output and severe restrictions in language comprehension.

Assessment and Treatment of Aphasia

Some of the newer creative approaches to long-term management of aphasia are referred to in Chapter 8, which discusses social models of intervention; in addition to music and art approaches which are increasing in professional practice, in particular Chapter 12 by Joanne Loewy and colleagues, "Music Therapy in Neurologic Dysfunction to Address Self-Expression, Language, and Communication: The Impact of Group Singing on Stroke Survivors and Caregivers." Commonly, a speech-language pathologist (SLP) with training in neurogenic communication disorders is the best qualified professional to provide assessment and remediation to individuals with aphasia. A speech-language pathologist may assess aphasia and communicative competence using a variety of formal testing instruments, clinical assessment, and family interviews. Foundational information can be found in Brookshire's *An Introduction to Aphasia* (1973) as well as current ongoing research examining the range of aphasia test batteries and their interpretation. Formal (standardized via norm-referenced criteria) evaluations, as well as informal assessments, are conducted in the areas of speech fluency and coordination, speech comprehension (in differing levels of complexity), and the overall expressive complexity and coherence of the patient's language output. Intervention strategies will vary based on the prevalence of symptomatology. In recent years, there has been a movement away from linguistic-based approaches to more functional communication approaches that address how a person can function in the real world. The functional approach was described by Sarno first in 1971, who then continued to update the research in 2004.

Living successfully with aphasia is an integral part of the Life Participation Approach to Aphasia (LPAA), developed by the LPAA Project Group (Chapey et al., 2001; Kagan & LeBlanc, 2002). Although individuals cannot change the course of a disease that may ultimately lead to stroke-related aphasia, they can adjust their coping skills and reactions to it. The LPAA emphasizes a support of individuals living with aphasia with a focus on "re-engagement in life" and "achieving immediate and longer term life goals" throughout assessment, intervention and continuing life-long support after hospital discharge (Chapey et al., 2001). This approach redirects the clinical support speech-language pathologists provide to be "consumer-driven" (Chapey et al., 2001). The clients themselves "participate in the recovery process" by determining with a speech-language pathologist what interventions and adjustments are meaningful to them personally. This focus on life adjustments of the individual in order to live successfully with aphasia is something the World Health Organization champions as a way of measuring extent of disability (Gold, Stevenson, & Fryback, 2002). Some of the primary coping skills promoted include adjusting to the environment, maximizing social integration despite of disability, looking forward to remainder of one's life. The coping skills advocated demonstrates a diagnosis of wellness rather than a diagnosis of illness. Kagan et al. (2008), influenced by and applying the value-based approach presented by the LPAA, produced an aphasia framework for outcome measurement: *Living with Aphasia: Framework for Outcome Measurement* (A-FROM). This framework integrates "aphasia severity, participation in life situations, communication and language environment, and personal identity, attitudes and feelings" as overlapping factors that make up an individual's life with aphasia (Kagan et al., 2008, p. 266). These are all factors that are then used to measure outcomes such as quality of life.

In a pilot research study conducted by Carozza and Miraglia (2013), discharged aphasia patients who were enrolled in an optional "after-care" social conversation group reported greater communication confidence and improved overall quality of life on formal self-study questionnaires. The idea of adapting to the limitations of a disorder and reacquiring personal identity is behind the drive to help patients with chronic disease. This draws from the existing social models of therapy (Aten, Caligiuri, & Holland, 1982; Cruice, Hill, Worrall, & Hickson, 2010; Worrall & Yiu, 2000). Regaining social identity is part of a continuum of care as a patient moves from inpatient to outpatient to the community. After care creates a model of readjustment in a quasi-therapeutic plan that supports and promotes reentry into the community.

Additional Considerations

Additional areas that the clinician will assess or seek special consultation for include higher-level academic skills (specifically reading and writing abilities), as well as feeding/swallowing skills. In subsequent sections the strategies that may address these areas, particularly for the chronic patient, will be described. However, in general, it can be stated that there is evidence from scientific investigations that speech-language interventions assist people in recovery both during initial stages as well as long term. The reader may refer to website of The Academy of Neurologic Communication Disorders and Sciences (ANCDS) for published information on evidence-based treatment paradigms for individual assessment, treatment and group strategies. For the purposes of this book, the emphasis will be on the social model and group treatment approaches that assist patients in real-world applications. Reading and writing abilities of individuals with chronic aphasia are not addressed in terms of rehabilitation within community groups, but rather the functional use of these abilities are addressed. While the focus of the community groups may not be rehabilitation in terms of these particular skills, there are carryover activities that call on these maintained, even though impaired, higher-level academic skills.

Social Communication: Pragmatics

The use of language in interpersonal contexts is an important area of evaluation. Social communication (sometimes referred to as pragmatics) is the use of all our language functions to negotiate life and learning. This is a highly integrated use of language, with correlations to education and cognition. Since language in the real world is dynamic and involves partnership with other speakers and listeners, the social model of intervention (as opposed to a medical model) is especially fruitful in aphasia rehabilitation. Social models of intervention are especially important because they can focus on teaching compensation strategies for communication in a real-world context, such as including use of gestures, writing, computer-assisted devices, and so forth. These strategies can then be practiced with either attending caregivers/family members, or other patients, until their level of comfort increases to a point of being able to carryover these skills into the real world. The social model includes practice in therapeutic group settings and community speaking opportunities in a variety of settings, and has been demonstrated to be effective (Elman & Bernstein-Ellis, 1999).

For this reason, there are specific assessments designed for the practical implications of the aphasia disorders. One of these is the "Aphasia Needs Assessment," developed by Kathryn Garrett and David Beukelman in 1997. In addition, the patient may have a very specific need related to premorbid occupation. For example, the use of language for higher-order reasoning when constructing a court argument, in the case of an attorney, is an instance of the integrated function of many levels of language ability. This is distinct from social language in which many environmental supports may exist.

In the same way, for the general public and nonprofessional patient, this is also true of the ability to understand humor, poetry, conversational nuances, and even appropriate turn-taking. None of these skills is taught per se, but they develop out of a lifetime of learning and experience. The use of social language will be further discussed in Chapter 8, as it underlies a good deal of competence in social settings and every day problem-solving.

Group Therapy

The scope and practice of speech-language pathology includes specialized training in acquired and neurogenic disorders. Increasingly, however, there has been a lack of proper reimbursement for the provision of in-depth services. This has, in part, led to various strategies that attempt to provide effective, low cost, and meaningful services in a naturalistic setting with other members of the community. Two types of group interventions have been reported on in speech literature. One is the formal therapy group in which didactic training takes place with specific training goals and outcomes designed to carry out therapy agendas in a group model. Another is the "community group," which is much less formal and is designed for socialization and the practice of learned skills without the therapeutic programming and modeling that systematic therapy entails. Student volunteers of an aphasia support group have informed me that the groups engender feelings of deep commitment to its members as well as feelings of success and satisfaction from the natural setting in which the students feel they can provide support to individuals with aphasia.

Let us consider the formal group first. According to specific information provided by ASHA,

> The person may participate in group therapy settings to practice conversational skills with other persons with aphasia. The speech-language pathologist (SLP) may lead the group through structured discussions, focusing on improving initiation of conversation, turn-taking, and repairing conversational breakdowns. Group members may role-play common communication situations that take place in the community and at home, such as talking on the telephone, ordering a meal in a restaurant, and talking to a salesperson at a store. (ASHA, 2014)

Response behavior is examined and supported through known strategies to assist patients achieve more functional independence, and is typically monitored via behavioral interventions consisting of formal goal planning and achievement criteria. Various influential research projects have been carried out that have examined the efficacy of group communication treatment for adults with chronic aphasia. Roberta Elman and Ellen Bernstein-Ellis' (1999) work specifically examines the impact group therapy has on linguistic and communicative performance for individuals with chronic aphasia. After examining two groups, one receiving group treatment and a second group not receiving group treatment, the researchers discover significant improvements in the participants with chronic aphasia who received group treatment. In addition, family members of those individuals reported noticeable positive life changes as well as psychosocial benefits after the participation in group therapy. Carly Cermak (2011) similarly examined the effect group therapy has on adults with chronic aphasia but by providing an analysis a variety of existing literature. Ultimately, she discovered a relationship between group therapy and an improvement in functional communication and psychological well-being across the data she examined.

On the other hand, community groups, as conceived many years ago, are designed to have patients function in a close to real-life setting with other individuals living with aphasia to achieve a greater return to personal social identity, which can often be lost when people lose the ability to express themselves (Worrall & Frattali, 2000). A community group allows similarly affected individuals to gradually take steps toward community independence, and share their experiences in a way that allows fellow patients to see that they can adjust to aphasia and go on to live relatively independent lives. There are many such programs that have been an outgrowth of this philosophy, (Klein, 1995) with both anecdotal and empirical evidence to support and substantiate evidence of their success.

In the work of Carozza and Miraglia (2013), a pilot study revealed that patients consistently reported increased quality of satisfaction with activities related to external communication events after participating in a community group. In this sense, the goal of community reintegration is being met as patients attend outings, share anecdotes, and feel the support and comfort of like-minded individuals. The idea of shared experience and "calculated risk-taking" in a community group setting helps prepare individuals for encounters in their day-to-day settings.

The ultimate goal of any successful rehabilitation program is to maximize community reintegration (M. Sarno, personal communication, 2013). The path to reintegration in life and the community comes through building increased confidence in external situations in a series of steps over time.

CEASRS

A preliminary study by Carozza and colleagues examined how patient reactions affected their use of language behaviors, depending on their perceived stress level in the context of a variety of communication events. Circumstances such as hailing a cab or ordering in a restaurant were described to patients and judged as being stress related and communicatively effective. This tool, the Communicative Effectiveness and Stress Rating Scale (CEASRS) (which is still under field-testing via various student-faculty collaborations) is unique in that it provides a pictorial scale so that patients with language restrictions can make a scaled choice in terms of differential response (Carozza, Olea-Santos, & Abesamis, 2005a, 2005b). The implications are that the natural stress level of certain communication events that we all experience should be taken into account in planning activities for patients with aphasia, in addition to the requisite language demands. The functional activities of daily life are compounded when a person has communication deficits in addition to natural performance anxiety. It is a challenge to perform activities of daily living with difficultly in communication. This relates to the social model in that it considers the real world implications for patients who may receive therapy but not practice their goal behaviors in the real world. This may have further implications for building such strategies into the community group models.

Creative Aftercare

A further approach by Carozza (2008) appeared in the ASHA Leader. The idea that patients with aphasia can benefit from indirect interventions as a way of overcoming language and life participation restrictions underlies the strategy of this particular creative arts program, which was presented at the Speaking Out Conference in NYC in 2008 (Carozza, 2008). Within this program, patients created art projects with art therapy and speech therapy students. Through this indirect intervention, the participants found more ease of communication and art as an alternative means of communication. It was profound that patients with the loss of speech experienced this nonverbal means of communication satisfying and effective, which was additionally highly satisfying to their families and the clinicians as well. People with aphasia benefit from an interdisciplinary approach involving art and other nonspeech strategies that encourage patients to communicate via other than verbal means. This program and others like it are similar to the dementia programming that will be described by Volkmer later in the text. The use of alternative socially relevant material in "aftercare" rather than in traditional therapy may be a strong strategy by which to enrich community participation for individuals who can participate in alternative modalities.

Other Clinical Applications

Therapeutic recreation and many other creative sources of life participation are enjoyed by patients and their families who become educated in alternative paths to recovery. The Adler Center in New Jersey is a leader in this domain, providing many unique and effective opportunities for families with a full range of opportunities to interact. There are many similar concepts on the therapeutic horizon including those of virtual realities that, as technology advances, will become more accessible through practical applications and creative providers.

An additional thrust to the community group movement has been the trend to employ a "social model" of aphasia management. Many prominent aphasiologists now focus on increasing the involvement of aphasic individuals in their social environment and subscribe to the *social and life-participation approaches* to aphasia management (Byng & Duchan, 2005; Chapey et al., 2001; Simmons-Mackie, 2001). These writers and clinicians have borrowed notions from the World Health Organization International Classification of Function (World Health Organization, 2014) and the SF-36 Health Survey Scoring (Medical Outcomes Trust, 2014) which pertain to activities related to participation in life, with the goal of reengaging in life by strengthening daily participation in activities of the individual's choice at the center of the philosophy. This includes attention to the creation of supportive environments, (e.g., joining community activities, dealing with strangers and the community at large, maintaining friendships) primarily from the standpoint of reducing emotional pain, which is thought to interfere with social and emotional adjustment in the chronic phase.

The *social and life-participation* model suggests that the primary task of the poststroke patient, after medical stability is regained, is the renegotiation of social identity within a social context. Shadden and Agan (2004) emphasize this concern and that the primary focus of support groups in aphasia should be the renegotiation of social identity, which they maintain is an integral part of the coping process. Astrom, Asplund, and Astrom (1992) identified the importance of a social network for patients with chronic conditions and found that individuals who are 3 years poststroke have more psychiatric symptoms and depression than other nonstroke elderly persons. It stands to reason that individuals with communication disabilities are more vulnerable to the effects of social isolation since conversation with others is the primary way people connect with one another (Carozza & Shafi, 2013).

IMPORTANT TRENDS

In dealing with patients with chronic communication disabilities, there can be a commonality of purpose that the speech-language pathologist finds. In the aphasia patient, the goal will be around patient support as the aphasia improves and/or stabilizes and in the patient with dementia, the goal will be on family education as the disease progresses (Hinckley, Bourgeois, & Hickey, 2011). Some commonalities may include the need for conversational approaches and training of caregivers. This is modified according to the client need and clinical expertise and draws on ongoing research. Typically, the speech-language pathologist moves from delivery of specific strategies to counseling around expectations and family education and support, depending on etiology and severity. Ultimately, in many cases, it is the skill of the individual practitioner that drives movement from step to step at different stages and the effective use of available therapeutic information.

From my perspective, the goals of patients and families, as opposed to "curriculum-driven materials," are of paramount importance. It is critical to identify the specific communication needs of the patient and match those with his/her preserved skills to enhance probability of improvement. The support of the patient, no matter what the underlying etiology, is the prime concern in any planned reintegration. A careful dynamic assessment, using informal and formal batteries coupled with clinical intuitions based on a philosophy of quality of life, is central to a standardized approach to long-term care.

Specifically for aphasia management, several methodologies that may be incorporated include the need for visual and verbal augmentation of communication. As soon as possible, patients should be given alternative supports to help them engage and participate in the outside community. The patients with complex diagnoses, for example a person with comprehension and cognitive-linguistic deficits, will similarly require a breakdown of activities that help bypass issues of factors such as cognitive rigidity and egocentricism, (Garrett & Beukelman, 1997). Additionally, the use of strategies suggested by evidence-based practice and supported by meta-analyses will have the greatest research data. This includes the work by Wisenburn, Donahue, and Sobrinski (2010) regarding use of strategies in the complex agrammatic patient.

The field of long-term aphasia management is a complex area of study, with input from many different sources. A review of recent literature continues to support the general tenets that the overall aim is for "functional" as opposed to linguistic recovery. The overarching factors that will affect recovery have to do with many factors that will focus on issues that are not directly related to communication per se. Art appreciation themes used in groups, for example, focus on a nonverbal form of communication. Art is a nonverbal modality that can change and evolve over time during aphasia recovery (Resch, 2012). Over time, the individual's personality and adjustment to the change in status secondary to aphasia is of utmost importance. This includes individual attitudes toward hope for recovery, the social network, and important cognitive strengths that support retraining, such as attention, memory, and recall. The traditional cognitive linguistic approach, for example, considers these, particularly attention, some of the primary goals of its approach to treatment.

To turn to the patients with dementia in this discussion, the use of nonpharmacological treatment has long been understood as meaningful (Olazaràn et al., 2010). Mary Mittelman has contributed a great deal to family and patient interventions, including those with creative arts influence (see "The Unforgettables" Chorus, http://www.med.nyu.edu/aging/research/chorus). The reduction of patient and family stress and burden is the result of these indirect interventions that allow patients to function maximally (see Mittleman, Haley, Clay, & Roth, 2006). A special note should be mentioned regarding the qualitative differences of the language changes in the different dementia profiles. In particularly, the fronto-temporal dementias have an aphasia-like symptom presentation in the initial stages. The patients may seek support around language decline but will also need family education and counseling regarding forthcoming cognitive deterioration. This patient group may need special considerations beyond the creative approach themes suggested in this section. At present, the best state of evidence can be obtained via The Association for Frontotemporal Degeneration (http://www.theaftd.org/) and via extensive studies conducted at Northwestern University's Cognitive Neurology and Alzheimer's Disease Center (http://www.brain.northwestern.edu).

All of these approaches are as creative as the individual clinician performing them, with attention to baselines and probes to ensure that a sustained and meaningful difference is occurring. The research literature is relatively scant regarding in the effectiveness of nonpharmacological management; however, there is a growing body of evidence that will become increasingly meaningful as patient numbers increase and medical economies become more stringent.

CONCLUSIONS

Language production and processing are at the heart of the psychosocial personhood of an individual. When we can no longer communicate our daily wants and needs, along with higher-level abstract language, we become restricted in meeting the demands of daily living, as well as in the expression and appreciation of interpersonal communication in all forms. Therefore, individuals who suffer conditions that affect communication are among society's most vulnerable. Understanding normal communicative changes, as well as "abnormal" change brought on by conditions such as aphasia and dementia, is critical to effective care and overall well-being. This is crucial in understanding the neurogenic language changes and differentiation that individuals may suffer on a chronic basis which call for extended care options stated in related sections of the book.

REFERENCES

Alzheimer's Association. *Types of dementia*. Retrieved from http://www.alz.org/dementia/types-of-dementia.asp

Alzheimer's Foundation of America. (2014). *About dementia*. Retrieved from http://www.alzfdn.org/AboutDementia/definition.html

American Speech-Language Hearing Association. (2014). *Aphasia*. Retrieved from http://www.asha.org/public/speech/disorders/Aphasia/

Association for Frontotemporal Degeneration (AFTD). Retrieved from http://www.theaftd.org/understandingftd/disorders

Astrom, M., Asplund, K., & Astrom, T. (1992). Psychosocial function and life satisfaction after stroke. *Stroke, 23*, 527–531.

Aten, J. L., Caligiuri, M. P., & Holland, A. L. (1982). The efficacy of functional communication therapy for choronic aphasic patients. *Journal of Speech and Hearing Disorders, 47*(1), 93–96.

Baddeley, A. (2003). Working memory and language: An overview. *Journal of Communication Disorders, 36*, 189–208.

Brookshire, R. (1973). *An Introduction to aphasia*. Minneapolis, MN: BRK.

Byng, S., & Duchan, J. (2005). Social model philosophies and principles: Their applications to therapies for aphasia. *Aphasiology, 19*, 906–922.

Camp, C., & Stevens, A. (1990). Spaced-retrieval: A memory intervention for dementia of the Alzheimer's type. *Clinical Gerontologist: The Journal of Aging and Mental Health, 10*(1), 58–61.

Capilouto, G. J., Wright, H. H., & Srinivasan, C. (2009). *Cognitive changes in healthy aging: Impact on relaying main events. Convention Presentations*. Retrieved from http://www.asha.org/events/convention/handouts/2009/1898_capilouto_gilson/

Carozza, L. S. (1995). *Automatic and controlled information processing in Alzheimer's disease* (Doctoral dissertation). City University of New York, New York, NY.

Carozza, L. S. (2008). *Creative after care: An interdisciplinary approach to aphasia rehabilitation*. Presented at Speaking Out! National Aphasia Association Regional Conference, New York, NY.

Carozza, L. S., & Miraglia, R. (2013). *Addressing quality of life outcomes in aphasia community groups.* Presentation at the NYC Speech-Language-Hearing Association, New York, NY.

Carozza, L. S., Olea-Santos, T., & Abesamis, T. M. (2005a). *CEASRS: Communicative Effectiveness and Stress Rating Scale.* Presentation at the ASHA 2006 Convention Poster Session, Miami, FL.

Carozza, L. S., Olea-Santos, T., & Abesamis, T. M. (2005b). *CEASRS: Communicative Effectiveness and Stress Rating Scale.* Presentation at the ASHA 2007 Convention Poster Session, Boston, MA.

Carozza, L. S., & Shafi, N. (2013). Quality of life in aphasia community group members: A social model of clinical treatment. *ACTA Neuropsychologica, 10*(4).

Cermak, C. (2011). The efficacy of group therapy for adults with chronic aphasia. *School of Communication Sciences and Disorders, U.W.O.* Retrieved from https://www.uwo.ca/fhs/csd/ebp/reviews/2010-11/Cermak.pdf

Chapey, R., Duchan, J., Elman, R. J., Garcia, L. J., Kagan, A., Lyon, J. G., & Simmons-Mackie, N. (2001). Life participation approach to aphasia: A statement of values for the future. In R. Chapey (Ed.), *Language intervention strategies in aphasia and related neurogenic communication disorders* (4th ed.). Philadelphia, PA: Lippincott Williams & Wilkins.

Cruice, M., Hill, R., Worrall, L., & Hickson, L. (2010). Conceptualising quality of life for older people with aphasia. *Aphasiology, 24*(3), 327–347.

Elman, R. J., & Bernstein-Ellis, E. (1999). The efficacy of group communication in adults with chronic aphasia. *Journal of Speech, Language, and Hearing Research, 42*, 411–419.

Fridriksson, J., Holland, A., Beeson, P., & Morrow, L. (2005). Spaced retrieval treatment of anomia. *Aphasiology, 19*(2), 99–109.

Garrett, K. L., & Beukelman, D. R. (1997). *Aphasia needs assessment.* Retrieved from http://aac.unl.edu/screen/screen.html

Gold, M. R., Stevenson, D., & Fryback, D. G. (2002). HALYS and QALYS and DALYS, Oh my: Similarities and differences in summary measures of population Health. *Annual Review of Public Health, 23*(1), 115–134.

Hinckley, J. J., Bourgeois, M. S., & Hickey, E. M. (2011). *Treatments that work for both dementia and aphasia.* Convention presentation at the ASHA 2011 Session, San Diego, CA.

Hopper, T., Mahendra, N., Kim, E., Azuma, T., Bayles, K., Cleary, S., & Tomoeda, C. (2005). Evidence-based practice recommendations for working with individuals with dementia: Spaced retrieval training. *Journal of Medical Speech Pathology, 13*(4), xxvii–xxxiv.

Kagan, A., & LeBlanc, K. (2002). Motivating for infrastructure change: Toward a communicatively accessible, participation-based stroke care system for all those affected by aphasia. *Journal of Communication Disorders, 35*(2), 153–169.

Kagan, A., Simmons-Mackie, N., Rowland, A., Huijbregts, M., Shumway, E., McEwen, S., . . . Sharp, S. (2008). Counting what counts: A framework for capturing real-life outcomes of aphasia intervention. *Aphasiology, 22*(3), 258–280.

Kempler, D. (1991). Language changes in dementia of the Alzheimer type. In R. Lubinski (Ed.), *Dementia and communication* (pp. 98–115). Philadelphia, PA: Mosby.

Klein, K. (1995). *Aphasia Community Group Manual.* New York, NY: National Aphasia Association.

Medical Outcomes Trust. (2014). *Health Survey.* Retrieved from http://www.sf-36.org/

Mittleman, M. S., Haley, W. E., Clay, O. J., & Roth, D. L. (2006). Improving caregiving well-being delays nursing home placement of patients with Alzheimer disease. *Neurology, 67*(9), 1592–1599.

Myers, P. S. (1994). Communication disorders associated with right-hemisphere brain damage. In R. Chapey (Ed.), *Language intervention strategies in adult aphasia* (pp. 513–534). Baltimore, MD: Williams & Wilkins.

National Aphasia Association. (2011). *Aphasia FAQ.* Retrieved from http://www.aphasia.org/content/aphasia-faq

Nebes, R. (1989). Semantic memory in Alzheimer's disease. *Psychological Bulletin, 106,* 377–394.

Northwestern University. (n.d.). *Cognitive neurology and Alzheimer's disease center.* Retrieved from http://www.brain.northwestern.edu

Olazaràn, J., Reisberg, B., Clare, L., Cruz, I., Peña-Casanova, J., del Ser, T., . . . Muñiz, R. (2010). Nonpharmacological therapies in Alzheimer's disease: A systematic review of efficacy. *Dementia and Geriatric Cognitive Disorders, 30,* 161–178.

Owens, R., Farinella, K., & Metz, D. E. (2011). *Introduction to communication disorders: A lifespan evidence-based perspective* (5th ed.). Harlow, UK: Pearson.

Resch, R. C. (2012). *Without utterance: Tales from the other side of language.* Everett, WA: Starseed.

Rogalski, Y., Fleming, V., Bourgeois, M., Key-DeLyria, S., & Quintana, M. (2013). Mild cognitive impairment and healthy aging: Characteristics, evaluation and treatment. *Convention Presentations.* Retrieved from http://www.asha.org/events/convention/handouts/2013/1412-rogalski/

Sarno, J. E., Sarno, M. T., & Levita, E. (1971). Evaluating language improvement after completed stroke. *Archives of Physical Medicine of Rehabilitation, 52*(20), 73–78.

Sarno, M. (2004). Aphasia therapies: Historical perspectives and moral imperatives. In *Challenging aphasia therapies: Broadening the discourse and extending the boundaries* (pp. 19–32). Hove, UK: Psychology Press.

Shadden, B., & Agan, J. (2004). Renegotiation of identity: The social context of aphasia support groups. *Topics in Language Disorders, 24*, 174–186.

Simmons-Mackie, N. (2001). Social approaches to aphasia intervention. In *Language intervention strategies in adult aphasia and related disorders* (4th ed.). Baltimore, MD: Lippencott, Williams, & Wilkins.

Stead, A. L, Donovan, N., & Hoffman, P. (2011). Time of day effects on language discourse in healthy aging and dementia. *Convention Presentations.* Received from http://www.asha.org/events/convention/handouts/2011/stead-donovan-hoffman/

"The Unforgettables" Chorus. (n.d.). *Chorus: People with dementia and their caregivers join in harmony.* Retrieved from http://www.med.nyu.edu/aging/research/chorus

Wisenburn, B., Donahue, C., & Sobrinski, M. (2010). *A meta-analysis of therapy efficacy for agrammatism due to aphasia.* Presentation at the American Speech-Language-Hearing Association Annual Convention, Philadelphia, PA.

World Health Organization. (2014). *International classification of functioning, disability, and health.* Retrieved from http://www.who.int/classifications/icf/en/

Worrall, L., & Yiu, E. (2000). Effectiveness of functional communication therapy by volunteers for people with aphasia following stroke. *Aphasiology, 14*, 911–924.

Worrall, L. E., & Frattali, C. M. (2000). (Eds.), *Neurogenic communication disorders: A functional approach* (pp. 247–259). New York, NY: Thieme Medical.

CHAPTER 5 RECOMMENDED ADDITIONAL SOURCES

Carozza, L. S. (2012). Facilitated narratives in dementia: A conversational analysis approach. *Journal of Intercultural Disciplines, 10*, 103–111.

Carozza, L. (2014). *Communication and aging: Creative approaches to improving the quality of life*. San Diego, CA: Plural.

Fox, C., Morrison, C., Ramig, L., & Sapir, S. (2002). Current perspectives on the LeeSilverman Voice Treatment (LSVT) for individuals with idiopathic Parkinson's disease. *American Journal of Speech Language Pathology, 11*, 111–123.

Heffinger, M., D'Amico, G., Dasilva, M., & Carozza, L. S. (2014). Assessing the effects of cognitive decline on the speech rate of demented and healthy elderly speakers. *The Journal of the Acoustical Society of America, 135*(4), 2293.

Kent, R. D., Kent, J. F., & Weismer, G. (2000). What dysarthrias can tell us about the neural control of speech. *Journal of Phonetics, 28*, 273–302.

Vickers, C. P. (2010). Social networks after aphasia: The impact of aphasia group attendance. *Aphasiology, 24*(6–8), 902–913.

CHAPTER 6

Hearing and Aging

Abbey L. Berg and Yula C. Serpanos

The intersect in human communication that is at the crossroads of hearing and speech communication is of profound importance in understanding many aspects of our behavior as a species, both in development as well as in decline. The study of hearing behavior is essential in understanding one of the most prominent issues facing a "graying" population, that is sensory acuity and accuracy. Audition and perception are challenge areas for people as they move through life changes and deficits in these areas can be extremely self-limiting to an individual whose needs are left unaddressed. This chapter brings forth this important information.

—Linda S. Carozza

"An untreated hearing loss is more noticeable than hearing aids."

—Sergei Kochkin

INTRODUCTION

Over one in every eight (13.3%) adults living in the United States is 65 years of age or older and this number is increasing (Administration on Aging [AOA], 2012; Desai, Pratt, Lentzner, & Robinson,

2001). Adults in the 80 to 84 and 85 years and older range are projected to be the fastest growing population (Desai et al., 2001). In 2011, the number of older adults reached 41.4 million, an increase of 6.3 million or about 18% since 2000 (National Institute on Deafness and Other Communication Disorders [NIDCD], n.d.). Adults who do reach age 65 years can expect to live on average an additional 19.2 years, 20.4 years for females and 17.8 years for males (AOA, 2012; Desai et al., 2001).

Of these adults, approximately 18% of those 45 to 64 years of age, 30% of those 65 to 74 years, and 47% of those 75 years of age or older living in the United States have hearing loss (NIDCD, n.d.). Onset of age-related hearing loss, or presbycusis, is gradual. Presbycusis affects the sensory and/or neural components of the inner ear, auditory nerve, and central auditory system and is characterized by sensorineural hearing loss (SNHL). A typical audiometric configuration is sloping with better hearing sensitivity in the lower frequencies than high frequencies, of mild to moderate degree, and symmetrical in both ears (Howarth & Shone, 2006). Initially, the hearing loss is observed around 4000 Hz with gradual involvement of the mid to lower frequencies.

Chien and Lin (2012) estimated that 23 million adults 50 years and older in the United States have untreated hearing loss and that only one in seven uses a hearing instrument. Reasons why so few older adults use hearing aids include that they are not recommended, that are costly, and/or that there is the perception they are not needed (Gopinath et al., 2011). Unaddressed and uncorrected hearing loss in older adults not only has consequences regarding communication, but also contributes to reduced quality of life (QoL), poor psychosocial well-being, depression, and cognitive dysfunction (Arlinger, 2003).

This chapter addresses the anatomic and physiologic auditory alterations that occur due to presbycusis; the effect of presbycusis on speech perception, particularly in noise; QoL, psycho-social well-being, and depression; cognitive function; assessment of auditory function in the older adult; audiologic rehabilitation; and clinical implications and interventions. An in-depth discussion of these topics is beyond the scope of this chapter; thus the reader is encouraged to examine the reference section for deeper exploration.

ANATOMIC AND PHYSIOLOGIC AUDITORY ALTERATIONS DUE TO PRESBYCUSIS

It is difficult to separate the effects of auditory peripheral pathology (hearing sensitivity or acuity) from the central auditory system, which is responsible for interpretation of the spoken message. With age, the auditory system changes, as do other bodily systems. Thus, the effects of auditory peripheral pathology typically coexist with the effects of biologic aging (Willott, 1996). For example, the ability to perceive speech given the level of hearing sensitivity is often more impaired than expected in the older adult. This phenomenon is known as phonemic regression and does not occur in younger individuals with hearing loss (Tyberghein, 1996).

Anatomic and Physiologic Changes in the Outer and Middle Ear (Conductive Mechanism)

Although the effect on hearing acuity is minor, differences in the older individuals' pinna, external auditory meatus and ossicles have been noted (Howarth & Shone, 2006). Specifically, the cartilaginous portion of the external auditory canal often collapses (Chandler, 1964) and there is also stiffening or lack of elasticity of the tympanic membrane (Rossenwasser, 1964) and ossicular chain can occur (Belal, 1975).

Anatomic and Physiologic Changes in the Sensory (Cochlea/Inner Ear) and Neural Mechanisms

As previously noted, the high-frequency outer hair cells, located at the basal end of the cochlea, are first impaired, with involvement eventually extending to the mid- to low-frequency regions. The outer hair cells amplify sounds and enhance auditory sensitivity. In addition, the outer hair cells contribute to cochlear nonlinearities as well as efferent system function, important for auditory feedback and the reduction of background noise to the auditory system (Frisina, 2001).

The tonotopic organization or frequency mapping of the outer hair cells to structures in the higher auditory pathway is disrupted. For example, the high-frequency region of the outer hair cells located on the basal end of the cochlea must accurately connect to the ventral (high-frequency region) of the inferior colliculus (IC). When the high-frequency outer hair cells are damaged, neural input to the ventral region of the IC is weakened (Willott, 1996). In addition, the ventral region of the IC begins to respond to low- and mid-frequency sounds, thus "over-amplifying" these frequencies. This is an example of a negative effect of neural plasticity; the reorganization of the ventral region of the IC occurs as a result of the elimination or interruption of the now damaged high-frequency outer hair cells (Kaas, 1991).

Loss of neural cell bodies of the auditory nerve, the spiral ganglion cells, occurs. The stria vascularis degenerates with age, reducing the production of endolymph, which contributes to and is necessary for the transmission of sounds to the auditory nerve (Schuknecht et al., 1974).

Important in the neural coding of sounds is the interaction between the excitatory and inhibitory synapses. Impaired inhibitory circuits due to age-related cochlear pathology and/or age-related central auditory dysfunction results in increased difficulty perceiving speech in less than advantageous listening environments. The inhibitory synapses activated by the inhibitory neurotransmitter glycine, found in the cochlear nucleus, have been shown to decrease with age in mice bred with age-related cochlear pathology (Willott, Carlson, Brownfield, & Bross, 1995). Another inhibitory neurotransmitter, GABA, as well as GABA presynaptic terminals and receptors found in the IC, have also been found to be reduced in aging Fischer 344 rats (Caspary, Milbrandt, & Helfert, 1995). Loss of neuronal cell volumes in structures in the higher auditory pathways (i.e., anteroventral cochlear nucleus, the octopus cell area of the posteroventral cochlear nucleus, and layer III of the dorsal cochlear nucleus) has been observed (Willott, Bross, & McFadden, 1992). Each region of the central auditory system contributes to different neural circuits that support specific auditory functions; thus any alteration will have an impact on auditory perception (Willott, 1996).

Age-related hearing loss typically involves alterations in both the peripheral and central auditory systems. Biochemical and metabolic changes, administration of ototoxic medications, heredity and previous exposure to noise all contribute to structural changes in hearing. Tonotopic reorganization or remapping of the peripheral and higher auditory structures, loss of neurons, presynaptic terminals and receptors, reduced cell volumes, and disruption of the excitatory-inhibitory neural circuits result in negative consequences regarding hearing and speech perception in older individuals that do not occur in younger individuals with hearing loss.

Gender Differences

Jerger, Chmiel, Stach, and Spretnjak (1993) found that males had greater high-frequency hearing losses above 1000 Hz compared to females, attributed to greater cardiovascular disease observed in older males compared to older females. Of interest is that elevated (poorer) low-frequency hearing thresholds have been observed with increasing age in females relative to males (Erdman & Demorest, 1998; Hayes & Jerger, 1979; Megighian, Savastano, Salvador, Frigo, & Bolzan, 2000; Pearson et al., 1995). Several explanations have been posited. First, microvascular disease often involves the stria vascularis. The low frequencies would be the most affected as the blood supply is distal at the apical end of the cochlea (Gates, Cobb, D'Agostino, & Wolf, 1993). Second, cardiovascular disease may have a more pronounced effect on hearing in women than men (Lee, Matthews, Mills, Dubno, & Adkins, 1998a, 1998b). Although the most pronounced auditory difference between males and females is observed in pure-tone thresholds, effects of medications and genetics have also demonstrated differential effects (Helfer, 2001).

Gender differences regarding the effects of hearing loss have been found, which may have a gender-specific impact regarding QoL.

THE EFFECT OF PRESBYCUSIS ON SPEECH PERCEPTION

Older adults often note that the inability to understand speech is most frustrating even when the hearing loss is mild. The loss of cochlear neurons with concomitant progressive loss of speech recognition abilities with a stable pure-tone audiogram is not uncommon (Howarth & Shone, 2006).

Speech recognition in the presence of background noise poses greater difficulties for the older adult than for the young adult (Working Group on Speech Understanding and Aging, 1988). Frisina and Frisina (1997) recruited young and old adults to perform a variety of speech recognition tasks in quiet and noisy conditions. Older participants were assigned to different subgroups based on their degree of hearing loss. One subgroup of older adults, "the golden ears," had pure-tone hearing sensitivity in a quiet condition similar to younger participants. Despite the equivalence in pure-tone findings, "the golden ears" subgroup of older adults had significantly poorer speech recognition abilities in the presence of background noise compared to the younger participants (Frisina & Frisina, 1997). This finding was attributed to deficits in auditory temporal processing not present in the young participants (Snell, 1997).

Schneider and Pichora-Fuller (2001) found that the difficulty older adults often experience perceiving speech in typical listening environments, even with intact hearing sensitivity, could partially be attributed to loss of neural synchrony, which (1) compromises the coding of the temporal fine structure of speech, (2) contributes to poorer frequency discrimination at low frequencies, and (3) is important in maintaining the harmonic structure of speech sounds to separate speech from background noise. Disruptions in temporal processing could also account for the difficulty older adults experience perceiving rapid speech and speech in reverberant conditions (Schneider & Pichora-Fuller, 2001; Willott, 1996).

Studies have indicated that the performance of older adults, independent of hearing loss, on binaural and spatial separation tasks is poorer relative to young adults (Abel, Giguere, Consoli, & Papsin, 2000; Cranford, Andres, Piatz, & Reissig, 1993; Strouse,

Ashmead, Ohde, & Grantham, 1998). Koehnke and Besing (2001) matched a young and an old adult, both with normal hearing sensitivity through 2000 Hz, dropping to a precipitous loss for frequencies above. In a reverberant condition the older adult had higher (poorer) speech thresholds when speech and noise were both at 0 degrees azimuth (the front of the face); and slightly lower (better) thresholds when the speech signal and noise were separated 180 degrees (Koehnke & Besing, 2001). Although the young adult had lower (better) thresholds when the speech signal and noise were separated 180 degrees than at 0 degrees, lower (better) thresholds were observed relative to the older adult in this condition. This study is consistent with what was observed by McFadden and Willott (1994) who examined spatial separation in C57 mice—mice bred with peripheral pathology. In their study, young and middle-aged C57 mice were presented with a signal that was fixated at +90 degrees azimuth and the noise was presented at +90 degrees (signal and noise at same location, the left side), 0 degrees (signal to the left side and noise in front of the face), and −90 degrees (signal to the left side and noise to the right side). For both the young and middle-aged mice, thresholds were higher (poorer) with the noise; however, the young mice had lower (better) thresholds than the older mice when the signal and noise were separated. In other words, the young C57 benefited from the spatial separation of the signal from the noise; the older C57 mice did not (McFadden & Willott, 1994). This is yet another example of how age-related hearing loss manifests itself differently than hearing loss in younger individuals, even when hearing thresholds are similar.

Most recently, Wöstmann and colleagues (2015) examined the brain's alpha waves in hearing tasks administered to young adults (20–30 years of age) and older adults (60–70 years of age). Listening effort by the listener is measured by the strength of these waves. Both the young and older adults listened to two numbers presented in background noise to simulate a noisy environment typically encountered. By pressing a button, participants indicated whether the second number was higher or lower than the first. While the participants were focused on the number task, the researchers manipulated the acoustic quality of the speech signal and measuring their alpha waves. Older adults benefited more from a better quality of acoustic speech signal in background noise than the younger adults as reflected by their perception of the difficulty of the task and their alpha waves. These researchers indicated that hearing aids adapted to listeners' brain activity might improve speech comprehension in less than advantageous listening environments (Wöstmann et al., 2015).

> Speech perception abilities in the older adult in noisy or less than advantageous listening environments are poorer than what younger adults with hearing loss experience. Increased speech perceptual difficulties will have an impact on the older persons' QoL as greater communication effort is required.

HEARING LOSS AND COGNITIVE CHANGES IN NORMAL AGING AND DEMENTIAS

Especially challenging for the older adult is the ability to divide their attention and quickly divert it between simultaneous mental activities (Anderson, Craik, & Naveh-Benjamin, 1998) and to ignore distracting and irrelevant stimuli (Barr & Giambra, 1990). The ability to divide attention and/or simultaneously attend to multiple stimuli and tune out extraneous stimuli is known as executive control and is a function of working memory (Baddeley, 1996).

With age, a general slowing of perception and cognition occurs, along with reduced working memory capacity and efficiency of executive function regarding attention (Wingfield & Tun, 2001). Reduced auditory stimulation that results from longstanding untreated hearing loss appears to alter central brain function, which would have an impact on cognitive processes. Lin, Ferrucci, Metter, An, Zonderman, and Resnick (2011) observed an independent association of severity of hearing loss and poorer performance in mental status, memory, and executive function in a study of 347 individuals over 55 years of age. A more recent prospective investigation of 1,984 older adults (mean age = 77 years) revealed a greater risk for cognitive dysfunction in those with hearing loss with as much as a 40% faster rate of cognitive decline compared to normal hearing counterparts (Lin et al., 2013).

Speed of Speech Processing

By nature, speech is rapid and this has a greater impact on the older adult than younger individuals. Speech varies and is influenced by the speaker (both inter- and intraspeaker) as well as linguistic context. A challenge for the older adult, even with good hearing, is to "normalize" speech so that speech perception independent of the speaker can occur (Wingfield & Tun, 2001). For the older adult this task takes more effort than for a young individual (Sommers, 1997). And in fact, Wingfield and Ducharme (1999) demonstrated that older adults preferred and selected slower speech rates than young adults.

An additional constraint facing the older adult is the determination of word boundaries, which requires knowledge of linguistic context. In natural speech, words tend to run together. In highly predictable or redundant contexts, such as, "He is going to the store," speech is even more underarticulated, resulting in additional difficulty for older adults. As speech is often articulated, and underarticulated at that, at a rate of 2.3 to 3 words per seconds, the older adult must also identify words, their meanings, and the syntactic and semantic structures of the intent of the message at the phrase, sentence, and discourse levels (Wingfield & Tun, 2001).

> Attending to the rapid speech signal requires greater effort for older individuals than younger. This additional effort may contribute to reduced QoL as increased attention, requests for clarifications, and fatigue occur.

Working Memory

A multicomponent definition of working memory includes the temporary or short-term storage and manipulation of information in an episodic buffer system and retention of speech for incorporation with what was heard (Baddeley, 2003; Wingfield & Tun, 2001). Wingfield, Stine, Lahar, and Aberdeen (1988) found that young and older adults performed similarly when the memory task was simple. With age, however, significant differences occurred. As the memory task became more complex, multiple cognitive processes were required. Three types of memory span tests—digit, word, and sentence—were administered to three groups of participants: young adults (mean age = 19 years), young-older adults (mean age = 65 years), and old-older adults (mean age = 75 years) (Wingfield et al., 1988). All three groups performed similarly on the digit memory span task; they recalled the same number of digits. Group differences occurred for the word memory span test. The young adults performed best (recalled a greater number of words) compared to the young-older and old-older adults; the young-older adults recalled a greater number of words than the old-older participants. Both the digit and word memory span tasks are considered tests of short-term memory because these tasks require the individual to hold temporarily and recall without manipulating the information required of working memory (Wingfield et al., 1988). For the sentence memory span task, all three groups performed more poorly than on the digit and word memory span tasks. The pattern of performance, however, remained the same. That is, the young adults performed better than both the young-older and old-older adults, and the young-older adults performed better than the old-older adults. The sentence span task taps working memory. Participants were required to listen to a set of sentences, indicate if the sentence made sense, to ensure participants were attending to its meaning, and then finally to recall the final word of each sentence (Wingfield et al., 1988). To perform this task correctly, the individual must hold the final word of the sentence in memory while processing subsequent sentences for meaning (Daneman & Carpenter, 1980). Evidence exists that indicates that older adults experience greater difficulty comprehending and recalling syntactically complex and/or syntactically ambiguous sentences that tax working memory (Kemtes & Kemper, 1997; Zurif, Swinney, Prather, Wingfield, & Brownell, 1995).

> Syntactically complex sentences tax working memory in the older adult.

Linguistic Knowledge and Context

When sentences are syntactically correct and meaningful, older adults can use their linguistic knowledge to compensate somewhat for speech that is rapid or presented in noise or distractions (Wingfield, Poon, Lombardi, & Lowe, 1985). This ability is attributed to contextual support for memory (Wingfield et al., 1985). For example, Wingfield, Aberdeen, and Stine (1991) presented recorded words that varied in word-onset (gating) duration to young and old participants. In other words, participants heard the first 50 to 100 msec of the word until it was correctly identified. Without the benefit of context, young and old adults performed similarly; that is both groups correctly identified the word after only hearing 50% to 60% of the word onset information. In contrast, when these words were embedded in a sentence with context, the older adults performed better than the young adults; specifically, the older adults only required 20 to 30% of the word onset information to identify correctly the target word. This study is an example of how linguistic context, even when limited (Grosjean, 1996), can compensate for the acoustical deficits in the speech signal often encountered by the older adult (Wingfield et al., 1985).

A caveat exists, however. Although older adults are able to use quite knowledge and context quite effectively, this appears not to hold true in some situations. Specifically, when the word cannot be identified until the speaker speaks more of the sentence, the older adult must retain the unclear elements until clarified by the speaker. As older adults often have a limited temporary or short-term memory capacity, they may still be less effective than young adults in using linguistic context (Wingfield & Tun, 2001). Wingfield, Alexander, and Cavigelli (1994) presented young and older adults with computer-edited words that were difficult to identify in isolation (low-context). When such a word was presented along with an additional one, two, three, and four words of prior context, the older adults performed better (made better use of context) than the younger adults. However, when the word was presented with the one, two, three, and four words from a sentence that followed the word that was difficult to identify, the older adults made less use of this form of context than the younger adults. These results indicate that although older adults with presbycusis can often correctly identify and recall words with linguistic assist, enormous effort is required (Wingfield et al., 1994). This extra effort needed for speech perceptual processing prevents the older adult with presbycusis to expend the effort required for encoding words in memory for later use (Pichora-Fuller, Schneider, & Daneman, 1995; Rabbitt, 1991; Tun, 1998).

Studies have also found that older adults can effectively use syntactic prosody to aid in sentence comprehension (Shattuck-Hugnagel & Turk, 1996), recall (Kjelgaard, Titone, & Wingfield, 1999), and individual word recognition (Wingfield, Lindfield, & Goodglass, 2000). Exaggerated prosody and/or an excessively slower rate of speech, however, have been found to have a negative impact on communication. This type of speech can be interpreted as demeaning or patronizing and is sometimes used by health professionals and caregivers when speaking to older individuals (Kemper & Harden, 1999).

> Older adults' linguistic knowledge can compensate for rapid speech and/or speech perceptual abilities in some conditions and environments.

Hearing Loss and Dementias

A higher prevalence of hearing loss among individuals with dementia, and greater incidence of dementia with increased severity of loss, has been found (Herbst & Humphrey, 1980; Weinstein, 1986). Lin, Metter, O'Brien, Resnick, Zonderman, and

Ferrucci (2011) conducted a longitudinal prospective study of hearing on 639 adults 36 to 90 years without initial diagnosis of dementia. Over a median follow-up period of nearly 12 years, 58 individuals were diagnosed with incident all-cause dementia with hearing loss present in more than one-third of those older than 60 years. These investigators also found that hearing loss was independently associated with incident all-cause dementia and a linearly increased risk of all-cause dementia with severity of loss. Unknown is whether hearing loss is an early modifiable indicator for early stage dementia (Lin et al., 2011).

In a cohort of 100 individuals with dementia compared to a cohort of matched controls, an association between the severity of hearing loss and cognitive dysfunction as measured by the Mini-Mental State Examination (MMSE) was found (Uhlmann, Larson, Rees, Koepsell, & Duckert, 1989). Lin and colleagues (2013) found that of 1,162 individuals with hearing loss greater than 25 dB HL at the beginning of their study, cognitive decline was 41% greater than those with normal hearing as measured by their MMSE scores, a measure of global function (Lin et al., 2013). Furthermore, individuals with hearing loss had rates of cognitive decline 32% greater than those with normal hearing on the Digit Symbol Substitution test, a measure of executive function. These authors also noted that individuals with hearing loss at the beginning of their study had a 24% greater risk of developing cognitive impairment than individuals with normal hearing, supporting findings by other studies (Herbst & Humphrey, 1980; Weinstein, 1986). No statistically significant association between hearing-aid use and rate of cognitive decline or risk of cognitive impairment were found, also supporting findings by Allen and colleagues (2003). Following hearing-aid fitting in older individuals with primary dementia and mild hearing loss, Allen and colleagues (2003) found improvements in speech intelligibility and hearing handicap over a 6-month period, but no benefit was noted in cognitive function or activities of daily living.

An association between dementia and hearing loss has been found.

Visual Acuity and Auditory Function

It would be remiss not to address the effect of dual-sensory impairments (DSI), specifically vision and hearing, on cognition. Visual impairments are not uncommon in the older adult and include macular degeneration, cataracts, and glaucoma. Macular degeneration is prevalent, occuring in over 1.75 million older adults in the United States and is estimated to increase to over 3 million by the year 2020 (Friedman et al., 2004). The overall prevalence of cataracts increases with age with rates of 40% and 60% in older adults over age 70 and 75 years respectively (Acosta et al., 2006). In 2010 the prevalence of glaucoma reached over 2.7 million adults and is projected to reach over 4.2 million by 2030; the most dramatic increase occurs in adults 75 years and older (National Eye Institute, n.d.).

An estimated 1 in 9, or 11.3%, of all adults 80 years or older has a DSI (Swenor, Ramulu, Willis, Friedman, & Lin, 2013). Already noted is the increased rate of cognitive decline in individuals with hearing loss (Lin et al., 2011; Lin et al., 2013) and DSI may accelerate cognitive impairment, decline, or dementia (Swenor et al., 2013). Also not well understood or researched are effective evidence-based audiologic rehabilitative strategies and interventions to treat and/or intervene for the older adult with DSI.

> Dual-sensory impairments are not uncommon in the older adult and must be taken into account when designing rehabilitation and intervention strategies. The loss of yet another sense can contribute to reduced QoL.

Psychosocial Implications

Unaddressed and uncorrected hearing loss in older adults not only has consequences for communication, but also contributes to poor psychosocial well-being, depression, and cognitive dysfunction. Older hearing-impaired individuals who do not use amplification exhibit characteristics of reduced social activity, and present increased reports of sadness, worry, and depression, leading to a reduced perception of well-being and QoL (Arlinger, 2003; Gates & Mills, 2005). In a large-scale study of 2,688 older adults (mean age = 69 years), Dalton et al. (2003) found a relationship between the severity of hearing loss and reduced QoL based on measures of hearing handicap, self-reported communication difficulty, and health-related activities of daily living including physical, social, emotional, and mental health.

In addition to stress, depression, sadness, and reduced perception of well-being, researchers at Johns Hopkins found that individuals with hearing deficits were significantly more likely to be hospitalized and to have prolonged periods of physical illness or injury than individuals with normal hearing (Genther, Frick, Chen, Betz, & Lin, 2013). Data were analyzed from 1,140 men and women aged 70 and older with hearing loss and 529 normal hearing controls (Genther et al., 2013).

In summary, perceptual and cognitive slowing occurs with age. Evidence exists that hearing loss appears to be associated with greater and more rapid cognitive decline and impairment in older adults with hearing loss than older adults with normal hearing. The added attention required to "hear" the acoustic speech signal, speaker, and message limits the available resources that can be allocated to other cognitive tasks. A reduction of working memory capacity and executive function in allocating and sharing attention then results (Pichora-Fuller, Schneider, & Daneman, 1995; Rabbitt, 1991; Tun, 1998). The ability to apprehend, encode, store, recall, and understand speech, especially in less than advantageous listening environments, pose even greater challenges for the older adult with age-related hearing loss than for younger individuals with hearing loss. Presbycusis and cognitive decline and impairment may share a neuropathologic basis that has yet to be identified (Lin et al., 2013). Finally, hearing loss that results in communication difficulties also can lead to social isolation, a known contributor to cognitive decline and impairment, and reduced QoL.

Not well understood is whether or not audiologic rehabilitation and use of amplification would stave off cognitive decline and impairment. A positive finding is that linguistic knowledge and context, as well as the ability to use prosody effectively, are often well preserved in the normal aging older adult and can help to facilitate speech recognition.

ASSESSMENT OF AUDIOLOGIC
ACUITY AND FUNCTION

The concomitant changes of the aging auditory, cognitive, visual, and physical systems in older adults require that special consideration be given to this population during audiologic assessment and rehabilitation services. An important initial factor for the practitioner to consider is the residential status of the older adult. Approximately 4% of adults 65 years and older live in facilities such as adult care, assisted living, or nursing homes, while only about 29% of noninstitutionalized older adults live alone (Administration on Aging, 2013). The American Speech-Language-Hearing Association (ASHA) 1997 Guidelines for Audiology Service Delivery in Nursing Homes (ASHA, 1997b) recommends accommodations in the delivery of services and comprehensive audiologic management for adults in these settings. For example, since sound-treated test booths may not be available in these facilities, the omission of lower frequencies (i.e., 250 Hz, 500 Hz) and use of insert earphones should be considered to offset the influence of background ambient noise on hearing threshold outcomes.

Older individuals are likely to be accompanied by family/caretakers during audiologic services in clinical settings. It is important, therefore, to include relevant parties in obtaining information during the case history, in counseling sessions regarding audiologic outcomes and recommendations, and during hearing-aid and hearing assistive technology (HAT) fitting and orientation appointments. In addition to auditory and speech perception difficulty often experienced by older adults, factors such as memory loss, diminished visual acuity, and physical limitations will need to be considered. Depending on the needs of the individual, audiologists may need to reinstruct during assessment procedures, repeat and rephrase information about hearing loss or hearing device operation, and allow more time during service appointments (DeBonis & Donohue, 2008).

Otoscopy should be conducted with a careful focus on potential ear canal collapse when using headphones, and presence of excess cerumen or hair in the outer ear canal. Ear canal collapse and impacted cerumen may inflate hearing threshold outcomes, leading to an inaccurate diagnosis of conductive hearing loss. Randolph and Schow (1983) determined that up to 16% of adults 60 to 79 years have collapsible ear canals when tested with headphones, and reports indicate that a higher prevalence (~41%) exists among older nursing home residents 80 years or older (Schow & Goldbaum, 1980).

Excess cerumen and hair growth in the outer ear canal can hinder accurate measurements in amplification fittings such as during real ear testing or earmold impressions. Cerumen impaction is a common occurrence among individuals over age 65 years, with estimates ranging from 19% to 65% and older adults in nursing homes at the upper range of prevalence reports (Roland et al., 2008). In older men, excess hair growth is often found around the pinna and tragus portion, in addition to the lateral lining of the ear canal, which can impede normal cerumen migration and lead to impaction (Hawke & McCombe, 1995).

During pure-tone threshold testing, older adults may be more cautious and slower to respond to the signals (Rees & Botwinick, 1971). Longer response times during pure-tone audiometry and reinstruction when necessary are recommended to avoid potential suprathreshold outcomes. In older individuals, it may be best to perform threshold and suprathreshold speech recognition tasks prior to pure-tone measures to gauge better the degree of loss (DeBonis & Donohue, 2008). Due to the noted effects of presbycusis on speech perception, particularly in the presence of background noise (see section above on The Effect of Presbycusis on Speech Perception), speech-in-noise recognition tasks should be included in the audiologic assessment protocol for the older adult.

Self-assessment scales on communicative function and the social and emotional effects of hearing loss are essential components of the assessment and rehabilitative process in older adults. There are several adult functional diagnostic tools (e.g., Hearing Performance Inventory [HPI; Giolas, Owens, Lamb, & Schubert, 1979]; Hearing Handicap Inventory for the Elderly [HHIE; Ventry & Weinstein, 1982; Weinstein & Ventry, 1983]; Communication Profile of Hearing Impaired [CPHI; Walden, Demorest, & Hepler, 1984]; Speech, Spatial and Qualities of Hearing Scale [SSQ; Gatehouse & Noble, 2004]) as well as screening tools (e.g., HHIE-S [Ventry & Weinstein, 1983]; Self-Assessment of Communication [SAC] and Significant Other Assessment of Communication

[SOAC; Schow & Nerbonne, 1982]) that help to identify hearing disability or handicap, and are beneficial for counseling the older adult, their family members/caregivers, and help to guide the practitioner in planning services (ASHA, 1997a, 1998).

Modifications and adjustments in testing procedures with the older adult are often necessary. Functional measures (e.g., self-reports, questionnaires) are important components to include in audiologic assessments to understand and address those listening situations that have a negative effect on QoL.

AMPLIFICATION SYSTEMS AND HEARING ASSISTIVE DEVICES

Audiologic rehabilitation (AR) for adults with presbycusis consists of varied and combined intervention strategies using devices as well as evaluative or therapeutic services geared to improve overall communication. Electronic personal amplification systems including hearing aids or implantable devices, and HAT, are considered the best treatment options for remediating the hearing loss resulting from presbycusis, as it is not medically correctable at this time (Sprinzl & Riechelmann, 2010). Hearing-aid use among adults decreases the psychological, social, and emotional effects of SNHL and improves QoL (Chisolm, Noe, McArdle, & Abrams, 2007). In a survey of close to 4,000 hearing impaired adults age 50 years of age and older and their friends and family, Kochkin and Rogin (2000) reported that those fit with hearing aids showed benefit in areas of physical, emotional, mental, and social well-being.

Garstecki and Erler (1998) found gender differences related to hearing aid use attributed to the degree of loss, social support, personal reaction to instrument use, comfort, expectations, motivation, and perceived value of improved communication. A survey of 131 hearing aid candidates 65 years of age and older revealed that males fit with hearing aids perceived the instruments as less stigmatizing, were less likely to fault others for ineffective communication, and were more accepting of hearing loss than males who did not acquire amplification. Females fitted with amplification displayed less hearing handicap and depressive symptoms than females not fitted with hearing aids. Though further study is indicated, gender differences may require consideration in the hearing management of older individuals (Garstecki & Erler, 1998).

A comprehensive rehabilitative plan for hearing-aid fitting in adults must include family and/or caregivers and incorporates assessment, treatment planning, selection, verification, orientation, and validation. The use and choice of hearing technology is determined by many considerations such as the degree and type of loss, instrument features of the amplification systems(s) and HAT, as well as individuals' motivation, lifestyle, cosmetic preference, device cost, and user ability (ASHA, 1998). For example, older adults with diminished visual acuity or limited manual dexterity may be unable to manipulate the batteries or controls in small devices.

Hearing aids refer to removable amplification devices intended to be worn daily in all listening conditions throughout the waking hours of the user. Instruments vary in style, power, technology, and wearing options (i.e., extended wear, disposable). Traditional hearing aid styles include behind-the-ear (BTE) and variations of custom in-ear devices (in-the-ear [ITE], in-the-canal [ITC], and completely-in-the-canal [CIC]). The many component options to consider include the type of signal processing (digital, analog), microphone directionality, response channels and program memories, noise reduction or compression circuits to improve listening in background noise or to loud signals, and telecoil controls (T-coil, T-switch) for telephone use. (For more detailed information on hearing aids, see Dillon, 2012; Valente, Hosford-Dunn, & Roeser, 2007.)

Surgically implanted amplification devices such as middle ear implants or cochlear implants offer distinct advantages to individuals who may not benefit from conventional hearing aids. Middle-ear implants incorporate an implanted transducer on the ossicular chain to enhance sound transmission to the cochlea without occlusion of the outer ear, providing cosmetic appeal and reduction of acoustic feedback for candidates with moderate to severe SNHL (Gangadhara Somayaji & Aroor, 2013). Cochlear implants embed electrodes in the temporal lobe region to stimulate the auditory nerve, beneficial for those with significant (severe-to-profound) cochlear hearing impairment with concomitant poor speech recognition abilities (Clark, 2003; Zeng, 2004).

Binaural amplification fitting is considered standard care for individuals with bilateral symmetric SNHL and is typically presented in presbycusis. The benefits of binaural amplification particularly in the elderly include improved sound localization and speech perception in noise, tinnitus suppression, and prevention of auditory deprivation (Arlinger, 2003; Holmes, 2003). However, for some older adults binaural amplification may not be beneficial. Age-related changes in the central auditory nervous system may cause an inefficient transfer of interhemispheric auditory information leading to asymmetry in dichotic listening and binaural interference (Baran, 2002). Walden and Walden (2005) evaluated unilateral and bilateral aided speech recognition in noise measures using the Quick Speech-in-Noise test (QuickSIN) in 28 older adults (mean age = 75 years). For the majority of individuals, results indicated better aided speech-in-noise performance in the monaural condition. The authors concluded that binaural amplification might not always be the best fitting strategy in background noise situations for all older adults (Walden & Walden, 2005). These findings support a patient-centered approach to hearing-aid fitting. Alternative strategies, including monaural fitting and HAT, are options to consider in the older adult.

Hearing aids may not benefit users in all communicative situations and can be limited in compromised listening conditions such as in distance or noisy distracting backgrounds. Thus, HAT should be considered separately or in combination with a hearing aid or implantable amplification. Examples of HAT include listening (e.g., frequency modulated [FM] or infrared systems, telephone amplifiers), communication (e.g., closed-captioning, texting devices, captioned telephones), alerting and/or signaling devices (e.g., visual or vibrating alarms, door signalers; ASHA, n.d.). HATs are used independently or with hearing aids and/or implantable instruments to enhance audibility in situations including personal communication, broadcast or electronic media, on the telephone, and to environmental stimuli. FM systems improve speech audibility by transmitting the speech signal picked up by a microphone near the speech source directly to a receiver worn by the user. Potential communicative breakdowns caused by distance, background noise, or room reverberation are often decreased or eliminated.

Assistive listening technology can be helpful for the older adult with hearing impairment living independently or in an assistive care facility, and may be a more appropriate and beneficial alternative to unsuccessful hearing-aid use (Valente et al., 2006). Frequency modulated (FM) systems in particular have been shown to improve sound quality and speech recognition performance, as well as reduce perceived handicap in older adults (Chisolm, Johnson, et al., 2007; Jerger, Chmiel, Florin, Pirozzolo, & Wilson, 1996).

A number of self-assessment scales specifically address perception of hearing-aid benefit pre- and postfitting, including the Profile of Hearing Aid Performance (Cox & Gilmore, 1990), Abbreviated Profile of Hearing Aid Benefit (APHAB; Cox & Alexander, 1995), Client Oriented Scale of Improvement (COSI; Dillon, James, & Ginis, 1997), the SSQ (Gatehouse & Noble, 2004), the International Outcome Inventory for Hearing Aids (IOI-HA; Cox, Alexander, & Beyer, 2003) and the Satisfaction with Amplification in Daily Life (SADL; Cox & Alexander, 1999). Outcomes gleaned from these assessments can assist the examiner in determining adjustments necessary in the fitting and provide insight on the individual's expectations with amplification to guide counseling and intervention efforts. Post-hearing aid functional measures also illustrate to the individual that ease of hearing in many situations is much better with the hearing aids than without.

The APHAB evaluates the listener's level of communicative difficulty with 24 items in four categories: ease of communication; communication in reverberant environments; communication in background noise; and aversiveness to environmental sounds. Cox (1997) reported that scores indicating the amount and pattern of disability using the unaided APHAB might be predictive of success with amplification in adults. An example of two hearing aid candidates with similar audiometric profiles illustrated the value of administering the questionnaire. Though audiometric findings would have suggested a similar potential for success with amplification, a higher percentage of reported difficulty was obtained on the unaided APHAB for one of the individuals (Cox, 1997). Hosford-Dunn and Halpern (2000) evaluated outcomes from 375 adults (mostly over age 60 years) on the SADL one year post hearing-aid fitting. Results supported use of the SADL to validate hearing aid satisfaction with applicability to older adults. In a follow-up investigation evaluating the predictive validity of the SADL on the same individuals, Hosford-Dunn and Halpern (2001) concluded that SADL scores yield specific patterns of satisfaction and dissatisfaction that assist in management planning and are predictive of hearing aid fitting success.

> Hearing aids and/or HATs improve QoL in the majority of older adults. The older adult's environment, physical and cognitive capabilities, and auditory requirements need to be considered when recommending and prescribing amplification and/or HATs.

AUDIOLOGIC REHABILITATION (AR) STRATEGIES

The fitting of an amplification system and HAT is just the first step in the AR process. Of equal importance in remediating hearing loss in older adults and to successful hearing-aid fitting is effective education, counseling, and participation in AR services geared to improving communication skills (ASHA, 2006; Boothroyd, 2007). Hearing loss affects not only the older individual with the hearing loss but family and friends as well. Thus, educating and counseling the older adult and family/caregiver(s) on the effects of hearing loss, the benefits and limitations of amplification, and communication strategies are necessary and can prevent unrealistic expectations regarding hearing aid performance (ASHA, 1998; Saunders, Lewis, & Forsline, 2009). In a prospective study of 98 new hearing-aid users, Vuorialho, Karinen, and Sorri (2006) determined that counseling was a cost-effective service that significantly improved hearing-aid use and benefit.

Recently, a shift has emerged in AR paradigm from the main focus on hearing technology to a more person-centered approach

(Hickson, 2012; Hickson & Worrall, 2003). Although advances in hearing- aid technology have occurred, Kochkin (2007) found that 26% of adults with hearing aids wore them less than 4 hours per day and Davis, Smith, Ferguson, Stephens, and Gianopoulis (2007) found that 22% of adults fitted with hearing aids discontinued wearing them. Hearing-aid dissatisfaction stems mainly from the difficulty the older adult with hearing loss experiences hearing in challenging listening environments. Thus, greater emphasis has resulted on self-management programs, such as the Listening and Communication Enhancement (LACE) program (Sweetow & Sabes, 2006) and the Active Communication Education (ACE) program (Hickson, Worrall, & Scarinci, 2007).

The LACE program is completed at home on a computer for 30 minutes per day, 5 days per week for 4 weeks. The three communication domains addressed by this interactive, adaptive computer program are degraded speech, cognitive skills, and compensatory strategies (Sweetow & Sabes, 2006). In contrast, the ACE program involves face-to-face group interactions 2 hours per week for 5 weeks and includes not only the adult with the hearing loss but their significant others. This program is designed to teach problem-solving skills to the older adult to better manage their communication difficulties (Hickson et al., 2007).

Individual and/or group AR services need to include hearing-aid orientation and training in communication strategies, speechreading, and listening (Tye-Murray, 2014). Formal training can be supplemented with home-based, interactive adaptive computerized auditory retraining programs such as the LACE or ACE, which has demonstrated improvements in communication performance in adults (Sweetow & Sabes, 2006; Hickson et al., 2007). Effective communication strategies for instructing the older adult with hearing loss include: (1) watching the speaker's face (speechreading) and body language; (2) asking the speaker specific questions to repair the communication breakdown (e.g., "Did you say you were going the *store*?"); (3) acknowledging the hearing loss (e.g., "I have a hearing loss and it would be helpful if you spoke a bit slower and closer to me."); (4) asking the speaker or group of people the topic of the conversation to bring appropriate vocabulary to the forefront (e.g., the vocabulary for conversing about a sporting event is different than the vocabulary needed to converse about the latest theatre performance); (5) arriving early to a lecture to ensure seating is most conducive for hearing (e.g., in the front, closer to the speaker, not behind a column); and finally (6) consumer awareness of self-help groups, literature, and direction to professional websites for resources that empower, support and provide information for the older adult with hearing loss and their families (Hearing Loss Association of America, n.d.).

In addition to the programs described above, narratives have emerged in which older adults with hearing loss describe their journey to ascribe meaning to their disability (Gregory, 2012). Narratives allow the audiologist to focus on the communication difficulties important to the older adult to ensure better outcomes and understanding of the complexity of their hearing loss, which will hopefully lead to increased acceptance and satisfaction of amplification and AR (Gregory, 2012). The Communication Rings tool was developed to help the older adult with hearing loss identify communication networks, the people important in their lives and the impact of hearing loss on those relationships (Montano & Almakadma, 2012). The intent of the Communication Rings is to increase, develop, and appreciate relevant communication goals for the person with hearing loss and their significant others' needs, and the environments that pose the greatest challenges. Individuals with hearing loss who have strong social networks and support manage their hearing loss better than individuals who do not (Montano & Almakadma, 2012).

Another aspect of AR is working with significant others in their speaking to maximize successful communication outcomes. Acoustic parameters of clear speech include slower speaking rate, stop bursts of almost all word-final consonants released and alveolar flapping reduced, both consonants and vowels lengthened, consonant-to-vowel intensity increased, acoustic space between vowels increased, first formant of vowels is higher, mean and range of fundamental frequency are greater, and speech volume 5 to 8 dB sound pressure level greater in intensity (Caissie & Tranquilla, 2010).

Caissie et al. (2005) trained two groups of spouses in clear speech versus conversational speech. Group 1 consisted of spouses who received formal clear speech training (one 45-minute session) and Group 2 spouses were just instructed to speak clearly. Spouses recorded sentences at three different time periods; before intervention, 1 week after intervention, and 1 month after intervention. Sentences were played to a group of individuals with normal hearing and individuals with hearing loss (65 dB HL loss; not their spouses) in the presence of a multitalker babble noise at a signal-to-noise ratio of +10 dB. Participants with hearing loss who asked speakers to speak clearly received clearer speech. However, the speakers trained in clear speech used more of the acoustic parameters of clear speech, had more stable speech, and participants had higher speech recognition scores than speakers just told to speak more clearly. Of note, participants with hearing loss performed just as well as normal hearing participants on speech recognition tasks.

In summary, comprehensive rehabilitative plans that involve not just the older adult with hearing loss but their significant others' as well, have a strong impact on hearing-aid success (Kochkin et al., 2010). In an evidence-based review of the literature, Hawkins (2005) found that adults who participated in group AR programs that focused on communication strategies with counseling showed better use of hearing aids and communication strategies, and a reduction in self-perceived hearing handicap. (For more in-depth information on counseling and AR services, see Clark & English, 2013; Montano & Spitzer, 2013.)

> In addition to hearing aids and/or HATs use of clear speech, implementation of conversational repair and anticipatory strategies will enhance successful communication, reduce isolation, frustration, and empower the older adult with hearing loss, thus improving their QoL.

CLINICAL IMPLICATIONS AND INTERVENTIONS

Based on the information presented in this chapter, the strategies listed below have been found to help the older adult with hearing loss to communicate more easily:

- *Linguistic knowledge:* As linguistic knowledge often remains well preserved and is often better in older adults than younger adults, context-based communication to facilitate comprehension has been shown to be beneficial. Informing the older adult of the topic of conversation and rephrasing have also been shown to be effective strategies for improving communication.

■ *Prosody:* Use of *appropriate* prosody (e.g., pitch contour, word stress) and slower rate of speech can help the older adult mark syntactic boundaries. Training the older adults' family members/caregivers in a "clear" speech program demonstrated improved communication.

■ *Amplification:* Hearing aids and HAT are beneficial. The advantages and limitations of these instruments requires explanation if the older adult with hearing loss is to benefit the most from their use and to avoid unrealistic expectations. Unaided and aided self-assessment scales identify and provide insight as to the psychosocial effects of the hearing loss and assist in treatment planning geared to the older adults' audiologic challenges.

■ *AR strategies that include counseling:* Hearing loss affects the entire family. The auditory difficulties experienced by the older adult with hearing loss are frustrating for both the person with the hearing loss and their communication partners. Audiologic rehabilitation strategies must address the frustrations of both the person with the hearing loss and their family members/caregivers. Communication repair strategies require implementation by both parties. Specifically, the older adult with hearing loss must guide and convey to their communication partner where the communication breakdown occurred (e.g., "Did you say . . . "). The communication partner needs to make sure the older adult knows the topic to take advantage of context and linguistic knowledge. These strategies improve communication even in challenging listening environments.

In summary, presbycusis is different from the hearing loss that occurs in younger individuals. Age-related hearing loss is complex and involves alterations in the peripheral and central auditory systems as well as challenges regarding cognition and working memory. Amplification and auditory rehabilitation must account for and address these differences and capitalize on the older adults' linguistic knowledge and ability to use effectively linguistic context. Specifically, assessments that target the auditory structures impaired in older individuals need to be developed. Amplification that can account for inter- and intraspeaker variability warrants consideration. Audiologic rehabilitation that includes not only strategies and training for the speaker but also provides guidance for the older individual with the hearing loss to communicate and accommodate better his or her communicative needs has been shown to be most effective. These strategies will best address and have a positive impact on improving the QoL for older individuals with hearing loss.

REFERENCES

Abel, S. M., Giguere, C., Consoli, A., & Papsin, B. C. (2000). The effect of aging on horizontal plane sound localization. *Journal of the Acoustical Society of America, 108,* 743–752.

Acosta, R., Hoffmeister, L. Roman, R., Comas, M., Castillas, M., & Castells, X. (2006). Systematic review of population-based studies of the prevalence of cataracts. *Archivos de la Sociedad Española de Oftalmología, 81,* 509–516.

Administration on Aging. (2013). A profile of older Americans: 2013. *U.S. Department of Health and Human Services.* Retrieved July 20, 2014, from http://www.aoa.gov/Aging_Statistics/Profile/index.aspx

Administration on Aging–Administration for Community Living. (2012). A profile of older Americans: 2012. *U.S. Department of Health and Human Services.* Retrieved July 8, 2014, from http://www.aoa.gov/Aging_Statistics/Profile/2012/docs/2012profile.pdf

Allen, N. H., Burns, A., Newton, V., Hickson, F., Ramsden, R., Rogers, J., . . . Morris, J. (2003). The effects of improving hearing in dementia. *Age and Ageing, 32*(2), 189–193.

American Speech-Language-Hearing Association. (n.d.). *Hearing assistive technology.* Retrieved July 29, 2014, from http://www.asha.org/public/hearing/hearing-assistive-technology/

American Speech-Language-Hearing Association. (1997a). *Guidelines for audiologic screening.* Retrieved July 23, 2014, from http://www.asha.org/policy/GL1997-00199.htm

American Speech-Language-Hearing Association. (1997b). *Guidelines for audiology service delivery in nursing homes.* Retrieved July 20, 2014, from http://www.asha.org/policy

American Speech-Language-Hearing Association. (1998*). Guidelines for hearing-aid fitting for adults.* Retrieved July 19, 2014, from http://www.asha.org/policy

American Speech-Language-Hearing Association. (2006). *Preferred practice patterns for the profession of audiology.* Retrieved July 19, 2014, from http://www.asha.org/policy

Anderson, N. D., Craik, F. I. M., & Naveh-Benjamin, M. (1998). The attentional demands of encoding and retrieval in younger and older adults. *Psychology and Aging, 13,* 405–423.

Arlinger, S. (2003). Negative consequences of uncorrected hearing loss: A review. *International Journal of Audiology, 42,* 2S17–2S20.

Baddeley, A. (2003). Working memory and language: An overview. *Journal of Communication Disorders, 36*(3), 189–208.

Baddeley, A. D. (1996). The concept of working memory. In S. Gathercole (Ed.), *Models of short-term memory* (pp. 1–28). Hove, UK: Psychology Press.

Baran, J. A. (2002). Auditory processing disorders can negate the benefits of binaural amplification. *The Hearing Journal, 55*(8), 60.

Barr, R. A., & Giambra, L. A. (1990). Age-related auditory selective attention. *Psychology and Aging, 3,* 597–599.

Belal, A. (1975). Presbyacusis: Physiological or pathological. *Journal of Laryngology and Otology, 89*(10), 1011–1025.

Boothroyd, A. (2007). Adult aural rehabilitation: What is it and does it work? *Trends in Amplification, 11*(2), 63–71.

Caissie, R., Campbell, M. M., Frenette, W. R., Scott, L., Howell, I., & Roy, A. (2005). Clear speech for adults with hearing loss: Does intervention with communication partners make a difference? *Journal of the American Academy of Audiology, 16*(3), 157– 171.

Caissie, R., & Tranquilla, M. (2010). Enhancing conversational fluency: Training conversation partners in the use of clear speech and other strategies. *Seminars in Hearing, 31*(2), 95–103. doi:10.1055/s-0030-1252101

Caspary, D. M., Milbrandt, J. C., & Helfert, R. H. (1995). Central auditory aging: GABA changes in the inferior colliculus. *Experimental Gerontology, 30,* 349–360.

Chandler J. R. (1964). Partial occlusion of the external auditory meatus: Its effect upon air and bone conduction hearing acuity. *Laryngoscope, 74,* 22–45.

Chien, W., & Lin, F. R. (2012). Prevalence of hearing aid use among older adults in the United States. *Archives of Internal Medicine, 172*(3), 292–293.

Chisolm, T. H., Johnson, C. E., Danhauer, J. L., Portz, L. J., Abrams, H. B., Lesner, S., . . . Newman, C. W. (2007). A systematic review of health-related quality of life and hearing aids: Final report of the American Academy of Audiology Task Force on the Health-Related Quality of Life Benefits of Amplification in Adults. *Journal of the American Academy of Audiology, 18*(2), 151–183.

Chisolm, T. H., Noe, C. M., McArdle, R., & Abrams, H. (2007). Evidence for the use of hearing assistive technology by adults: The role of the FM system. *Trends in Amplification, 11*(2), 73–89.

Clark, G. (Ed.). (2003). Preoperative selection. *Cochlear implants: Fundamentals and applications* (pp. 550–586). New York, NY: Springer-Verlag.

Clark, J. G., & English, K. M. (2013). *Counseling-infused audiologic care.* Needham Heights, MA: Allyn & Bacon.

Cox, R. M. (1997). Administration and application of the APHAB. *The Hearing Journal, 50*(4), 32–35.

Cox, R. M., & Alexander, G. C. (1995). The abbreviated profile of hearing aid benefit. *Ear and Hearing, 16*, 176–183.

Cox, R. M., & Alexander, G. C. (1999). Measuring satisfaction with amplification in daily life: The SADL scale. *Ear and Hearing, 20*(4), 306.

Cox, R. M., Alexander, G. C., & Beyer, C. M. (2003). Norms for the International Outcome Inventory for Hearing Aids. *Journal of the American Academy of Audiology, 14*(8), 403–413.

Cox, R. M., & Gilmore, C. (1990). Development of the Profile of Hearing Aid Performance (PHAP). *Journal of Speech, Language, and Hearing Research, 33*(2), 343–357.

Cranford, J., Andres, M., Piatz, K., & Reissig, A. (1993). Influences of age and hearing loss on the precedence effect in sound localization. *Journal of Speech and Hearing Research, 36*, 437–441.

Dalton, D. S., Cruickshanks, K. J., Klein, B. E., Klein, R., Wiley, T. L., & Nondahl, D. M. (2003). The impact of hearing loss on quality of life in older adults. *The Gerontologist, 43*(5), 661–668.

Daneman, M., & Carpenter, P. A. (1980). Individual difference in working memory and reading. *Journal of Verbal Learning and Verbal Memory, 19*, 450–466.

Davis, A., Smith, P., Ferguson, M., Stephens, D., & Gianopoulis, I. (2007). Acceptability, benefit and costs of early screening for hearing disability: A study of potential screening tests and models. *Health Technology Assessment, 11*, 1–294

DeBonis, D. A., & Donohue, C. L. (2008). Assessment and management of special populations. *Survey of audiology: fundamentals for audiologists and health professionals* (2nd ed., pp. 337–374). Boston, MA: Pearson.

Desai, M., Pratt L. A., Lentzner, H., & Robinson, K. N. (2001). Trends in vision and hearing among older Americans. *Aging Trends, 2,* 1–8. Hyattsville, MD: National Center for Health Statistics. Retrieved July 8, 2014, from http://www.cdc.gov/nchs/data/ahcd/agingtrends/02vision.pdf

Dillon, H. (2012). *Hearing aids* (2nd ed.). New York, NY: Thieme.

Dillon, H., James, A. M., & Ginis, I. (1997). Client Oriented Scale of Improvement (COSI) and its relationship to several other measures of benefit and satisfaction provided by hearing aids. *Journal of the American Academy of Audiology, 8,* 27–43.

Erdman, S. A., & Demorest, M. E. (1998). Adjustment to hearing impairment II: Audiological and demographic correlates. *Journal of Speech Language and Hearing Research, 41,* 123–136.

Friedman, D. S., O'Colmain, B. J., Munoz, B., Tomany, S. C., McCarty, C., De Jong, P. T., . . . Kempen, J. (2004). Prevalence of age-related macular degeneration in the United States. *Archives of Ophthalmology, 122*(4), 564–572.

Frisina, D. R., & Frisina, R. D. (1997). Speech recognition in noise and presbycusis: Relations to possible neural mechanisms. *Hearing Research, 106,* 95–104.

Frisina, R. D. (2001). Possible neurochemical and neuroanatomical bases of age-related hearing loss—Presbycusis. *Seminars in Hearing, 22*(3), 213–226.

Gangadhara Somayaji, K. S., & Aroor, R. (2013). Middle ear implants. *Archives of Medicine and Health Sciences, 1*(2), 183.

Garstecki, D. C., & Erler, S. F. (1998). Hearing loss, control, and demographic factors influencing hearing-aid use among older adults. *Journal of Speech, Language, and Hearing Research, 41*(3), 527–537.

Gatehouse, S., & Noble, W. (2004). The Speech, Spatial and Qualities of Hearing Scale (SSQ). *International Journal of Audiology, 43*(2), 85–99.

Gates, G. A., Cobb, J. L., D'Agostino, R. B., & Wolf, P. A. (1993). The relation of hearing in the elderly to the presence of cardiovascular disease and cardiovascular risk factors. *Archives of Otolaryngology, Head, and Neck Surgery, 118,* 221–227.

Gates, G. A., & Mills, J. H. (2005). Presbycusis. *The Lancet, 366*(9491), 1111–1120.

Genther, D. J., Frick, K. D., Chen, D., Betz, J., & Lin, F. R. (2013). Association of hearing loss with hospitalization and burden of disease in older adults. *Journal of the American Medical Association, 309*(22), 2322–2324. doi:10.1001/jama.2013.5912

Giolas, T. G., Owens, E., Lamb, S. H., & Schubert, E. D. (1979). Hearing performance inventory. *Journal of Speech and Hearing Disorders, 44,* 169–195.

Gopinath, B., Schneider, J., Hartley, D., Teber, E., McMahon, C. M., Leeder, S. R., & Mitchell, P. (2011). Incidence and predictors of hearing-aid use and ownership among older adults with hearing loss. *Annals of Epidemiology, 21*(7), 497–506.

Gregory, M. (2012). A possible patient journey: A tool to facilitate patient-centered care. *Seminars in Hearing, 33*(1), 9–15.

Grosjean, F. (1996). Gating. *Language and Cognitive Processes, 11*(6), 597–604. doi:10.1080/016909696386999

Hawke, M., & McCombe, A. (1995). *Diseases of the ear: A pocket atlas.* Hamilton, Canada: Manticore Communications.

Hawkins, D. B. (2005). Effectiveness of counseling-based adult group aural rehabilitation programs: A systematic review of the evidence. *Journal of the American Academy of Audiology, 16*(7), 485–493.

Hayes, D., & Jerger, J. (1979). Low-frequency hearing loss in presbycusis. *Archives of Otolaryngology, 105*, 9–12.

Hearing Loss Association of America. (n.d.). *Mission.* Retrieved July 13, 2014, from http://www.hearingloss.org/content/mission

Helfer, K. S. (2001). Gender, age, and hearing. *Seminars in Hearing, 22*(3), 271–286.

Herbst, K. G., & Humphrey, C. (1980). Hearing impairment and mental state in the elderly living at home. *British Medical Journal, 281*, 903–905.

Hickson, L. (2012). Defining a paradigm shift. *Seminars in Hearing, 33*(1), 3–8.

Hickson, L., Worrall, L. (2003). Beyond hearing aid fitting: Improving communication for older adults. *International Journal of Audiology, 42*(S2), 84–91.

Hickson, L., Worrall, L., & Scarinci, N. (2007). *Active Communication Education (ACE): A program for older people with hearing impairment.* London, UK: Speechmark.

Holmes, A. E. (2003). Bilateral amplification for the elderly: Are two aids better than one? *International Journal of Audiology, 42*, 2S63–2S67.

Hosford-Dunn, H., & Halpern, J. (2000). Clinical application of the satisfaction with amplification in daily life scale in private practice I: Statistical, content, and factorial validity. *Journal of the American Academy of Audiology, 11*(10), 523–539.

Hosford-Dunn, H., & Halpern, J. (2001). Clinical application of the SADL scale in private practice II: Predictive validity of fitting variables. Satisfaction with Amplification in Daily Life. *Journal of the American Academy of Audiology, 12*(1), 15–36.

Howarth, A., & Shone, G. R. (2006). Ageing and the auditory system. *Postgraduate Medical Journal, 82*(965), 166–171. doi:10.1136/pgmj.2005.039388

Jerger, J., Chmiel, R., Florin, E., Pirozzolo, F., & Wilson, N. (1996). Comparison of conventional amplification and an assistive listening device in elderly persons. *Ear and Hearing, 17*(6), 490–504.

Jerger, J., Chmiel, R., Stach, B., & Spretnjak, M. (1993). Gender affects audiometric shape in presbyacusis. *Journal of the American Academy of Audiology, 4,* 42–49.

Kaas, J. H. (1991). Plasticity of sensory and motor maps in adult mammals. *Annual Review of Neuroscience, 14,* 137–167. doi:10.1146/annurev.ne.14.030191.001033

Kemper, S., & Harden, T. (1999). Experimentally disentangling what's beneficial about elderspeak from what's not. *Psychology and Aging, 14,* 656–670.

Kemtes, K. A., & Kemper, S. (1997). Younger and older adults' on-line processing of syntactically ambiguous sentences. *Psychology and Aging, 12*(2), 362–371. doi:10.1037/0882-7974.12.2.362

Kjelgaard, M. M., Titone, D. A., & Wingfield, A. (1999). The influence of prosodic structure on the interpretation of temporary syntactic ambiguity by young and elderly listeners. *Experimental Aging Research, 25,* 187–207.

Kochkin, S. (2007). MarkeTrak VII: Obstacles to adult non-user adoption of hearing aids. *Hearing Journal, 60,* 24–51.

Kochkin, S., Beck, D. L., Christensen, L. A., Compton-Conley, C., Fligor, B. J., Kricos, P. B., . . . Turner, R. (2010). MarkeTrak VIII: The impact of the hearing healthcare professional on hearing-aid user success. *Hearing Review, 17*(4), 12–34.

Kochkin, S., & Rogin, C. M. (2000). Quantifying the obvious: The impact of hearing instruments on quality of life. *Hearing Review, 7*(1), 6–34.

Koehnke, J., & Besing, J. M. (2001). The effects of aging on binaural and spatial hearing. *Seminars in Hearing, 22*(3), 241–253.

Lee, F. S., Matthews, L. J., Mills, J. H., Dubno, J. R., & Adkins, W. Y. (1998a). Analysis of blood chemistry and hearing levels in a sample of older persons. *Ear and Hearing, 19*(3), 180–190.

Lee, F. S., Matthews, L. J., Mills, J. H., Dubno, J. R., & Adkins, W. Y. (1998b). Gender-specific effects of medicinal drugs on hearing levels of older persons. *Archives of Otolaryngology-Head and Neck Surgery, 118*(2), 221–227.

Lin, F. R., Ferrucci, L., Metter, E. J., An, Y., Zonderman, A. B., & Resnick, S. M. (2011). Hearing loss and cognition in the Baltimore Longitudinal Study of Aging. *Neuropsychology, 25*(6), 763.

Lin, F. R., Metter, E. J., O'Brien, R. J., Resnick, S. M., Zonderman, A. B., & Ferrucci, L. (2011). Hearing loss and incident dementia. *Archives of Neurology, 68*(2), 214–220.

Lin, F. R., Yaffe, K., Xia, J., Xue, Q. L., Harris, T. B., Purchase-Helzner, E., . . . Health ABC Study Group. (2013). Hearing loss and cognitive decline in older adults. *JAMA Internal Medicine, 173*(4), 293–299.

McFadden, S. L., & Willott, J. F. (1994). Responses of inferior colliculus neurons in C57BL/6J mice with and without sensorineural hearing loss: Effects of changing the azimuthal location of a continuous noise masker on responses to contralateral tones. *Hearing Research, 78,* 132–148.

Megighian, D., Savastano, M., Salvador, L., Frigo, A., & Bolzan, M. (2000). Audiometric and epidemiological analysis of elderly in the Veneto region. *Gerontology, 46,* 199–204.

Montano, J. J., & Almakadma, H. (2012). The Communication Rings: A tool for exploring the social networks of individuals with hearing loss. *Seminars in Hearing, 33*(1), 46–52.

Montano, J. J., & Spitzer, J. B. (2013). *Adult audiologic rehabilitation* (2nd ed.). San Diego, CA: Plural.

National Eye Institute. (n.d.). Retrieved July 19, 2014, from https://www.nei.nih.gov/eyedata/glaucoma.asp#4

National Institute on Deafness and Other Communication Disorders (NIDCD). (n.d.). Retrieved July 8, 2014, from http://www.nidcd.nih.gov/health/statistics/pages/quick.aspx

Pearson, J. D., Morrell, C. H., Gordon-Salant, S., Brant, L. J., Metter, E. J., Klein, L. L., & Fozard, J. L. (1995). Gender differences in a longitudinal study of age-associated hearing loss. *Journal of the Acoustical Society of America, 97,* 1196–1205.

Pichora-Fuller, M. K., Schneider, B., & Daneman, M. (1995). How young and old adults listen to and remember speech in noise. *Journal of the Acoustical Society of America, 97,* 593–607.

Rabbitt, P. (1991). Mild hearing loss can cause apparent memory failures which increase with age and reduce IQ. *Acta Otolaryngologica Supplement, 476,* 167–176.

Randolph, L. J., & Schow, R. L. (1983). Threshold inaccuracies in an elderly clinical population: Ear canal collapse as a possible cause. *Journal of Speech, Language, and Hearing Research, 26*(1), 54–58.

Rees, J. N., & Botwinick, J. (1971). Detection and decision factors in auditory behavior of the elderly. *Journal of Gerontology, 26*(2), 133–136.

Roland, P. S., Smith, T. L., Schwartz, S. R., Rosenfeld, R. M., Ballachanda, B., Earll, J. M., . . . Wetmore, S. (2008). Clinical practice guideline: Cerumen impaction. *Otolaryngology-Head and Neck Surgery, 139*(3 suppl. 1), S1–S21.

Rosenwasser, H. (1964). Otic problems in the aged. *Geriatrics, 19,* 11–17.

Saunders, G. H., Lewis, M. S., & Forsline, A. (2009). Expectations, prefit-ting counseling, and hearing-aid outcome. *Journal of the American Academy of Audiology, 20*(5), 320–334.

Schneider, B. A., & Pichora-Fuller, M. K. (2001). Age-related changes in temporal processing: Implications for speech perception. *Seminars in Hearing, 22*(3), 227–239.

Schow, R. L., & Goldbaum, D. E. (1980). Collapsed ear canals in the elderly nursing home population. *Journal of Speech and Hearing Disorders, 45*(2), 259–267.

Schow, R. L., & Nerbonne, M. A. (1982). Communication screening profile: Use with elderly clients. *Ear and Hearing, 3*(3), 135–147.

Schuknecht, H. F., Watanuki, K., Takahashi, T., Belal, A., Kimura, R. S., & Jones, D. D. (1974). Atrophy of the stria vascularis, a common cause of hearing loss. *Laryngoscope, 84*, 1777–1821.

Shattuck-Hufnagel, S., & Turk, A. E. (1996). A prosody tutorial for inves-tigators of auditory sentence processing. *Journal of Psycholinguistic Research, 25*, 193–247.

Snell, K. B. (1997). Age-related changes in temporal gap detection. *Journal of the Acoustical Society of America, 101*, 2214–2220.

Sommers, M. S. (1997). Stimulus variability and spoken word recogni-tion. II. The effects of age and hearing impairment. *Journal of the Acoustical Society of America, 101*, 2278–2288.

Sprinzl, G. M., & Riechelmann, H. (2010). Current trends in treating hearing loss in elderly people: A review of the technology and treat-ment options—A mini-review. *Gerontology, 56*(3), 351–358.

Strouse, A., Ashmead, D. H., Ohde, R. N., & Grantham, D. W. (1998). Temporal processing in the aging auditory system. *Journal of the Acoustical Society of America, 104*, 2385–2399.

Sweetow, R. W., & Sabes, J. H. (2006). The need for and development of an adaptive listening and communication enhancement (LACE™) pro-gram. *Journal of the American Academy of Audiology, 17*(8), 538–558.

Swenor, B. K., Ramulu, P. Y., Willis, J. R., Friedman, D., & Lin, F. R. (2013). The prevalence of concurrent hearing and vision impairment in the United States. *Journal of the American Medical Association, 173*(4), 312–313. doi:10.1001/jamainternmed.2013.1880

Tun, P. A. (1998). Fast noisy speech: Age differences in processing rapid speech with background noise. *Psychology and Aging, 3*, 424–434.

Tyberghein, J. (1996). Presbycusis and phonemic regression. *Acta Oto-rhinolaryngology Belgium, 50*(2), 85–90.

Tye-Murray, N. (2014). Aural Rehabilitation Plans for Adults. *Foun-dations of aural rehabilitation: Children, adults, and their family members* (4th ed., pp. 385–432). Stamford, CT: Cengage Learning.

Uhlmann, R. F., Larson, E. B., Rees, T. S., Koepsell, T. D., & Duckert, L. G. (1989). Relationship of hearing impairment to dementia and cognitive dysfunction in older adults. *Journal of the American Medical Association, 261*(13), 1916–1919.

Valente, M., Abrams, H., Benson, D., Chisolm, T., Citron, D., Hampton, D., & Sweetow, R. (2006). Guidelines for the audiologic management of adult hearing impairment. *Audiology Today, 18*(5), 32–37.

Valente, M., Hosford-Dunn, H., & Roeser, R. J. (2007). *Audiology treatment* (2nd ed.). New York, NY: Thieme.

Ventry, I., & Weinstein, B. (1982). The Hearing Handicap Inventory for the Elderly: A new tool. *Ear and Hearing, 3,* 128–134.

Ventry, I., & Weinstein, B. (1983). Identification of elderly people with hearing problems. *American Speech-Language-Hearing Association, 25,* 37–42.

Vuorialho, A., Karinen, P., & Sorri, M. (2006). Counselling of hearing aid users is highly cost-effective. *European Archives of Oto-Rhino-Laryngology and Head & Neck, 263*(11), 988–995.

Walden, B. C., Demorest, M. E., & Hepler, E. L. (1984). Self-report approach to assessing benefit derived from amplification. *Journal of Speech and Hearing Research, 27,* 49–56.

Walden, T. C., & Walden, B. E. (2005). Unilateral versus bilateral amplification for adults with impaired hearing. *Journal of the American Academy of Audiology, 16*(8), 574–584.

Weinstein, B. E. (1986). Hearing loss and senile dementia in the institutionalized elderly. *Clinical Gerontologist, 4*(3), 3–15.

Weinstein, B., & Ventry, I. (1983). Audiometric correlates of the Hearing Handicap Inventory for the Elderly. *Journal of Speech and Hearing Disorders, 48,* 379–384.

Willott, J. F. (1996). Anatomic and physiologic aging: A behavioral neuroscience perspective. *Journal of the American Acadamy of Audiology, 7,* 141–151.

Willott, J. F., Bross, L. S, & McFadden, S. L. (1992). Morphology of the dorsal cochlear nucleus in young and aging C57BL/6J and CBA/J mice. *Journal of Comparative Neurology, 321,* 666–678.

Willott, J. F., Carlson, S., Brownfield C., & Bross, L. S. (1995). Effect of hearing loss on short-latency sound-evoked inhibition of startle: Behavioral and immunocytochemical findings. *Association for Research in Otolaryngology Abstracts, 18,* 61.

Wingfield, A., Aberdeen, J. S., & Stine, E. A. L. (1991). Word onset gating and linguistic context in spoken word recognition by young and elderly adults. *Journal of Gerontology, 46*(3), 127–129. doi:10.1093/geronj/46.3.P127

Wingfield, A., Alexander, A. H., & Cavigelli, S. (1994). Does memory constrain utilization of top-down information in spoken word recognition? Evidence from normal aging. *Language and Speech, 37,* 221–235.

Wingfield, A., & Ducharme, J. L. (1999). Effects of age and passage difficulty on listening-rate preferences for time-altered speech. *Journal of Gerontology B Psychology Science, 54B,* 199–202. doi:10.1093/geronb/54B.3.P199

Wingfield, A., Lindfield, K. C., & Goodglass, H. (2000). Effects of age and hearing sensitivity on the use of prosodic information in spoken word recognition. *Journal of Speech, Language, and Hearing Research, 43,* 915–925.

Wingfield, A., Poon, L. W., Lombardi, L., & Lowe, D. (1985). Speed of processing in in normal aging: Effects of speech rate, linguistic structure, and processing time. *Journal of Gerontology, 40,* 579–585.

Wingfield, A., Stine, E. A. L., Lahar, C. J., & Aberdeen, J. S. (1988). Does the capacity of working memory change with age? *Experimental Aging Research, 17,* 103–107.

Wingfield, A., & Tun, P. A. (2001). Spoken language comprehension in older adults: Interactions between sensory and cognitive change in normal aging. *Seminars in Hearing, 22*(3), 287–301.

Working Group on Speech Understanding and Aging. (1988). *Journal of the Acoustical Society of America, 83,* 859–895.

Wöstmann, M., Herrmann, B., Wilsch, A., & Obleser, J. (2015). Neural alpha dynamics in younger and older listeners reflect acoustic challenges and predictive benefits. *The Journal of Neuroscience, 35*(4), 1458–1467.

Zeng, F. G. (2004). Trends in cochlear implants. *Trends in amplification, 8*(1), 1–34.

Zurif, E. B., Swinney, D., Prather, P, Wingfield, A., & Brownell, H. (1995). The allocation of memory resources during sentence comprehension: Evidence from the elderly. *Journal of Psycholinguistic Research, 24,* 165–182.

CHAPTER 7

Swallowing Functions Across the Lifespan

Matina Balou

The ability to manage secretions and relatedly, to chew and swallow properly is integral to quality of life of all individuals. Challenges in these areas provide a distinct barrier to many of the life participation activities central to many interactions and settings. This chapter helps readers gain a clear understanding of swallowing and swallowing-related deficits, an understanding that is essential to enhancing quality of life and independence.

—Linda S. Carozza

DYSPHAGIA AS A PROBLEM

Dysphagia can be considered an abnormality of bolus flow from the lips to the stomach (McCullough, Wertz, Rosenbek, & Dinneen, 1999). Flow of the bolus (food or liquid) through the oropharyngeal mechanism can be either stopped, as in oropharyngeal residue, or misdirected, as in penetration or aspiration of material into the airway. Dysphagia is not a primary medical diagnosis but a symptom of an underlying disease or medical diagnosis. The increased incidence of disease, neurological in nature, does contribute to the increased incidence of the swallowing and feeding disorders. There are occasions that the normal swallow physiology is altered due to the aging process, often referred as "presbyesophagus" or "presbyphagia." These subtle and subclinical related to age changes make older adults more vulnerable to dysphagia during disease insults (Wang et al., 2014). Overt signs of dysphagia include weight loss, aspiration pneumonia, and difficulty maintaining necessary nutrition and hydration. The diagnosis is often difficult and is based on the medical history and clinical examination in addition to various diagnostic tests. Its management is multidisciplinary, leaving only little room for medications or surgery.

NORMAL SWALLOWING

The swallowing mechanism is divided into four stages for simplification purposes: oral preparatory stage, oral stage, the pharyngeal stage, and the esophageal stage. During the oral preparatory stage, the food bolus is prepared in the oral cavity by chewing behaviors. Movement patterns and preparation time vary, depending on the volume and consistency of the bolus. From the time the bolus is placed in the oral cavity, labial seal is sustained to avoid anterior spillage. The tongue positions the bolus on the teeth and when the upper and lower teeth meet, the food falls medially toward the tongue, which moves the bolus back onto the teeth. Then, the tongue moves the food laterally to the molar ridges with repetitive movements of the jaw. The trigeminal nerve innervates muscles responsible for chewing (masseter, temporalis, and pterygoid muscles) and the facial nerve innervates the muscles of the mandible and the maxillae including the buccinators muscles. The intrinsic muscles of the tongue are innervated by the hypoglossal nerve (Groher & Crary, 2010, p. 22).

When the bolus propulsion begins posteriorly by the tongue, the oral stage is initiated. The tongue creates a propulsive anterior to posterior wave as it presses up and back against the hard palate, moving the bolus to the back of the mouth. The bolus is propelled into the oropharynx and then to hypopharynx, at the moment of swallow response (Groher & Crary, 2010, p.18).

During this pharyngeal phase, the soft palate rises, the hyoid bone and larynx move upward and forward, the vocal folds move to midline, the epiglottis folds backward to protect the airway, and the tongue pushes backward and downward into the pharynx to propel the bolus. The pharyngeal musculature (superior, middle, and inferior constrictors) contract to push the bolus through the pharynx in coordination with relaxation of the upper esophageal sphincter (UES), which relaxes and is pulled open by the forward movement of the larynx and hyoid bone. After the bolus passage, the UES closes and the pharyngeal structures return to reference position. The pharyngeal swallow response involves the motor and sensory tracts from the trigeminal (V), facial (VII), glossopharyngeal (IX), vagus (X), and hypoglossal (XII) cranial nerves and lasts 1 second (Paik, 2008).

In the esophageal phase, the bolus is propelled downward by peristalsis of circular and longitudinal smooth muscle coordinated by Auerbach's plexus. At the distal end, the lower esophageal sphincter relaxes (LES), allows the bolus to pass into the stomach, and closes again. This phase can be measured from the point the bolus passes the UES until it enters the stomach. According to Logemann (1998, p. 35), normal esophageal transit time varies from 8 to 20 seconds.

SWALLOWING IMPAIRMENT AND DYSPHAGIA EVALUATION

Dysphagia has been defined as any difficulty moving food or liquid from the mouth to the stomach (Logemann, 1986). It can be considered, therefore, an abnormality of bolus flow (McCullough, Wertz, Rosenbek, & Dinneen, 1999). Flow of the bolus (food or liquid) through the oropharyngeal mechanism can be either stopped, as in oropharyngeal residue, or misdirected, as in laryngeal penetration or aspiration of material into the airway. Food and liquid remaining in the oropharynx (residue) reduces the amount of food and liquid reaching the gut and increases the risk of dehydration and malnutrition. People who aspirate food and liquid increase their risk of developing pneumonia more than seven times compared to nonaspirating individuals (Schmidt, Holas, Halvorson, & Reading, 1994).

To swallow safely and efficiently, muscles of the tongue and pharynx must create sufficient pressures to propel the bolus through the pharynx while maintaining opening of the UES, allowing the bolus to move it into the esophagus (Castell & Castell, 1997). Impairment in the timing of oropharyngeal events, the magnitude of pharyngeal propulsive force, or the extent of UES relaxation and opening can lead to varying amounts of pharyngeal residue (material left in the pharynx after the swallow) and aspiration (material that is misdirected into the larynx and passes below the vocal folds into the trachea).

CLINICAL SWALLOW EVALUATION

Clinical swallow evaluation is the most common examination to diagnose dysphagia in numerous settings but it should be confused with swallow "screen." It is the first step to obtain information regarding diagnostic and therapeutic process and determine whether further evaluation is needed. Speech language therapists present small volumes of various consistencies to the patient and they watch for overt signs of laryngeal penetration or aspiration or any sign for abnormal swallowing function, such as anterior spillage, facial weakness, reduced hyolaryngeal elevation, coughing/throat clearing, and/or changes in voice quality after swallow. The main limitation of this assessment is that it relies on findings that are subjective and clinician dependent (Singh & Hamdy, 2006). Several investigators have tried to create objective and reliable scoring systems for the bedside assessment.

Videofluoroscopic Swallow Study

The videofluoroscopic swallow study (VFSS) is the most commonly used technique to evaluate oropharyngeal swallowing (Logemann, 1998). There are various terms that are used for the examination depending on the institution: modified barium swallow (MBS), videofluoroscopic swallow evaluation (VFSE), swallow study. VFSS provides information on bolus flow and the biomechanical movements of oral and laryngopharyngeal structures affecting bolus flow. This procedure enables visualization of the oral activity during chewing and oral bolus propulsion, the triggering of the pharyngeal swallow in relation to position of the bolus, and the biomechanics of the pharyngeal swallow, including movement of the larynx, hyoid, tongue base, pharyngeal walls, and cricopharyngeal region. It also enables the clinician to scan the esophagus in the anterior–posterior plane. In addition to diagnosing dysphagia, VFSS provides a means for examining the effects of various compensatory strategies to improve the efficiency of swallow. The clinician can obtain direct evidence of the efficacy for various methods of bolus presentation, sensory input prior to the swallow, head positioning, and swallow maneuvers.

VFSS has the advantages of clear visualization of barium through the oral cavity, oropharynx, as well as the pharynx and esophagus. It can easily be recorded and played back in slow motion many times if needed to identify laryngeal penetration or aspiration penetration of barium into the airway and below the true vocal cords, respectively.

Disadvantages of VFSS include the exposure to radiation. The procedure is carried out in very "controlled" conditions that may not reflect the patient's eating and swallowing habits during a meal. Barium's density is different compared to normal liquid and solid consistencies. There is no standard protocol for the volumes tested or the consistencies delivered (Singh & Hamdy, 2006).

Fiberoptic Endoscopic Evaluation of Swallowing (FEES)

Like the VFSS, the fiberoptic endoscopic evaluation of swallowing is another instrumental swallow evaluation intends to provide an objective assessment of the swallowing anatomy and physiology. It is a newer examination in the field compared with the swallow study but steadily it gets more popular in medical centers and nursing homes. It was first described as flexible endoscopic evaluation of swallowing safety (FEESS) by Langmore, Schatz, and Olsen in 1988. The fiberoptic endoscopic evaluation of swallowing (FEES) term was recommended by the American Speech-Language-Hearing Association (ASHA) but other terms have been used in the past such as videoendoscopic evaluation of dysphagia VEED (Bastian, 1991) and flexible endoscopy with sensory testing (FEEST) (Aviv, Martin, Keen, Debell, & Blitzer, 1993). The purpose of the examination, the materials used, and the process of the evaluations are similar with the videofluoroscopic examination (Groher & Crary, 2010). FEES is indicated in case there is an interest in evaluating nasopharyngeal and oropharyngeal anatomy, alterations in the anatomy of the larynx or pharyngeal symmetry, the ability of the patient to maintain airway protection during a longer period of time, also to provide feedback to the patient while using various compensatory strategies.

FEES does require a skilled therapists and technical equipment that may not be available in all settings. The oral and oropharyngeal phase of swallowing is not visualized and there is a "whiteout" as the bolus passes through the pharynx (Singh & Hamdy, 2006).

Esophageal Manometry

Esophageal manometry has historically been used to diagnose motility disorders of the esophagus and, specifically, intraluminal pressures and coordination of muscular contractions within the esophagus. Recent technological advances with this procedure, such as solid-state intraluminal transducers capable of rapid data collection, have resulted in renewed interest in manometry (Castell & Castell, 1994). Solid-state manometry has made it possible to obtain accurate manometric profiles of the pressures and durations of events associated with the pharynx and UES, as well as the esophagus (Hatlebakk et al., 1998; Hila, Castell, & Castell, 2001).

The solid-state intraluminal manometry catheter is a soft, flexible catheter with microtransducers which are in contact with the pharyngeal or esophageal wall. Unlike the older water-perfused catheters, solid-state intraluminal catheters measure contractions directly and without respect to the relative positions of the patient and the equipment. In this manner, studies can be performed with the participant in an upright position, which allows testing of various food consistencies and volumes as well as different head positions.

Despite advances, the use of manometry in clinical evaluations of pharyngeal dysphagia remains controversial. Malhi-Chowla, Anchem, Stark, and DeVault (2000) argued that UES and pharyngeal manometry should not be included as a routine procedure for patients undergoing esophageal manometry. The authors reviewed 435 complete manometry evaluations and found that only six of the patients were offered an intervention based on abnormal findings of the UES. Only three of the patients presented with dysphagia. However, the authors did not specifically select patients with complaints of dysphagia, which could explain the low incidence of UES and pharyngeal abnormalities. Xue, Katz, Castell, and Castell (2000) examined manometry records for 114 individuals diagnosed with dysphagia and compared the findings with the recordings of 80 patients with complaints of chest pain. In their study, dysphagic patients demonstrated significantly higher UES residual pressures, weak pharyngeal contractions, and UES/pharyngeal incoordination compared with participants presenting with chest pain. Seventy one percent of participants with dysphagia had at least one UES and pharyngeal manometric abnormality.

SWALLOW FUNCTION AND NORMAL AGING

After the 65 years of age, changes in swallow physiology are commonly noted that may be attributable to decreased muscle speed and strength, and/or sensory perception. A degree of muscle atrophy may occur in several structures of the anatomy which clinically is not easy to outline (Groher & Crary, 2010). These changes may alter the durations of swallowing but they would still be considered normal. According to Groher and Crary (2010), these changes may not be enough to indicate dysphagia but in case of causative diagnosis for dysphagia, they may intensify conditions. In other words, presbyphagia is the term that represents the physiological aging of swallowing function.

The tongue plays a key role in bolus propulsion, Nicosia and colleagues (2000) investigated the possible age effects on the magnitude and timing of lingual pressure generation. They described that decreased lingual strength with age combined with unchanging swallowing pressure leads to a decreased "pressure reserve," and concluded that older individuals may be at risk for dysphagia. Additionally, they also noted that swallowing appears to be slower with age changing the bolus flow.

Fei and colleagues (2013) reported that both tongue endurance and strength are found to decline in healthy aging, while the term sarcopenia has been used to describe age-related changes in function of the tongue. Studies have shown that the maximum isometric pressure (MIP) of the tongue is usually declining in older adults (Fei et al., 2013; Robbins et al., 2005). It is important to mention that these age-related changes appear to be seen only in certain tasks like swallowing honey thick liquid and puree but not during swallowing saliva or thin liquid (Robbins et al., 2005; Robbins, Levine, Wood, Roecker, & Luschei, 1995; Youmans & Stierwalt, 2006).

Aging: Oral Phase

Changes in taste and smell are common in the elderly and result from normal aging, medications, medical and surgical interventions, and environmental exposure. A number of studies have been conducted investigating these changes. Murphy and colleagues (2002) studied the prevalence of impaired olfaction in elderly and found that the mean was 24.5% (1.7%) while the prevalence increased with age. It was also found that the olfactory impairment was more prevalent among men. Other investigators support that tongue hypertrophy may result in reduced tongue isometric pressures (Robbins et al., 1995) and others argue that there is not a significance difference in tongue pressure generation (Nicosia et al., 2000; Youmans & Stierwalt, 2006). Problems caused by loss of the sense of smell and/or taste may result in malnutrition and weight loss due to loss of appetite, social isolation and depression. Until now the loss of olfactory function and taste changes has received relatively little attention compared to other disorders acquires with aging such as hearing loss.

Aging: Pharyngeal Phase

Changes in swallowing physiology seen with normal aging include slower oral transit time, delayed swallow initiation, and decreased pharyngeal propulsion (Logemann et al., 2000). In a study conducted by Logeman and colleagues (2000), the C2 to C4 distance of older men was found to be significantly shorter than that of younger men, and laryngeal position at rest was lower than in younger men. Older men had a significantly longer pharyngeal delay than younger men and significantly faster onset of posterior pharyngeal wall movement in relation to first cricopharyngeal opening. The authors also noted that older men exhibited significantly reduced maximum vertical and anterior hyoid movement as compared to the younger men. Older men also exhibited less width of cricopharyngeal opening than younger men at 10 ml volumes. That finding may explain increased higher pharyngeal contraction pressures (peak pressures) in order to compensate for the reduced UES relaxation (Groher & Crary, 2010).

Videofluoroscopic swallow evaluations comparing older and younger male participants showed that penetrations were significantly more frequent after age 50 and thick viscosities penetrated only in subjects age 50 and over. In addition, for participants under 50 years old, 7.4% of swallows exhibited penetration, while for people age 50 and over, 16.8% of swallows showed penetration (Daggett, Logemann, Rademaker, & Pauloski, 2006). The authors also noted significantly more penetration that occurred on larger liquid boluses; however they found no relationship between gender and frequency of penetration.

Robbins and colleagues (1992) have shown that in older persons, the airway closure and laryngeal vestibule closure was longer in duration compared to younger persons. The authors conclude that since the oral and pharyngeal transit times are slower in older individuals, there are protective reflexes to maintain airway closure to avoid laryngeal penetration/aspiration (Groher & Crary, 2010). Aviv and colleagues (1994) carried out 672 trials of calibrated puffs of air to the supraglottic larynx in 56 healthy adults divided into three age groups: 20 to 40, 41 to 60, and 61 to 90 years of age. The authors found that laryngeal closure as a response was not as evident in older participants compared to the younger ones until the pressure levels of the air puffs were higher. There was a statistically significant difference between the 41- to 60-year and 61- to 90-year age groups. Progressive reduction in pharyngeal and supraglottic sensitivity with increasing age might be a contributing factor in the development of dysphagia and aspiration in the elderly.

The elevation of the hyoid bone is essential for swallowing and is controlled by the suprahyoid muscles in order for the bolus to enter the UES and then the esophagus. In a more recent study, Iida and colleagues (2013) investigated the effects of aging on suprahyoid muscle strength. They analyzed the effects of aging on suprahyoid muscle strength by comparing the jaw opening functions of healthy adults and elderly adults. The mean jaw opening force of healthy adults was significantly greater than the mean of the healthy elderly subjects.

Increased incidence of diagnoses such as stroke, dementia, and other neurological diseases in older individuals results in higher incidence of swallowing disorders. It is fair to mention that aging alone should not result in dysphagia in individuals over the age of 65. On many occasions, individuals complain of dysphagia, which is mostly associated with grastroesophageal reflux and globus sensation (Lindgren & Janzon, 1991) (Table 7–1).

NEUROGENIC DYSPHAGIA

Neurogenic disorder is one of the most common etiologies of dysphagia. More than three quarters of cases of dysphagia are due to some kind of neurological disease. The underlying etiology determines the characteristics of the swallowing disorder and rules the rehabilitation strategies to prevent or treat the dysphagia (Leonard & Kendall, 2014).

Cerebrovascular Accident (CVA)

Many studies have tried to establish the incidence of dysphagia after stroke with numbers ranging from 23% to 50%; this represents a wide range. Other studies found that dysphagia is present in 29% to 80% of patients with an acute stroke (González-Fernández & Daniels, 2008). Persistent dysphagia is seen in

Table 7–1. Etiology that May Cause Neurogenic Dysphagia

Central		
Nondegenerative	*Degenerative*	
Stroke	Dementia	
Traumatic brain injury	Parkinson's disease	
Cerebral palsy	Multiple sclerosis	
Medication	Subranuclear palsy	
Neoplasm	Huntington's disease	
Peripheral		
Neuromuscular	*Myopathy*	*Neuropathy*
Poliomyelitis	Muscular dystrophy	Guillain-Barré syndrome
Myasthernia gravis	Polymyositis	
Amyotrophic lateral sclerosis	Dermatomyositis	
Other Conditions That May Cause Dysphagia		
Connective tissue	*Iatrogenic etiology*	*Structural etiology*
Scleroderma	Chemotherapy	Tumor
Sjögren's disease	Radiation therapy	
Progressive systemic sclerosis	Tracheostomy	
	Intubation	
	Anterior/posterior cervical spine fusion	
	Coronary artery bypass grafting	

Source: Adapted from Leonard & Kendall, 2014.

approximately 20% to 50% of those patients. The explanation for this lies in variations in study design and in the identification of dysphagia (Singh & Hamdy, 2006). Dysphagia after stroke is associated with the presence of silent aspiration (2–66%) and aspiration pneumonia that is considered one of the most common reasons for rehospitalization in acute strokes (Leonard & Kendall, 2014).

Some of the common swallowing deficits noticed in patients post-stroke are:

- Delayed pharyngeal swallow initiation
- Incoordination of oral movements and increased oral transit times
- Increased pharyngeal transit times
- Reduced pharyngeal constriction
- Aspiration
- Reduced upper esophageal sphincter relaxation and opening

DEMENTIA

Progressive diseases like dementia are also known to affect swallowing function. Dementia is characterized by the overall decline in cognition and memory. According to Easterling and Robbins (2006), in 2004 more than 12% of the population in the United States was aged 65 years or older. By 2030, this percentage is expected to increase to 20% of the population. Easterling and Robbins reported that the prevalence of swallowing disorders in older individuals ranges from 7% to 22% and dramatically increases to 40% to 50% in those who live in long-term care facilities. For older individuals with dementia, dysphagia can be a result of behavioral, sensory, or motor problems. It is estimated that 45% of institutionalized dementia patients have dysphagia. The high prevalence of dysphagia in patients with dementia is probably the result of age-related changes in sensory and motor function, in addition to those produced by neuropathology.

One-third of patients with Alzheimer's disease may exhibit aspiration, and pneumonia is the most common cause of death (González-Fernández & Daniels, 2008). Common swallowing disorders in patients with dementia are:

- Weight loss
- Oral bolus formation, A–P bolus propulsion, increased oral transit times

- Self-feeding difficulties
- Delayed swallow initiation
- Aspiration

PARKINSON'S DISEASE

Parkinson's disease is a slowly progressive disease and the main problem is the execution of voluntary movement. Many times these patients present with cognitive impairment and in some cases a form of dementia in addition to dysphagia (Groher & Crary, 2010). Solid consistencies are usually more challenging than liquids and González-Fernández and Daniels (2008) reported syprahyoid dysfunction. Aspiration pneumonia is also the leading cause of death in patients with Parkinson's disease. The cause of these infections is largely attributed to the presence of dysphagia with silent aspiration, or aspiration without an appropriate cough response.

Some of the common findings during VFSS in patients with Parkinson's disease are:

- Repetitive posterior–anterior tongue movement
- Piecemeal deglutition
- Oral residue
- Pharyngeal residue
- Decreased laryngeal elevation
- Laryngeal penetration/aspiration

AMYOTROPHIC LATERAL SCLEROSIS (ALS)

This is a progressive neurodegenerative disease that destroys nerve cells in the brain and spinal cord, and dysphagia is global over time due to progressive weakness leading to aspiration pneumonia in 15% of these patients (González-Fernández & Daniels, 2008). Ertekin and colleagues (2000) performed electromyography studies in 43 patients who exhibited decreased UES opening and prolonged hyolaryngeal excursion.

Swallowing deficits in patients with ALS are (Groher & Crary, 2010):

- Decreased oral bolus formation and A–P propulsion
- Anterior spillage
- Increased oral transit times
- Oral residue
- Pharyngeal residue
- Decreased airway clearance after laryngeal penetration/aspiration

MYASTHENIA GRAVIS

Myasthenia gravis is an autoimmune disorder resulting in inadequate acetylcholine and reduced muscle contraction. Dysphagia is a common symptom in myasthenia gravis and it eventually occurs in 15% to 40% of patients (Llabrés, Molina-Martinez, & Miralles, 2005). The authors pointed that the diagnosis in these patients may be difficult, especially if acetylcholine receptor antibodies are not present.

In patients with dysphagia, esophageal manometric studies have shown a progressive deterioration in the amplitude of pharyngeal contractions with repeated swallows. In patients with myasthenia gravis, initial movements of deglutition and swallowing are almost intact and the muscles get weaker with repeated use. Some patients have greater problems with chewing food or moving it in their mouth, whereas others have difficulties restricted to the pharyngeal phase. Several of these patients also have a nasal speech due to weakness of the soft palate, whereas other dysphagic patients may have dysphonia (Jaradeh, 2006).

CONCLUSION

Dysphagia is a common consequence of many medical conditions, including stroke, chronic and progressive neurological diseases that affect the nervous system, and surgeries that affect the head and neck. But swallowing difficulty can also be associated with aging alone. It has been estimated that as many as 20% of individuals over the age of 50 years, and most individuals by the age of 80 years, experience some degree of swallowing difficulty resulting in more referrals for swallowing evaluation in medical settings. The large and increasing population above 65 years of age leads us to understand all we can about how aging affects swallowing (Leonard, 2013).

Dysphagia referral rates doubled between 2000 and 2007, with increases of 20% per year. Over 70% of dysphagia referrals were for patients of 60 years and older, and over 42% of these were for patients over 80 years. Referrals for 80- to 89-year-old patients almost doubled and for patients over 90 years more than tripled between 2000 and 2007 (Leder & Suiter, 2009).

Some changes in swallowing function due to aging may be less obvious, but can increase the effort required to swallow, and can even interfere with swallowing safety and effectiveness (Leonard, 2013). These changes may be:

- Reduced vocal cord bulk and sensitivity that help protect the airway.
- Reduced bulk and strength of the muscles of the tongue and pharynx that propel foods and liquids from the mouth into the esophagus.
- Decreased upper esophageal opening and relaxation
- The pharynx is longer and dilated in older individuals. This means that the airway has to be protected longer in order for safe swallowing to occur.

Though increasing age facilitates subtle physiologic changes in swallow function, age-related diseases are significant factors in the presence and severity of dysphagia. Among elderly diseases and health complications, stroke, and dementia reflect high rates of dysphagia. In both conditions, dysphagia is associated with nutritional deficits and increased risk of pneumonia. Recent efforts have suggested that elderly community residents are also at risk for dysphagia and associated deficits in nutritional status and increased pneumonia risk.

REFERENCES

Aviv, J. E., Martin, J. H., Jones, M. E., Wee, T. A., Diamond, B., Keen, M. S., & Blitzer, A. (1994). Age-related changes in pharyngeal and supraglottic sensation. *Annals Otolaryngology, Rhinolology, & Laryngology, 103*(10), 749–752.

Aviv, J. E., Martin, J. H., Keen, M. S., Debell, M., & Blitzer, A. (1993). Air pulse quantification of supraglottic and pharyngeal sensation: A new technique. *Annals Otolaryngology, Rhinolology, & Laryngology, 102*(10), 777–780.

Bastian, R. W. (1991). Videoendoscopic evaluation of patients with dysphagia: An adjunct to the modified barium swallow. *Otolaryngology and Head & Neck Surgery, 104*(3), 339–350.

Castell, J., & Castell, D. (1994). Manometric analysis of the pharyngoesophageal segment. *Indian Journal Gastroenterology, 13*(2), 58–63.

Castell, J., & Castell, D. (1997). Recent developments in the manometric assessment of upper esophageal sphincter function and dysfunction. *Digestive Diseases, 15*(Suppl. 1), 28–39.

Daggett, A., Logemann, J., Rademaker, A., & Pauloski, B. (2006). Laryngeal penetration during deglutition in normal subjects of various ages. *Dysphagia, 21*(4), 270–274.

Easterling, C. S., & Robbins, E. (2008). Dementia and dysphagia. *Geriatric Nursing, 29*(4), 275–285.

Ertekin, C., Aydogdu, I., Yüceyar, N., Kiylioglu, N., Tarlaci, S., & Uludag, B. (2000). Pathophysiological mechanisms of oropharyngeal dysphagia in amyotrophic lateral sclerosis. *Brain, 123*(Pt. 1), 125–140.

Fei, T., Polacco, R. C., Hori, S. E., Molfenter, S. M., Peladeau-Pigeon, M., Tsang, C., & Steele, C.M. (2013). Age-related differences in tongue-palate pressures for strength and swallowing tasks. *Dysphagiam, 28*(4), 575–581.

González-Fernández, M., & Daniels, S. K. (2008). Dysphagia in stroke and neurologic disease. *Physical Medicine and Rehabilitation Clinics of North America, 19*(4), 867–888.

Groher, M., & Crary, M. (2010). *Dysphagia: Clinical management in adults and children.* St. Louis, MO: Elsevier.

Hatlebakk, J., Castell, J., Spiegel, J., Paoletti, V., Katz, P., & Castell, D. (1998). Dilatation therapy for dysphagia in patients with upper esophageal sphincter dysfunction: Manometric and symptomatic response. *Diseases of the Esophagus, 11*(4), 254–259.

Hila, A., Castell, J., & Castell, D. (2001). Pharyngeal and upper esophageal sphincter manometry in the evaluation of dysphagia. *Journal of Clinical Gastroenterology, 33*(5), 355–361.

Iida, T., Tohara, H., Wada, S., Nakane, A., Sanpei, R., & Ueda, K. (2013). Aging decreases the strength of suprahyoid muscles involved in swallowing movements. *The Tohoku Journal of Experimental Medicine, 231*(3), 223–228.

Jaradeh, S. (2006). Muscle disorders affecting oral and pharyngeal swallowing. *GI Motility online.* doi:10.1038/gimo35

Langmore, S., Schatz, K., & Olsen, N. (1988). Fiberoptic endoscopic examination of swallowing safety: A new procedure. *Dysphagia, 2*(4), 209–211.

Leder, S. B., & Suiter, D. M. (2009). An epidemiologic study on aging and dysphagia in the acute care hospitalized population: 2000–2007. *Gerontology, 55*(6), 714–718.

Leonard, R. (2013). *How aging affects our swallowing ability.* Retrieved August 15, 2014 from http://www.swallowingdisorderfoundation.com/how-aging-affects-our-swallowing-ability/

Leonard, R., & Kendall, K. (2014). *Dysphagia assessment and treatment planning: A team approach.* San Diego, CA: Plural.

Lindgren, S., & Janzon, L. (1991). Prevalence of swallowing complaints and clinical findings among 50- to 79-year-old men and women in an urban population. *Dysphagia, 6*(4), 187–192.

Llabrés, M., Molina-Martinez, F. J., & Miralles, F. (2005). Dysphagia as the sole manifestation of myasthenia gravis. *Journal Neurology Neurosurgery and Psychiatry, 76*(9), 1297–1300.

Logemann, J. A. (1986). Treatment for aspiration related to dysphagia: An overview. *Dysphagia, 1*(1), 34–38.

Logemann, J. A. (1998). *Evaluation and treatment of swallowing disorders.* Austin, TX: Pro-Ed.

Logemann, J. A., Pauloski, B. R., Rademaker, A. W., Colangelo, L. A., Kahrilas, P. J., & Smith, C. H. (2000). Temporal and biomechanical characteristics of oropharyngeal swallow in younger and older men. *Journal of Speech Language and Hearing Research, 43*(5), 1264–1274.

Malhi-Chowla, N., Achem, S., Stark, M., & DeVault, K. (2000). Manometry of the upper esophageal sphincter and pharynx is not useful in unselected patients referred for esophageal testing. *The American Journal of Gastroenterology, 95*(6), 1417–1421.

McCullough, G. H., Wertz, R. T., Rosenbek, J. C., & Dinneen, C. (1999). Clinicians' preferences and practices in conducting clinical/bedside and videofluoroscopic swallowing examinations in an adult, neurogenic population. *American Journal of Speech-Language Pathology, 8*(2), 149–163.

Murphy, C., Schubert, C. R, Cruickshanks, K. J., Klein, B. E., Klein, R., & Nondahl, D. M. (2002). Prevalence of olfactory impairment in older adults. *Journal of the American Medical Association, 288*(18), 2307–2312.

Nicosia, M. A., Hind, J. A., Roecker, E. B., Carnes, M., Doyle, J., Dengel, G. A., & Robbins, J. (2000). Age effects on the temporal evolution of isometric and swallowing pressure. *Journals of Gerontology Series A: Biological Sciences and Medical Sciences, 55*(11), 634–640.

Paik, N. J. (2008). *Dysphagia.* Retrieved March 21, 2009, from http://www.emedicine.medscape.com

Robbins, J., Gangnon, R. E., Theis, S. M., Kays, S. A., Hewitt, A. L., & Hind, J. A. (2005). The effects of lingual exercise on swallowing in older adults. *Journals of Gerontology Series A: Biological Sciences and Medical Sciences, 53,* 1483–1489.

Robbins, J.·, Hamilton, J. W., Lof, G. L., & Kempster, G. B. (1992). Oropharyngeal swallowing in normal adults of different ages. *Gastroenterology, 103*(3), 823–829.

Robbins, J., Levine, R., Wood, J., Roecker, E. B., & Luschei, E. (1995). Age effects on lingual pressure generation as a risk factor for dysphagia. *Journals of Gerontology Series A: Biological Sciences and Medical Sciences, 50*(5), M257–M262.

Schmidt, J., Holas, M., Halvorson, K., & Reading, M. (1994). Videofluoroscopic evidence of aspiration predicts pneumonia and death but not dehydration following stroke. *Dysphagia, 9*(1), 7–11.

Singh, S., & Hamdy, S. (2006). Dysphagia in stroke patients. *Postgraduate Medical Journal, 82*(968), 383–391.

Wang, C. M., Chen, J. Y., Chuang, C. C., Tseng, W. C., Wong, A. M., & Pei, Y. C. (2014). Aging-related changes in swallowing, and in the coordination of swallowing and respiration determined by novel non-invasive measurement techniques. *Geriatrics Gerontology International.* Advance online publication.

Xue, S., Katz, P. O., Castell, J. A., & Castell, D. O. (2000). Upper esophageal sphincter and pharyngeal manometry: Which patients? [abstract]. *Gastroenterology, 118,* A410.

Youmans, S. R., & Stierwalt, J. A. (2006). Measures of tongue function related to normal swallowing. *Dysphagia, 21*(2), 102–111.

CHAPTER 8

Social Language Enhancement in Dementia and Aphasia

Linda S. Carozza with contribution by Noel Shafi

Community reintegration is the ultimate goal of all rehabilitation and successful adjustment to life at different junctures takes courage and knowledge. Some strategies in this chapter will describe current state of the art approaches to fulfilling a productive social role under many circumstances. The access to participation in life is a right of all individuals. This chapter offers a unique window into life-enhancing communication-based strategies, research-based and meaningful in many settings, that support personal identity and interaction.

—Linda S. Carozza

INTRODUCTION

This chapter provides a unique perspective on some of the causes of communication failure in the context of aging, coupled with strategies and methods with which to handle the stages of aftercare. Aftercare refers to the stage in recovery and service delivery when no further direct services are provided, yet the client continues to make small gradual and meaningful gains. With the medical economy shrinking worldwide, and the increase of a "graying population," there will be fewer resources for more people, and many people are striving to live longer with the best possible quality of life. This applies to the healthy elderly as well as those with impairments who seek to participate in society to the best of their functional capacities. "Wellness" is for everyone, and this chapter will describe paths to community participation and social interaction for impaired individuals. Using communication strategies in an interpersonal context is key to living a more satisfactory and fulfilling life.

This chapter also extends the discussion of the pragmatic uses of language and speech communication, as well as the use of techniques such as those adapted from the study of conversational analysis (Carozza, 2012), among others. Within this work, a single subject was examined for the benefit obtained via different types of questions (open-ended versus closed). The purpose of the examination was to clarify caregiver communications with individuals with dementia. Statistical results revealed the patient benefited from closed question types with defined response parameters much more so than when asked open-ended questions. This corresponded with expectations of changes in language performance associated with dementia. Therefore, it is recommended as a strategy for dementia patients and should be studied further with larger patient groups and with different levels of dementia types. This is a demonstration of one of the many analyse focusing on the pragmatic uses of language. Practical approaches are important in a book of this nature because the focus is not on the traditional medical model therapy per se, but on real world applications. In this sense, we must take into account various methods of communication, not just verbal, including paralinguistic and nonverbal communication. For example, a patient may not be capable of verbal speech, but can still communicate using body language and facial cueing, both of which are part of the totality of human communication. The social use of language arises from a complexity of brain mechanisms and therefore can break down due to a variety of reasons. This may include injury to the parts of the brain that contribute to visual and spatial processing, among others.

INTRODUCTION TO COMMUNICATIVE BREAKDOWNS AND NEUROGENIC CONSIDERATIONS

The changes in function that accompany normal aging versus disordered language must be considered. Changes in adult language use, structure, and content over time have been studied extensively by language researchers, and are covered in detail in the cognitive chapters of this book. These are especially important areas of research in that normal functioning depends on a brain-based activity and a host of cues in everyday environments that go beyond mere words and allow us to perceive incoming messages of all kinds, verbal and nonverbal. Whereas the focus of this chapter will be on living successfully with neurogenic communication disorders such as aphasia and dementia, the overall challenge of communication in a fast-paced society is an experience with which all communicators can identify.

One aspect of this is the change in response times that may take place during the normal life span. Since language reception and expression are, in effect, the detection of a rapid and fixed code, communication can be seen as the ability to quickly detect the features of a communication instance such as tone of voice, eye gaze patterns, and other nonverbal accompaniments to actual words and sentences. One major contribution to the lack of an efficient information processing system may be the overall changes in response time and related accuracy that is generally experienced as a person ages. Therefore, a decline in processing speed or "cognitive slowing," is one variable that may account for the differences in response times of older adults in both online experimental language processing tasks and normal day-to-day interpersonal communication. A further explanation of the decline in response times arises out of an understanding of how language is perceived and processed from a neuroscientific point of view, or some of the so-called cognitive underpinnings that support language and contribute to a psycholinguistic explanation of how language may work.

The notion of an "inhibition" factor that allows us to block out or ignore distraction is a component of many theories of language activation and use (Carozza, 1995). It can be hypothesized that an older adult may have difficulty with competing stimuli and therefore be unable to ignore distractions. Nonetheless, in this vast area of semantic network studies, there have been a significant number of discrepant findings on how inhibition may account for language function and decline in older adults and impaired populations. One explanation for discrepant theories lies in the highly complex methodological components of assessing semantic theory in the normal aged mechanism, which makes it extremely challenging to determine if scientific findings in processing studies are due to one sole mechanism or a contribution of many factors. The main example of this complex research area is the semantic priming literature, which tries to clarify whether subjects' failure to correctly identify properties of word stimuli stems primarily from the erosion of language centers per se, or arises from a failure in the retrieval mechanisms in the brain that allow for speedy access to and interaction between areas of the brain during normal ongoing language production. The fact that this interoperational process takes place is undeniable can be seen simply by observing the speed and efficiency of everyday communication marked by the rapid production of generative and novel language generation in normal speakers.

In addition, working memory changes over time. According to Kemper and Anagnopoulos (1989), limitations in memory do have significant effects on language processing and understanding in older adults. One difficulty with clarifying this theory, however, is that natural language represents a kind of "moving target." It is constantly changing and even a simple back-and-forth conversation, with all of the various linguistic and paralinguistic cues, and information being exchanged at rapid rates, can make it difficult to quantify/measure due to the fact that it is not controlled. Therefore, studies have moved to looking at related communication targets such as eye tracking and other measures as factors that may contribute to differences in processing strategies, and for which other experimental designs may not have fully accounted.

An additional familiar construct that seeks to describe characteristics in the language of older adults has to do with the "tip-of-the-tongue" phenomenon. Although this is far more common in older speakers and is mimicked in certain pathological communication disorders, there is no clear evidence that transmission of a progressive deficit occurs in healthy aging. Proof of this is the fact that nonspecific tip-of-the-tongue phenomena does not progress in otherwise healthy individuals, as it would in certain neurologic conditions such as dementia; nor does word-finding status in evolving conditions such as stroke-related aphasia have the same overt characteristics as the more nonspecific naming errors seen in healthy elderly. There is reason to conclude that neurologically healthy older speakers maintain syntax throughout the lifespan, and retain and may even expand semantic base and vocabulary well into middle age. Therefore, it is reasonable to expect healthy elderly speakers to perform daily life communication tasks into their later years, unaffected by significant change beyond mild cognitive slowing and related decline.

THE NEED FOR LONG-TERM STRATEGIES FOR CHRONIC COMMUNICATION DISABILITIES

The two main disorders that will be discussed in this chapter are aphasia and dementia in relation to long-term strategies for individuals in chronic stages of disease. This is a critical area of need for patients who must continue to live with language restriction after stroke and in cases of dementia, who will continue to suffer language decline. The goal of this chapter is to provide an overview of the evidence basis for some of the language methodologies used to support these two disparate conditions, in addition to emphasizing the component of social models and language support and finally some future directions given present research. Social communication skills will assist patients with chronic aphasia to overcome some of the daily hurdles of high-paced community participation. In addition when considering patients with language loss due to dementia, knowledge of strategies by which to sharpen the communication between patients and their caregivers may contribute to increased participation and well-being.

THE IMPACT OF SPEECH-LANGUAGE PATHOLOGY TREATMENT ON APHASIA

Individuals with aphasia are made up of a very large segment of different onsets, sites of lesion, age at onset, and other highly pertinent factors that directly and critically affect medical rehabilitation in the acute stages. This rich area of practice is beyond the scope of this chapter, which focuses on strategies for patients who are no longer in active treatments as a whole. However, for purposes of a complete picture of the earlier stages of intervention, it is very important to note that the primary aphasia therapies have been examined intensively for efficacy and effectiveness. This research includes the results of a systematic review of approaches. Randall Robey (1998) provides leadership in conducting evaluations of level of evidence in this population. The outcome management of this complex patient population depends on defined expectations and outcomes, and therefore underscoring the relevance of the systematic review of literature describing primary patient approaches. In Robey's work, a meta-analysis of 55 reports of clinical outcomes substantiated the use of aphasia therapy as contributing to improved language recovery. The concept exists that amount of treatment, specific approach, as well as severity and type of aphasia, are crucial factors. This is important in underscoring that primary medical rehabilitation services in the formed of skilled speech-language clinicians trained specifically in neurogenic disorders has a proven effect in positive clinical expectations. In recent years there has been a shift toward therapies with the goal of helping clients with aphasia make life adjustments in order to "access everyday interactions and activities" via "practical strategies" (AphasiaAccess, 2014). AphasiaAccess, a network of individuals with the goal to "advance communicative access for people with aphasia," has greatly supported this life adjustment approach within therapies of people with aphasia. AphasiaAccess believes that "professionals who serve those with aphasia must strive to create environments people with aphasia can navigate" (AphasiaAccess, 2014). The long-term management of patients, however, who may no longer receive direct services of a speech specialist will be the following area of discussion in this chapter.

STRATEGIES FOR SOCIAL LANGUAGE ENHANCEMENT IN APHASIA

Strategies for independent learning on a long-term basis is a goal of many patients with aphasia, and their families. Anecdotal reports suggest that patients can make incremental gains long after formal individual and group therapies. For some individuals, aphasia community groups such as described in this chapter provide a consistent venue of fellowship and support. For others in which community participation may not be feasible, at home programs delivered via Skype or other applications may be appropriate. One such option is provided by the Lingraphica system (The Aphasia Company, http://www.aphasia.com), which has customized original icons that adult users may find comfortable and convenient. This is one of several systems available via laptop and smartphone application. Separately, low tech assistance is available to patients via the communication books which many clinicians make for clients as well as via systems of communication such as the Life Interest and Value Cards (Helm-Estabrooks & Whiteside, 2012) that help an individual maintain vital activities of daily living in a meaningful way.

Community Reintegration as Ultimate Aphasia Strategy

There has been a growth in the appreciation that language is by its very nature meant to be "communicated"; therefore, emphasis on communication strategies that employ training in supportive communication for caregivers and the all-important family and support systems of the patient is paramount. This is especially significant for the long-term aphasic patient who is learning to reintegrate into the community and may no longer be part of a formal service delivery system. Several authors have developed specific strategies that can be used as caregiver communication models, namely Cunningham and Ward (2003) and Simmons-Mackie and Kagan (2010). In general, it can be stated that partner education, including video sessions with feedback and role-play, can help increase communication supports such as gesture and "repairs" of communication attempts that help patients and partners in successful communication and satisfaction. This is very salient in the work that has been very transformative to me as a seasoned clinician. I have found that the focus on social connectivity in language support to individuals with aphasia is especially salient. That is, not only relearning language forms but also the meaningful interactions with others are extremely helpful in helping patients regain psychosocial identity and confidence.

The Importance of Social Connectivity

One of the areas of practice that combines the community reintegration notion and the importance of social connectedness is a social networks approach. Social networks are important to individual life satisfaction and fulfillment. Therefore, this type of intervention takes into account that individuals with aphasia may have reduced social contacts and connections. The overarching goal is to get patients to reconnect and communicate with their prior contacts in real-life scenarios. As an example of social connectedness challenges is described by Mosheim (2010), who speaks about aphasia and social media, which many patients may be eager to use. Furthermore, clinicians are beginning to use tools, such as the Communicative Effectiveness and Stress Rating Scale (CEASRS; Carozza, Olea-Santos & Abesamis, 2005a, 2005b) and the Quality of Communication Life Scale, published by the American Speech-Language-Hearing Association (Paul, Frattali, Holland, Thompson, Caperton, & Slater, 2005), to measure perceived and real social-language competencies in an effort to help clients begin to reach out to others in meaningful and satisfying ways, despite their residual aphasia. This particular unified set of goals aims at helping patients to regain confidence and re-enter communicatively challenging situations.

Caregiver Supports and Community Re-entry

The role of conversational partners is critical in making speech scenarios realistic and challenging at the same time. The use of trained nonspeech-clinicians to participate in carryover activities may be particularly effective in this model since this form of "guided rehearsal" may help patients take on the new small calculated communication attempts in a controlled environment with some support, but not at a therapeutic level. This helps patients begin to take the initial steps in a less challenging environment and gain the confidence of small gains, thereby helping them to take the next step in a calculated model of expanding social networks. Role-play, as an example, may form a bridge to outside communication scenarios in a more realistic way via engagement and practice. In this sense, lost social networks may begin to be broadened and regained. The fact that community re-entry and adjustment to disability is so important to long- term adjustment is underscored in the statement by Cynthia Vickers in the 2010 Mosheim article, that "It's often possible to demonstrate that offering an aphasia group program emphasizes the values of a medical facility concerned with the health and well-being of its community" (Mosheim, 2010). This statement speaks to the fact that groups, and after care community groups, are essential to taking part in real world interpersonal communication. These groups function as a paced introduction to real-world independent communication needs. The role of the community group versus a treatment group thereby takes on a highly critical role in the service delivery stream and affords meaningful and needed options for patients who are formally discharged from third-party payer outpatient settings and require continued support to fully integrate into the community. It is critical that patients see other individuals recovering and share experience and personal narratives as well as all the natural supports and dialogue that community membership brings.

The social communication approach reported in 1998 by Aura Kagan has had an impact around the world and has given new meaning to management in aphasia service delivery. The basic tenets of this standard training of volunteers as communication partners has demonstrated improvements in both patient and volunteer competencies. There are conceptual, technical, role-play, and evaluation components to the training. The affirmation of the patient in terms of expressions of verbal support as well as a standard of allowing time, materials, prompts, and verification of message are key components in the training paradigm. The patient with aphasia is a partner in this model and many treatment group and social model groups use components of this model.

Application of the Quality of Life Approach in Aphasia

In a very real way, the social networks expansion achieved via community group involvement is a real-life methodology by which to practice and enhance the quality of life for people with aphasia. Changes in self-acceptance and the ability to take on new communication challenges in a measured fashion are logical outcomes that can be measured by group leaders practicing application of a social model approach. One such methodology may include self-report scales such as the scales adapted for aphasic individuals to describe their communicative roles in real-life settings.

The Quality of Communication Life Scale (Paul et al., 2005) is a well-recognized measurement that captures information about the impact of a communication disorder on the social, emotional, psychosocial, and overall quality of life of an individual. In fact, quality of life (QoL) research is helpful for all patients and may help substantially improve the understanding of the sequelae of stroke and hence, clinical management and treatment outcomes of aphasia. Vickers (2010) found that people with aphasia are susceptible to both a reduction in social networks and social isolation, and that people with aphasia who attend aphasia community groups report increased social participation and a sense of social connectedness. These are important supports in terms of strengthening social communication strategies that help to improve quality of "communication life" in people with aphasia, separate and apart from linguistic outcomes. Furthermore, the utility of pre and post measures of community groups using scales such as this can contribute to improved outcome expectations and planning for clients' long-term social communication goals, as was piloted by Carozza and Miraglia and reported to the New York City Speech-Language-Hearing Association (2013).

Predictive Factors and Use of Quality of Life Approaches

The goal of social models using quality of life indicators can be enhanced by a closer look at related factors that contribute to positive outcome expectation. More fully understanding the predictive factors of quality of life in poststroke aphasia can help clinicians and researchers develop appropriate intervention programs (Hilari, Wiggins, Roy, Byng, & Smith, 2003). Cruice, Worrall, Hickson, and Murison (2003) emphasize that functional communication ability is linked to quality of life, alongside emotional and physical health. This is consistent with King (1996) who identified three predictive factors of quality of life in long-term poststroke survivors, including depression, social support, and functional status. Therefore, to participate fully in life, patients must learn and use newly adapted strategies in a self-driven manner, independent of face-to-face clinical interventions, which affords a pathway to interpersonal relations and a sense of well-being. One of the ways patients with restrictions in language expression may participate with others is in the many forms of creative self-expression that are not language bound, such as music, art, horticulture, and similar pursuits. This creative arts approach may form a natural complement to the social model and community group context in that the topics and themes have the potential to help patients regain mastery of areas of competence and enjoyment via fulfillment and engagement. As such, higher-level language functions and abstraction may be a way to engage patients with aphasia with lost areas of cultural fulfillment and life, and potentially other areas of personal expression and satisfaction via the arts. An example of this approach in action is one that capitalizes on the creative area of poetry and language. The following section highlights the use of poetry as a creative approach to language rehabilitation in the elderly. Poetry, along with music and art therapy, is described in greater detail as a creative therapeutic approach in Part II of this book.

Poetry: A Creative Arts Approach to Language Rehabilitation in the Elderly

The creative arts approach to speech and language rehabilitation for adults with neurogenic communicative disorders is based on the principles of recreation for the general geriatric population. Creative arts and psychotherapy have long been intertwined for cognitive rehabilitation. Creative arts therapies include poetry, art, and music therapies. Poetry therapy is of potential interest to speech-language pathologists working with the elderly. Mazza

(2003) describes many of the concepts related to poetry therapy guidelines and practice in different settings.

Poetry therapy is a complementary therapy technique used for cognitive and language stimulation. Using poetry as a method of language rehabilitation is an understudied approach in speech-language pathology. However, this method has been extensively used in other health-related disciplines. Professionals in the fields of nursing, social work, and psychiatry may point to the benefits of poetry in facilitating conversation and creative expression. Poetry reading, recitation, and reflection provide different aspects of language use and communication roles, and may promote divergent thinking and nonliteral language comprehension.

Poetry Therapy and Oral Language

Silvermarie (1988) conducted poetry therapy with nursing home residents to encourage and elicit the expression of memories and imagination. As per qualitative observation of social outcomes, she found that it facilitated resident bonding, emotional expression, and interpersonal relations with nursing staff. Similarly, Goldstein (1987) conducted poetry therapy with geriatric patients at a short-term psychiatric hospital, to encourage reminiscing. He found that it stimulated cognition, reduced isolation, and enhanced self-esteem. Poetry therapy is also applied as a medium for eliciting written expression, in addition to oral expression.

Poetry Therapy and Written Language

Getzel (1983) conducted poetry writing exercises with elderly clients in a social group work context. Some of the poetry samples included in his work revealed that the elderly used poetry as a tool to describe their life philosophy and existential meaning. Conversations around self-identity and life purpose seem to be invaluable to the geriatric population. Elderly people diagnosed with aphasia are no exception, and their desire to renegotiate their sense of identity and communal role cannot be disregarded. Poetry writing is one way in which the elderly can feel secure in expressing and documenting the full range of their emotions and personal evolution through aging, or their struggle in coping with health-related issues.

In this very real sense, a creative arts approach to language loss centering on language and imagery can support a life participation model in addition to the social discovery community groups that may drive fulfillment and engagement to encourage patients to live successfully with adjustment to aphasia and renewed quality of life post-acute disability.

Future Directions

As we strive for person-centered approaches in the rapidly advancing world, technological supports for communication therapy will be forthcoming, particularly in the area of aphasia. The combination of approaches will most likely yield richest resources for this complex area of rehabilitation. As an example, medical technological advances such as transcranial direct current stimulation studies are being undertaken which may have positive influence on language performance (Marangolo, Fiori, Calpagnano, et al., 2013). In fact, the use of this type of direct brain stimulation in addition to the "conversational therapies" similar to those discussed in this chapter may yield potential positive outcomes in patients with chronic aphasia (Marangolo, Fiori, Cipollari, et al., 2013). The view to the future of patient understanding is enhanced by looking at the patient as a whole as a member of a larger community, as well as capitalizing on technologies that may be developed for different disorders yet find strong applicability to aphasia rehabilitation. In this sense, full quality of life can be pursued by engaging all areas of therapeutic possibilities with central focus on the individual. In the following sections, the needs of a diverse patient group will be discussed within the framework of communication strategies for social communication enhancement in dementia populations.

STRATEGIES FOR SOCIAL LANGUAGE ENHANCEMENT IN DEMENTIA

Patients living with dementia of many underlying etiologies comprise one of the most challenging of diagnostic classes. Unlike the aphasic individual who will often have relatively preserved comprehension and other cognitive strengths, the patient with communication loss secondary to dementia has many comorbid issues that compound treatment challenges. These patients may well be verbose indeed; however, clarity of their exchange in terms of meaningfulness is lost on almost all except perhaps the most familiar and sensitive listener. Therefore, strategies are markedly different than those that may be successful for aphasia and involve a reorientation of the environment and familiarity and security of routine, both language and otherwise. A highly important contribution to research in this area is the systematic review of the literature of communication strategies for people with dementia provided by Vasse, Vermooij-Dassen, Spijker, Rikkert, and Koopmans (2010). "Best practice" in communication approaches assists patients in psychosocial adjustment, and as such is vital in caregiving and family training. One-to-one interactions, particularly those that involve life review as a strategy and emphasize attention to nonverbal communication, can be embedded into patient routines with positive results.

A systematic review of cognitive interventions for individuals with dementia was done by Hopper et al., 2013). Conclusions determined that evidence is accumulating that, at this point, is more focused on delivery variables than overall effectiveness. Approaches such as errorless learning, spaced retrieval methods, vanishing cues strategies and use of verbal instructions and cueing are all considered important in dementia care. There is a generally positive trend toward establishing the "best practices." To date, however, there remains a broad range of methodological factors that confounds more specific conclusions.

Meta-analyses of research that examine communication strategies for individuals with dementia should be on the frontier of research and is needed as a call for action in this population. It is true that communication strategies for individuals with dementia have been lagging but clinicians are looking to technology and even robotic interventions for environmental adaptations. As an example, the Dem@Care project (http://www.demcare.eu/) uses voice monitoring to aid in early diagnosis of dementia in the home. Researchers on this project discovered that "certain neurological and mental disorders can manifest themselves in voice" (IBM Research). Therefore, monitoring and conducting speech analyses on physical changes in speech from the home via simple equipment, such as microphones, can result in an earlier diagnosis of dementia. These physical changes in speech serve as warning signs of dementia and come before the memory loss symptom (IBM Research). While this new form of diagnosis is important for both practitioners and families because it impacts how diseases associated with aging are both diagnosed and treated in the home and in medical practice, more information is needed. While these technologies will greatly assist populations who have access to these latest approaches in graduate programs and research populations, access by the general public is still extremely limited for various reasons, not the least of which is a certain lack of understanding of the primacy of communication even in populations considered "demented." Therefore, this area of practice would benefit from initial systematic reviews of literature and forthcoming meta-analyses of research that examine similar populations and protocols. (See the Cochrane Database of Systematic Reviews and The Joanna Briggs Institute Library of Systemic Reviews for existing research and resources.)

As in other segments of the population, wellness and quality of life of these individuals as part of the elderly population is a "hot topic" in current society (De Luca D'Alessandro, Bonacci, & Giraldi, 2011). The authors stress the growing aging demographic that has increasing implications for health, society, epidemiology, and related costs. Aging involves not only changes in medical health but also in psychological, cognitive, and social statuses. The preparation for the needs of the elderly involves prevention of illness and slowing of exacerbation. This can include interventions to guide individuals stricken the many disorders of aging, including as an example, cancers that affect speech (Shafi & Carozza, 2012), and pertinently, as well as those afflicted with communication loss secondary to dementia and its related underlying conditions.

Meaningful Communication Approaches to Support Dementia

The way in which I envision answering the need for enhancement of dementia strategies is via quality of life strategies. A good deal of the value in quality of life approaches is contained in how well these methods are *communicated* to patients and families as the underlying clinical philosophy. Using a communication-sensitive approach is common to many disciplines and the quality of communication itself has been studied extensively for impact by specialists in the field of psychology and human relations (Liu, Chua, & Stahl, 2010). These particular authors developed and validated an instrument that measures important dimensions of communication quality. These dimensions are clarity, responsiveness, and comfort. Their findings in different settings support the notion that a higher degree of communication quality leads to better outcomes. The implications exist for practice in a diverse array of fields, particularly in allied health and integrative medicine, and in dementia care.

Using person-centered approaches to increase patient adjustment is a known concept. Phillips, Reid-Arndt, and Pak (2010) studied the effects of creative expression intervention on emotions, communication, and quality of life in persons with dementia. This study, which has also had broad implications for other populations and potential nonpharmacological interventions, focused on a methodology that is central to some of the important advances in dementia care. Similarly, as conducted by Carozza and Georgiou (2009), an adaptation of the TimeSlips Storytelling program, developed by Anne Basting (2003), shows tremendous promise for increasing positive affect in patients. The authors attribute some of the effects to the program intervention's reliance on interaction and verbalization. The engaging nature of the TimeSlips narrative stimuli and interaction with a narrator provide cohesion to the verbal interactions stimulated through this group story-telling approach, which emphasizes participation and ease rather than accuracy and timeliness.

It is therefore appropriate to consider other communication-driven approaches that can benefit patients' adjustment and overall acceptance of their language strengths and restrictions, thus yielding better quality of life via interpersonal acceptance and communication-enhanced approaches. Some other important advances in this area will be discussed in the subsequent sections and chapters regarding creative approaches that focus on communication-enhancement as a vehicle to improve quality of life via other channels. Neumann, Carozza, and Georgiou (2010) examined the role of the interplay between neurolinguistics and psycholinguistics in understanding healthy aging and dementia. In this project, patient diagnostic groups were reliably determinable based on their narrative responses to a free speech task. An important contribution in this case may be replicability, and that is where the importance of outcome expectations and management comes into play, so that patients may be approached in nonthreatening but still meaningful conversational exchanges that "weave" their story via shared interaction. With increasing application of observational and empirical research, concerned professionals can "modularize" the approaches that are the most successful in their particular environment and that capitalize on research information, client preferences, and clinician experiences.

Social Communication in Persons with Dementia by Acton, Yauk, Hopkins, and Mayhew (2007) describes an important aspect of communication enhancement in individuals with dementia. Acton et al. found that communication breakdowns tend to result in increased stress, which may lead to behavioral issues. Quality of life improves for both patients and caregivers when communication burdens are eased. A therapeutic communication plan developed for patients and caregivers, with strategies to help patients express needs, preferences, and ideas, may be critical to overall outcome satisfaction.

Suggestions: Limiting Communicative Breakdowns

Encouraging communication in individuals with dementia involves both interpersonal encouragement and close attention to proxemics, or body language and physical contact. The following are some important reminders for families and caregivers to keep in mind when speaking with a person with impaired communication abilities as the result of a stroke or other health-related condition. General strategies include: attention to speech rate with one thought per statement, allowing ample response time, asking for confirmation, and not presuming understanding, in addition to not using "baby talk," or acting dismissively. Additional supports include using visual cues of all kinds, and repeating what you think was stated to offer affirmation, and always in a demeanor that offers choice and respect. Tone and gesture are especially important, as is gaze and truly active listening. Competing background sounds should be minimized along with encouragement via being a compassionate and attentive conversation partner. Knowing familiar names and activities will help the person feel comfortable in the conversational context.

Future Directions

Future directions of dementia care are on the horizon. Bharucha et al. (2009) emphasize the triple-fold increase in the dementia population that is anticipated by the year 2050. As in aphasia, assistive technologies will be essential to alleviate the caregiver burden that will ensue, in addition to that which exists already. Communication applications, cognitive devices, as well as physiologic and environmental sensor systems will all contribute to new methodologies such as Smart Home technology and health monitoring devices, which are in turn all part of the Alzheimer's Association Working Group on Technologies that will contribute to meeting the needs of dementia patients and potentially all aging Americans.

The chronic needs for communication strategies to help in the well-being of this important core of our medical population will call on our strengths as practitioners to bring to the forefront compassionate care coupled with scientific advancement and evidence. The work of both Elman (2007) and Hinckley, Hasselkus, and Ganzfried (2013) demonstrates how practitioners can best serve their clients through compassionate understanding of what they need. In the case of Elman (2007), she examined the key role speech-language pathologists have in reconnecting individuals with aphasia to their family members and community via group treatment. This is an example of a therapeutic approach supported by scientific evidence that interacts with social and compassionate aspects of a person's life: their interpersonal relationships. Hinckley's work (2013), on the other hand, examines how individuals with aphasia feel regarding the accessibility of resources and services. She argues that speech-language pathologists can better aid individuals with aphasia if there was a better understanding of how their clients access information and what information and resources are important to them to access. The most important thing is that clinicians need to consider "goals that matter" in order to implement life participation approaches meaningfully to persons with aphasia. The field is forthcoming in activities that help identify "key life" activities in a coordinated fashion to allow for a full picture of patient and family needs.

I suggest that the modification and application of maintaining life participation is also highly meaningful when considering the patients with dementia-related communication needs. The levels of care of clinical, research, and education are highly and equally important. Professionals working in this area are concerned with research proposals in this area to be better able to suggest creative approaches to dementia care with greater evidence.

The work by Nan Bernstein Ratner (2006) underscores the notion that evidence-based approaches in social communication management is a growing field and calls upon the flexible clinician who can problem solve and tailor any program to meet the specific needs of the client, regardless of underlying etiology. The author states this clinical acumen can outweigh the specifics of any particular protocol. The importance of seeking information relative to creative approaches, and to try to benefit from the experience of others in order to effectively apply new strategies is of utmost importance in any arena of clinical care.

A final note concerns the possibility of communication-enhancing medications in dementia management: according to Ferris and Farlow (2013), emphasis must be placed on the language decline in Alzheimer's disease due to the centrality of language to cognition. The language decline in these patients is primarily in areas of semantic and pragmatic function, at least through the moderate stage of the disease. The authors report a new finding that acetylcholinesterace inhibitors may have a beneficial effect on patients' language abilities. This speaks to the future possibility of pharmacological interventions for the recovery/stabilization of language function in the moderate stages during which significant breakdown is evident.

CONCLUSIONS

It is important that medical professionals and the public in general be aware of the different patterns on communication accompanying healthy aging and the commonly associated disease states, particularly aphasia and dementia. Too often, the elderly get grouped together into one diagnostic class and because of this, primary and secondary diagnoses can be obscured without a careful understanding of what constitutes healthy aging and what does not. In addition, it is imperative to realize that "one size does not fit all," now more than ever. With a shrinking global society, the communicative competence of professionals is more important than ever. This extends from therapists working directly with patients and families to the understanding and training of caregivers. This latter group is critical in many instances in which aging individuals may be in the full time company of persons who are from different cultures. The earnest sharing of values and personhood can go a long way in bridging any intercultural gap, and is especially important in older populations that may have additional communication limitations.

Since our aging population encompasses both normal and diagnostic populations, it is important to include adaptations of known quality-of-life strategies so that all individuals can attain their own highest level of satisfaction. In the following chapters, there is particular emphasis on both aphasia and dementia programming as well as other issues relative to aging demographics. Next sections will focus on communication-based strategies that emphasize inclusion and satisfaction of quality of life, particularly those that have to do with appreciation of creative aspects of fulfillment that may not require "words" per se, but still can lift the human spirit in effective ways.

While waiting for larger studies to emerge, this author believes there is a need for case study research. Case studies exemplifying the lives of individuals living with disabilities will portray how creative approaches truly aid those individuals on a day-to-day basis. In a final tribute to the many individuals who have lived successfully with disabilities, I gratefully include this excerpt from an exceptional couple regarding their journey. I hope it inspires all readers as it has inspired me and many others to look forward to recovery and satisfaction at all junctures of life.

ART'S STORY—LIVING SUCCESSFULLY WITH APHASIA (SENT TO LINDA CAROZZA BY HIS LOVING WIFE)

2/1/11, Art was on the floor, having a seizure and stroke. It was found he had left frontoparietal intraparechimal hemorrhage and SDH with mass effect. Art underwent left hemicraniectomy for evacuation of intraparechimal hemorrhage and EVD. When Art awoke, he had global apraxia and aphasia. His hearing was extremely strong, often hearing nurses conversations in the hall, wanting his door closed. Art was left with limited movement on his right side with his right arm and right leg. Art's long-term memory was good, but he had limited short-term memory. It took time for his cognitive skills to improve over the last 2½ years. Today, Art is very alert and positive. He has learned how to communicate through gestures. He is now reading and writing continues to improve.

Prior to his stroke, Art liked music; the Beatles, symphony music, and rock from the 50s to 80s. After Art had a stroke, I had read that music helped connect both sides of the brain. Right from the beginning while in ICU, I had downloaded "Orchestral Rock Songs of the Beatles, by the London Orchestral Symphony." His toes would tap and he would point with his forefinger swaying to the beat. His nurse asked if he was a conductor in an orchestra. I said, "No, a retired firefighter, with a wonderful beat." Music continued to play during his entire hospital stay in both, acute and subacute. I asked friends for songs: about New York, songs from Brooklyn, and the top 100 rock songs from the 50s to 80s.

Art attends Adler Aphasia Center in Maywood, New Jersey, 2 to 3 days a week. He takes six classes, ranging from communicative strategies, computer technologies, exercise, cooking, travel, game shows, comedy, drama and acting and so forth. Also during the summer they perform a play; last summer it was, "Anne Get Your Gun" in which Art was a Sioux Indian and also the King of Europe. This past summer he performed in "Grease" as a student and as Frankie Avalon, Teen Angel, singing/lip synching "Beauty School Dropout." He also performed in a choir group called "The Inspirations." His first word I heard was "Hallelujah." I cried. This semester he also started attending one day a week, "Something Special," where he creates jewelry, desk, and serving pieces that are sold at Adler.

Today, Art is learning to speak with melodic intonation, to the tune of "Happy Birthday." His vowels are excellent and he is now learning his consonants. He is up to 25 short sentences. Practice, practice, practice is the most important thing. Pictures of family and friends, places we had been, and events he had experienced with me helped him in remembering the past. I put together a small album. He had kept very few photos prior to meeting me. We meet 26 years ago and are married for 25. At one time, Art was an excellent photographer. On Facebook, many of our friends posted inspirational sayings and jokes. I would print and bring them to him, taping them to the wall of his hospital room. We are lucky to have a very supportive group of friends and family. Each week while he in the hospital, someone visited. While at home, we meet every week for dinner at a restaurant or at someone's home. This is a happening we have done since we meet and continues today.

Art loves to travel. After graduating from college, Art bought a Triumph motorcycle in the UK and spent a year touring Europe. Then he continued to Japan and mainland China. He later ventured to New Zealand where he helicopter snow skied and bungee jumped, also stopping over in Fiji. Our first trip was 3 weeks after meeting, spending a weekend in New Orleans. This was followed by a three week vacation to the Seychelles Islands including one week in London. Our honeymoon, one year later, was in Indonesia; Bali, Jakarta, and Yogyakarta. Since then we have traveled to Chili, Mexico, Italy, and many of the Caribbean Islands. Right before his stroke, we had taken a transatlantic cruise from New York City to Venice, Italy, also visiting cities in Portugal and Spain.

Since Art came home, we have traveled many times to visit my family in California. We have taken two cruises to Bermuda and to the Caribbean. On weekends, we have driven to Washington, DC, upstate New York and to visit friends at the New Jersey shore. With each trip, Art has shown some type of improvement and has become more independent. Art has always been active and full of adventure. Prior to his stroke, he scuba dived, snow skied, skydived and belonged to a bicycling group. He has owned many power boats, as well as sail boats.

There are many wonderful outdoor activities offered for disabled people. Since his stroke, Art has been swimming, sailing, kayaking, waterskiing, learning how to scuba dive again, snow skiing, on a glider plane, on a hot air balloon, hand cycling, and recumbent cycling. They also offer indoor rock climbing, horseback riding, surfing, and skydiving—both indoor and outdoor.

REFERENCES

Acton, G., Yauk, S., Hopkins, B., & Mayhew, P. (2007). Increasing social communication in persons with dementia. *Research and Theory for Nursing Practice, 21*(1), 32–44.

AphasiaAccess: An Alliance of Life Participation Providers. (2014). *Our History and Mission*. Retrieved from http://www.aphasiaaccess.org/history-and-mission

The Aphasia Company. (n.d.) *Products & apps for aphasia*. Retrieved from http://www.aphasia.com

Basting, A. D. (2003). Reading the story behind the story: Context and content in stories by people with dementia. *Generations, 27*(3), 25–29.

Bernstein Ratner, N. (2006). Setting the stage: Some thoughts about evidence-based practice. *Language, Speech and Hearing Services in Schools, 37*, 1–11.

Bharucha, S., Anand, V., Forlizzi, J., Dew, M., Reynolds, C., Stevens, S., & Wactler, H. (2009). Intelligent assistive technology applications to dementia care: Current capabilities, limitations, and future challenges. *American Journal of Geriatric Psychiatry, 17*(2), 88–104.

Carozza, L. S. (1995). *Automatic and controlled information processing in Alzheimer's disease* (Doctoral dissertation). City University of New York, NY.

Carozza, L. S. (2012). Facilitated narratives in dementia: A conversational analysis approach. *Journal of Intercultural Disciplines, X*, 103–111.

Carozza, L. S., & Georgiou, A. (2009) *Techniques for eliciting and comparing narratives obtained within aphasia groups*. Presentation at the Academy of Aphasia 47th Annual Meeting, Boston, MA.

Carozza, L. S., & Miraglia, R. (2013). *Addressing quality of life outcomes in aphasia community groups*. Presentation at the NYC Speech-Language-Hearing Association, New York, NY.

Carozza, L. S., Olea-Santos, T., & Abesamis, T. M. (2005a). *CEASRS: Communicative Effectiveness and Stress Rating Scale*. Presentation at the ASHA 2006 Convention Poster Session, Miami, FL.

Carozza, L. S., Olea-Santos, T., & Abesamis, T. M. (2005b). *CEASRS: Communicative Effectiveness and Stress Rating Scale*. Presentation at the ASHA 2007 Convention Poster Session, Boston, MA.

Cruice, M., Worrall, L., Hickson, L., & Murison, R. (2003). Finding a focus for quality of life with aphasia: Social and emotional health, and psychological well-being. *Aphasiology, 17*(4), 333–353.

Cunningham, R., & Ward, C. (2003). Evaluation of a training programme to facilitate conversation between people with aphasia and their partners. *Aphasiology, 17*(8), 687–707.

De Luca d'Alessandro, E., Bonacci, S., & Giraldi, G. (2011). Aging populations: The health and quality of life of the elderly. *Clinica Terapeutica, 162*(1), e13–e18.

Dem@Care. *Dementia ambient care: Monitoring for intelligent remote management and decision support.* Retrieved from http://www.demcare.eu/

Elman, R. J. (2007). The importance of aphasia group treatment for rebuilding community and health. *Topics in Language Disorders, 27*(4), 300–308.

Ferris, S., & Farlow, M. (2013). Language impairment in Alzheimer's disease and benefits of acetylcholinesterace inhibitors. *Journal of Clinical Interventions in Aging, 8,* 1007–1014.

Getzel, G. (1983). Poetry writing groups and the elderly. *Social Work With Groups, 6*(1), 65–76.

Goldstein, M. (1987). Poetry: A tool to induce reminiscing and creativity with geriatrics. *Journal of Social Psychiatry, 7*(2), 117–121.

Helm-Estabrooks, N., & Whiteside, J. (2012). Use of Life Interests and Values (LIV) cards for self-determination of aphasia rehabilitation goals. *Perspectives on Neurophysiology and Neurogenic Speech and Language Disorders, 22,* 6–11.

Hilari, K., Wiggins, R., Roy, P., Byng, S., & Smith, S. (2003). Predictors of health-related quality of life (HRQL) in people with chronic aphasia. *Aphasiology, 17*(4), 365–381.

Hinckley, J. J., Hasselkus, A., & Ganzfried, E. (2013). What people with aphasia think about the availability of aphasia resources. *American Journal of Speech-Language Pathology, 22,* 310–317.

Hopper, T., Bourgeois, M., Pimentel, J., Qualls, C. D., Hickey, E., Frymark, T., & Schooling, T. (2013). An evidence-based systematic review on cognitive interventions for individuals with dementia. *American Journal of Speech-Language Pathology, 22,* 126–145.

IBM Research. (n.d.). *A new kind of dementia treatment: Using voice monitoring to help diagnose and treat dementia at home.* Retrieved from http://www.research.ibm.com/articles/dementia-treatment-diagnosis.shtml

Kagan, A. (1998). Supported conversation for adults with aphasia: Methods and resources for training conversation partners. *Aphasiology, 12*(9), 816–830.

Kemper, S., & Anagnopoulos, C. (1989). Language and aging. *Annual review of applied linguistics, 10,* 37–50.

King, R. B. (1996). Quality of life after stroke. *Stroke, 27*(9), 1467–1472.

Liu, L. A., Chua, C. H., & Stahl, G. K. (2010). Quality of communication experience: Definition, measurement, and implications for intercultural negotiations. *Journal of Applied Psychology, 95*(3), 469.

Marangolo, P., Fiori, V., Calpagnano, M., Campana, S., Razzano, C., Caltigirone, C. & Marini, A. (2013). TDCS over the left inferior frontal cortex improves speech production in aphasia. *Frontiers in Human Neuroscience*, 7, 1–10.

Marangolo, P., Fiori, V., Cipollari, S., Campana, S., Razzano, C., Di Paola, M., . . . Caltigorone, C. (2013). Bihemispheric stimulation over left and right inferior frontal region enhances recovery from paraxial of speech in chronic aphasia. *European Journal of Neuroscience, 38*, 3370–3377.

Mazza, N. (2003). *Poetry therapy: Theory and practice.* New York, NY: Brunner-Routledge.

Mosheim, J. (2010). *A social networks approach to aphasia: Incorporating principles of AAC into group therapy.* Retrieved from http://speech-language-pathology-audiology.advanceweb.com/Features/Article

Neumann, Y., Carozza, L. S., & Georgiou, A. (2010) Neurolinguistics and psycholinguistics: Contributions to understanding healthy aging and dementia. In S. Behrens & J. Parker (Eds.), *Language in the real world* (pp. 314–330). New York, NY: Routledge.

Paul, D. R., Frattali, C. M., Holland, A. L., Thompson, C. K., Caperton, C. J., & Slater, S. C. (2005). *Quality of communication life scale.* Rockville, MD: American Speech-Language-Hearing Association.

Phillips, L. J., Reid-Arndt, S. A., & Pak, Y. (2010). Effects of a creative expression intervention on emotions, communication, and quality of life in persons with dementia. *Nursing Research, 59*(6), 417.

Robey, R. (1998). A meta-analysis of clinical outcomes in the treatment of aphasia. *Journal of Speech, Language, and Hearing Research, 41*, 192–187.

Shafi, N., & Carozza, L. S. (2012). Treating cancer-related aphasia. *The ASHA Leader.* Retrieved from http://www.asha.org/Publications/leader/2012/120731/Treating-Cancer-Related-Aphasia.htm

Silvermarie, S. (1988). Poetry therapy with frail elderly in a nursing home. *Journal of Poetry Therapy, 2*(2), 72–83.

Simmons-Mackie, N., & Kagan, A. (2010). Communication strategies used by "good" versus "poor" speaking partners of individuals with aphasia. Aphasiology, *23*(9–11), 807–820.

Vasse, E., Vermooij-Dassen, M., Spijker, A., Rikkert, M., & Koopmans, R. (2010). A systematic review of communication strategies for people with dementia in residential and nursing homes. *International Psychogeriatrics, 22*(2), 189–200.

Vickers, C. P. (2010). Social networks after the onset of aphasia: The impact of aphasia group attendance. *Aphasiology, 24*(6–8), 902–913.

CHAPTER 8 RECOMMENDED ADDITIONAL SOURCES

American Speech-Language-Hearing Association. (2013). *Introduction to evidence-based practice*. Retrieved from http://www.asha.org/Members/ebp/intro/

American Speech-Language-Hearing Association. (2013). *Quality of communication life scale*. Retrieved from http://www.asha.org/eWeb/OLSDynamicPage.aspx?Webcode=olsdetails&title=Quality+of+Communication+Life+Scale+(ASHA+QCL)

Aphasia Online. (2013). *Blogs, group & therapy*. Retrieved from http://www.aphasia.org/aphasia_community/aphasiaonline.html

Babbit, E. M., & Cherney, L. R. (2010). Communication confidence in persons with aphasia. *Topics in Stroke Rehabilitation, 17*(3), 214–223.

Bloom, L. (1962). A rationale for group treatment of aphasic patients. *Journal of Speech and Hearing Disorders, 27*, 11–16.

The Canadian Cochrane Network and Centre. (2005). Retrieved from http://www.cochrane.uottawa.ca/presentations.asp

Chapey, R., Duchan, J. F., Elman, R. J., Garcia, L. J, Kagan, A., & Simmons-Mackie, N. (2001). Life participation approach to aphasia: A statement of values for the future. In *Language intervention strategies in aphasia and related neurogenic communication disorders* (4th ed.). Philadelphia, PA: Lippincott Williams & Wilkins.

Clarke, P., & Black, S. E. (2005). Quality of life following stroke: Negotiating disability, identity, and resources. *Journal of Applied Gerontology, 24*(4), 319–336.

Dalemans, R., de Witte, L. P., Lemmens, J., van den Heuvel, W. J. A., & Wade, D. T. (2008). Measures for rating social participation in people with aphasia: A systematic review. *Clinical Rehabilitation, 22*(6), 542–555.

Davis, G. A. (2007). *Aphasiology: Disorders and clinical practice* (2nd ed.). Boston, MA: Pearson/Allyn & Bacon.

Delcourt, C., Hackett, M., Wu, Y., Huang, Y., Wang, J., Heeley, E., . . . Anderson, C. S. (2011). Determinants of quality of life after stroke in China. *Stroke, 42*, 433–438.

Dollaghan, C. (2004). Evidence-based practice: Myths and realities. *The ASHA Leader, 12*, 4–5.

Duchan, J. F. (2011). Martha Taylor Sarno. *History of speech-language pathology*. Retrieved from http://www.acsu.buffalo.edu/~duchan/new_history/hist20c/sarno.html

Elman, R. J. (1999). The efficacy of group communication treatment in adults with chronic aphasia. *Journal of Speech Language and Hearing Research, 42*, 411–419.

Elman, R. J. (2010). The increasing popularity of aphasia groups: Some reasons why. *Perspectives on Neurophysiology and Neurogenic Speech and Language Disorders, 20,* 100–135.

Engell, B., Hütter, B-O., Willmes, K. & Huber, W. (2003). Quality of life in aphasia: Validation of a pictorial self-rating procedure. *Aphasiology, 17*(4), 383–396.

Fox, C., Morrison, C., Ramig, L., & Sapir, S. (2002). Current perspectives on the Lee Silverman Voice Treatment (LSVT) for individuals with idiopathic Parkinson's disease. *American Journal of Speech Language Pathology, 11,* 111–123.

Ganzfried, E. S. (2011). *Aphasia community groups and support systems: The nuts and bolts* [PowerPoint slides]. Retrieved from http://www.txsha.org/_pdf/Convention/2011Convention/2011Speaker Handouts/Ganzfried,%20Ellayne%20%20Aphasia%20Community%20Groups%20and%20Support%20Systems_The%20Nuts%20and%20Bolts.pdf

Kagan, A., Black, S. E., Duchan, J. F., Simmons-Mackie, N., & Square, P. (2001). Training volunteers as conversation partners using "supported conversation for adults with aphasia" (SCA): A controlled trial. *Journal of Speech, Language, and Hearing Research, 44,* 624–638.

Kagan, A., Simmons-Mackie, N., Rowland, A., Huijbregts, M., Shumway, E., McEwen, S., & Dickey, L. (2007). Assessment for living with aphasia. *International Journal of Speech-Language Pathology,* 1–13.

Kagan, A., Simmons-Mackie, N., Rowland, A., Huijbregts, M., Shumway, E., McEwen, S., . . . Sharp, S. (2008). Counting what counts: A framework for capturing real-life outcomes of aphasia intervention. *Aphasiology, 22*(3), 258–280.

Khanna, D., & Tsevat, J. (2007). Health-related Quality of Life—An introduction. *The American Journal of Managed Care, 13*(9), S218–S223.

Lanyon, L. E., Rose, M. L., & Worrall, L. (2013). The efficacy of outpatient and community-based aphasia group interventions: A systematic review. *International Journal of Speech-Language Pathology, 15*(4), 359–374.

Lomas, J., Pickard, L., Bester, S., Elbard, H., Finlayson, A., & Zoghaib, C. (1989). The Communicative Effectiveness Index: Development and psychometric evaluation of a functional communication measure for adult aphasia. *Journal of Speech and Hearing Disorders, 54,* 113–124.

Lyon, G. J. (1992). Communication use and participation in life for adults with aphasia in natural settings: The scope of the problem. *American Journal of Speech Language Pathology, 1,* 7–14.

Marshall, C. R. (1993). Problem-focused group treatment for clients with mild aphasia. *American Journal of Speech Language Pathology, 2*, 31–37.

Nicholas, M. (2012). The importance of aphasia community programs in supporting self-determination in people with aphasia. *Perspectives on Neuropsychology and Neurogenic Speech and language Disorders, 22*(1), 36–43.

Pederson, P. M., Vinter, K., & Olsen, T. S. (2001). Improvement of oral naming by unsupervised computerized rehabilitation. *Aphasiology, 15*(2), 151–169.

Penn, C., Milner, K., & Fridjhon, P. (1992). The communicative effectiveness index: Its use with South African stroke patients. *South African Journal of Communication Disorders, 39*, 74–82.

Purves, B. A., Petersen, J., & Puurven, G. (2013). An aphasia mentoring program: Perspectives of speech-language pathology students and of mentors with aphasia. *American Journal of Speech-Language Pathology, 22*, 370–379.

Raju, R. R., Sarma, P. S., & Pandian, J. D. (2010). Psychosocial problems, quality of life, and functional independence among Indian stroke survivors. *Stroke, 41*, 2932–2937.

Reistetter, T. A., & Abreu, B. C. (2005). Appraising evidence on community integration following brain injury: A systematic review. *Occupational Therapy International, 12*(4), 196–217.

Ross, K., & Wertz, R. (2003). Quality of life with and without aphasia. *Aphasiology 17*(4), 355–364.

Sackett, D., Straus, E. S., Richardson, W. S., Rosenberg, W., & Haynes, B. H. (2001). *Evidence-based medicine: How to practice and teach EBM* (2nd ed.). Edinburgh, UK: Churchill Livingstone.

Seligman, E. E. P. (1995). The effectiveness of psychotherapy: The Consumer Reports study. *American Psychologist, 30*(12), 965–974.

Simmons-Mackie, N. (2013). A systems approach to training potential communication partners of people with aphasia. *Perspectives on Augmentative and Alternative Communication, 22*(1), 21–29.

Stringer, E. T. (2013). *Action research* (4th ed.). Thousand Oaks, CA: Sage.

Trail, M., Fox, C., Ramig, L., Sapir, S., Howard, J., & Lai, E. (2005). Speech treatment for Parkinsons's disease. *Neurorehabilitation, 20*, 205–221.

Wallace, G. L. (2010). Profile of life participation after stroke and aphasia. *Topics in Stroke Rehabilitation, 17*(6), 432–450.

Wertz, R., Collins, M., Weiss, D., Kurtzke, J., Friden, R., Brookshire, R. H., . . . Ressurreccion, E. (1981). Veteran's administration cooperative study on aphasia: A comparison of individual and group treatment. *Journal of Speech and Hearing Research, 24*, 580–594.

Wilkinson, P. R., Wolfe, C. D., Warburton, F. G., Rudd, A. G., Howard, R. S., Ross-Russell, R. W., & Beech, R. (1997). Longer term quality of life and outcome in stroke patients: Is the Barthel Index alone an adequate measure of outcome? *Quality in Health Care, 6*, 125–130.
The World Health Organization. Quality of Life assessment (WHOQOL): position paper from the World Health Organization. (1995). *Social Sciences & Medicine, 41*, 1403–1409.

PART II

CHAPTER 9

Psychosocial and Creative Approaches to Dementia Care

Lauren Volkmer

The ability of an individual and family to cope with the life changes associated with the dementing conditions is one of the most profound challenges in the lifespan. This chapter provides rich insights into the current theories and applications that support affected individuals with the utmost of dignity, support, and professionalism. Quality of life interventions begin with the respect for the individual and personhood that this chapter describes and illustrates in detail.

—Linda S. Carozza

FOREWORD

As a social worker, I have long felt that a degree of flexibility and openness is essential to quality elder care, and in particular to quality dementia care. As a member of interdisciplinary teams,

I have found that when ideas, research findings, and attitudes cross disciplinary boundaries, care in all disciplines can benefit. In that spirit of collaboration, this chapter will present research, observations, and reflections on various psychosocial and arts-based approaches to dementia care.

These approaches are presented in the hope that the underlying principles and ideas may be transferable in ways that enrich speech-language pathology service provision for people with dementia, as well as for continued long-term care after formal therapy may have ended. Perhaps viewing therapy through a different lens can result in the formulation of new and creative approaches. These enhanced approaches and accompanying desired outcomes may differ from a strictly traditional view of therapy, but some small adaptations may increase the benefit to a person with dementia's quality of life.

Quality of life (QoL) is by definition a subjective and complex construct, made even more difficult to quantify due to the cognitive and functional limitations accompanying dementia. However, observational and qualitative measures of well-being and validated measurement scales are available for this population. Bowling et al. (2014) have provided an excellent summary and critique of measurement tools for dementia-related QoL, as have Algar, Woods, and Windle (2014), with a specific focus on tools relevant to measuring the effects of visual arts programming.

The chapter will begin with an introduction to a paradigm of dementia service provision based on a model of person-centered care. I will offer an overview of the literature regarding non-pharmacologic interventions for dementia, followed by a more detailed description of two subtypes of interventions: psychosocial and creative arts-based interventions. The chapter will conclude with descriptions of five arts-based programs that provide services in a variety of artistic modalities and settings, but that all share the goal of creative expression and increased quality of life.

Due to limitations in the evidence base, which will be discussed in this chapter, some interventions and theories included here will be described in an informal, even anecdotal manner. It is my opinion and the opinion of countless other professionals in the field that this work is nevertheless effective, vital, and worthy of further consideration. I invite the reader to consider these concepts for enhancing treatment and aftercare for people with dementia, as well as for possible replicability with other neurogenic populations.

PARADIGM SHIFT: MOVING BEYOND DEFICITS

The deficits of dementia are numerous and insidious, affecting nearly every aspect of function and communication. In therapeutic circles, the language of deficits tends to be the default language to describe observable changes from baseline behavior. Dementia is progressive and degenerative, generally rendering the observable changes from baseline slow but constant. Is it any wonder then, that the traditional paradigm of dementia care is deficits-based and nihilistic?

Professionals and family members alike often struggle to identify a sustainable desired outcome of a therapeutic experience for someone with dementia. Some quantitative outcome measures may seem irrelevant or inappropriate, while some qualitative methods may be dismissed as not adequately rigorous or overly subjective. Professionals may be discouraged by the person's diminished focus or lessened ability to demonstrate progress over time. Family members may be grieving the loss of the person's shared memories and former abilities. These reactions to loss are normal, but deficits are only part of the larger picture. A therapist's ability to identify remaining strengths and abilities, and to build upon those abilities to ease the detrimental effects of deficits and help the person achieve the greatest level of competence, is crucial.

People with Alzheimer's disease, the most common cause of dementia, live an average of 4 to 8 years after diagnosis and some live 20 years or more (Alzheimer's Association, 2014). This long time span of slow degeneration offers myriad opportunities for therapeutic interventions, to limit the adverse effect of excess disability and maintain quality of life. Sustainable outcomes over long periods of time may not be achievable due to the nature of the illness, but clinically and personally meaningful outcomes in

the moment are indeed possible and, some might argue, imperative to achieving high-quality care. High-quality care involves
turning the language of deficits to the language of connection,
repersonalizing the recipient of care from "patient" to "person."

SUPPORTING PERSONHOOD IN DEMENTIA

The concept of person-centered dementia care was popularized
with Tom Kitwood's seminal work *Dementia Reconsidered: The
Person Comes First* (1997). His model of person-centered care
was developed with an awareness of psychologist Carl Rogers'
work in client-centered and humanistic psychotherapy (Kitwood,
1997). A more in-depth discussion of the work of Rogers and
Kitwood is presented in Chapter 10. Nearly two decades later, the
paradigm of deficits still remains ingrained in the U.S. health care
system. However, much work is being done by both professionals and laypeople to shift the landscape of care to make room
for psychosocial and creative interventions that, if adopted on a
large scale, have enormous potential to improve quality of life for
millions of people living with dementia, across all care settings.

Perhaps the first step in moving past a deficits-only (or
deficits-heavy) model lies in approaching any kind of therapy or
basic care for a person with dementia in a holistic manner. This
involves becoming aware of the person's history, preferences,
and relationships with other people as well as the environment.
The key to supporting personhood in dementia, according to Kitwood, lies in embedding these concepts of person-centered care
in the attitudes of the people who interact with this population.
The person is only supported as a person if her social relationships treat her as such. She is supported if her psychological
needs are met, in addition to her basic physical needs. She then
responds to stimuli with all aspects of her self rather than solely
her deficits, which may be expressed in the form of challenging
behaviors. Her cognitive deficits become less debilitating when
her emotional experience is acknowledged and honored.

Kitwood emphasized the importance of relationship as
essential to quality care and the ultimate well-being of a person with dementia. In doing so, he implied that care practices

that enhance relationship can be therapeutic by virtue of being relationship-centered. In other words, supportive relationships can be more than simple gestures of kindness. They can be a form of nonpharmacologic intervention to address the symptoms of dementia. Individual or group therapies are valuable not only because of the knowledge and skill of the therapist, but also because they work in the context of relationship between human beings, in contrast to pharmacologic interventions, which occur outside of a social context.

NONPHARMACOLOGIC INTERVENTIONS FOR DEMENTIA: AN OVERVIEW

The body of research in the field of nonpharmacologic interventions in dementia is evolving. The evidence base is rich in its diversity of approaches, yet often admittedly (and in some cases unavoidably) imperfect in research design. Cohen-Mansfield and her colleagues (2014) enumerated the reasons why randomized controlled trials (RCT's) may be impractical, inappropriate, or even unethical when applied to studies of nonpharmacologic interventions with a dementia population. The establishment of double-blind designs, identification of control groups, and randomization of the sample are among potentially problematic issues that can affect the legitimacy and replicability of a study. Out of necessity and financial constraints, samples are often small and not randomized. See Cohen-Mansfield et al. (2014), Olazaràn et al. (2010), and Beard (2011) for a more in-depth description of these challenges. These authors and others (including de Medeiros & Basting, 2013) are calling for a shift away from the RCT standard to validate the effectiveness and further inform the replicability of these interventions.

Nonpharmacologic interventions are hardly new. For example, music has long been known anecdotally to be a powerful tool to connect with people with dementia. However, it has taken time for these interventions to gain legitimacy and recognition. They are generally used in tandem with pharmacologic interventions. Note the choice of wording here is "interventions," rather than "treatments," to emphasize the fact that no currently available interventions (pharmacologic or nonpharmacologic) have been proven to alter the course of the *underlying disease process* in the brain. Instead, these treatments are aimed at improving the *symptoms* of dementia (Alzheimer's Association, 2014).The U.S. Food and Drug Administration has approved only five medications to treat the cognitive symptoms of Alzheimer's disease by acting on neurotransmitter levels in the brain, and these medications tend to vary widely in their effectiveness (Alzheimer's Association, 2014). Psychotropic medications are often prescribed off-label to treat the behavioral and psychological symptoms of dementia, and may carry a risk of adverse side effects (Cohen-Mansfield, 2001).

Many challenging behavioral symptoms of dementia are most effectively addressed in a nonpharmacologic manner, especially as a first line of response. Behavior may be a person's attempt to communicate an unmet need within his physical or social environment, which is then resolved when the environment is altered accordingly (Camp, Cohen-Mansfield, & Capezuti, 2002). Nonpharmacologic interventions can be individualized to accommodate for personal preference and history, which Cohen-Mansfield, Libin, & Marx (2007) found to significantly reduce agitated behavior. These practices may even replace pharmacology in some cases, as Fossey et al. (2006) found that antipsychotic use decreased in nursing homes when staff received training in person-centered care techniques. Nonpharmacologic interventions can also be an integral part of palliative care, combining medical and psychosocial approaches to manage behavioral symptoms, and monitor and control pain appropriately (Volicer & Simard, 2014).

Olazaràn and colleagues (2010) reviewed randomized controlled trials of nonpharmacologic interventions for people with dementia and their caregivers. The therapies being examined included cognitive training, cognitive stimulation, reminiscence, music, massage, exercise, and caregiver education and support. The researchers found that despite methodological challenges in many studies, there was a demonstrated level of effectiveness across a wide variety of domains. Notably, high-quality trials of multicomponent interventions for caregivers were found to significantly delay institutionalization of people with dementia. Institutional delay has potential to translate into enormous savings for the long-term care system, not to mention the increase of dignity and quality of life that comes from being able to stay safely in the home environment as long as possible.

Outcomes of nonpharmacologic interventions include improved verbal communication, improved mood, improved cognitive function, decreased number or severity of challenging behaviors, and improved motor skills. Slightly more difficult to operationalize, but equally as important, are outcomes of enhanced personhood, quality of life, well-being, and sense of self. de Medeiros and Basting (2013) conducted an integrative review, examining outcomes from pharmacologic studies alongside psychosocial and cultural arts interventions. They compared the three types of interventions in three outcome domains: cognition, behavioral symptoms, and quality of life. Their analysis suggested that nonpharmacologic intervention subtypes of psychosocial and arts-based interventions were far more effective than pharmacology in quality of life outcomes, with positive effect in cognition and behavior as well.

PSYCHOSOCIAL INTERVENTIONS IN DEMENTIA CARE

Psychosocial interventions, a general term encompassing a wide variety of approaches, are a class of nonpharmacologic interventions that are increasingly popular in the dementia care field. The interventions can be delivered by credentialed professionals, including social workers and recreational therapists, as well as by trained paraprofessionals, volunteers, and family members. These interventions can supplement and enhance speech, physical, and occupational therapy techniques. They can be used in clinical settings, residential facilities, and private homes. They can also enhance adult day care settings, which will be discussed in more detail in Chapter 10. The different types of psychosocial interventions are not mutually exclusive and can be tailored to the specific needs, abilities, cultural background, and personal preferences of a person with dementia. Interventions can also be specifically targeted to people of different genders, ages, types of diagnosis (Alzheimer's disease versus other types of dementia), and stage of dementia (early, middle, or late) (Van Mierlo, Van der Roest, Meiland, & Dröes, 2010).

Interventions can be highly complex, or as simple as purposeful changes in caregiver communication. (See the discussion in Chapter 8 on communication adaptations for dementia.) Such changes can be facilitated through formalized training, as in the excellent person-centered care work of Teepa Snow for family caregivers and professionals (see Snow, 2003). In other words, psychosocial interventions are valuable because they are *personalized*. In dementia care, they are often most effective in one-on-one delivery, though small group delivery can be used successfully as well, given proper training for practitioners and agency or institutional support. What follows is a description of a few examples of psychosocial approaches that are grounded in a variety of disciplines.

Bourgeois: Cueing Systems

As people progress through dementia, they need more and more cues to help them succeed at tasks and communicate their needs. Psychosocial interventions can enhance the physical environment to help the person be as independent and successful as possible. Michelle Bourgeois is a speech-language pathologist who has spent years developing memory aids and cueing systems for this purpose. Her book *Memory Books and Other Graphic Cuing Systems: Practical Communication and Memory Aids for Adults with Dementia* (2007) provides caregivers with practical tools for enhancing conversation and orientation, helping people with dementia communicate their basic needs and wants, making adjustments for safety, increasing levels of engagement, and decreasing negative behavioral symptoms. She suggests the production and use of memory books and memory wallets, reminder cards, and pictorial or written representations of multistep tasks, such as getting dressed or doing laundry.

Camp: Spaced Retrieval

Another psychosocial intervention with direct links to speech therapy practice is spaced retrieval, a memory-enhancement technique adapted for use with people with dementia by researcher Cameron Camp, also discussed in Chapter 5 of this book. The spaced retrieval method uses repetition of simple information at increasing time intervals to enable people with dementia to learn and retain new information (Camp & Stevens, 1990). The type of information repeated varies widely based on personalized assessment of need: perhaps a therapist's or caregiver's name, or the location of an item such as dentures or glasses, or the time at which a family member will visit. A small study by Brush and Camp (1998) showed that spaced retrieval could be incorporated successfully into traditional speech therapy sessions with this population. The intervention gave participants the opportunity to succeed at learning and retaining information with minimal effort, which increased their likelihood to participate actively in therapy. Because it was integrated and normalized within a speech therapy and social context, the intervention did not trigger the common types of stress and frustration that tend to occur when a patient feels as if he is being tested or quizzed.

Psychosocial Intervention in the Environment

Activities that are tailored to individual needs and preferences are considered a form of psychosocial intervention. The educational methods and practical activity designs of educator Maria Montessori have been adapted for adults with dementia with much success (Camp, 2010; Camp, 1999). Montessori-based activities have been shown to reduce agitation and increase positive affect and engagement in this population, particularly in people with dementia who have never spoken, or who have lost fluency in, the language spoken by their caregivers (van der Ploeg et al., 2013).

It is also notable that the design of the environment itself may lend itself to meaningful activity, sense of purpose, comfort, and independence within the bounds of safety (Zeisel, 2013). The physical environment is also a factor in managing negative behavioral symptoms of dementia including agitation, aggression, withdrawal, and psychotic symptoms (Zeisel et al., 2003). For example, the potentially problematic behavior of wandering can be controlled by environmental adaptations such as camouflaging exits, creating a safe path for those who are inclined to wander, and providing engaging sights or activities along that path (for example, a hallway that ends in an inviting space such as a library or sitting room).

ARTS-BASED INTERVENTIONS IN DEMENTIA CARE

Similar in many ways to psychosocial approaches, arts-based interventions have shown particular promise with dementia populations. For the purposes of this chapter, the term "arts-based interventions" will refer to approaches to dementia care that use cultural experiences and/or creative arts of all disciplines (visual art, music, poetry, dance, drama, or storytelling) as central to a therapeutic or relationship-affirming experience. The interventions may be those provided by credentialed creative arts therapists, professional artists, other professionals, or family members. They may be expressive (creating art or making music) or receptive (looking at art or listening to music). They generally include an element of social interaction, either in a one-on-one or group setting. They build on strengths of what each person can do, whether that strength is to imagine, perform, create, observe, reflect, describe, or emote.

While most interventions are flexible enough to take place in a private home or residential setting, there is also benefit to bringing people with dementia out into the community to experience cultural events that have been tailored to their needs (Zeisel, 2009). By diversifying the artistic modalities and types of exposure, and by including personal and family accounts of history and preference in the selection of interventions, the activities can be truly individualized and made meaningful across a wide range of educational, linguistic, and cultural backgrounds.

Participation in arts programs has been shown to improve both physical and mental health among older adults (Castora-Binkley, Noelker, Prohaska, & Satariano, 2010), but arts-based interventions for dementia are set apart from approaches by virtue of often being centered in the imagination or in the subjective experience of meaningfulness (de Medeiros & Basting, 2013). This makes them especially difficult to quantify and evaluate according to the standards of double-blind randomized controlled trials, though as previously discussed, many argue that the standard models are not appropriate for adequately measuring the effect of these interventions (e.g., Beard, 2011; de Medeiros & Basting, 2013). I present here for consideration three potential theoretical frameworks, or lenses through which to view arts-based interventions: mediating objects, product versus process, and creation of narrative.

Mediating Objects

Researcher and dementia expert John Zeisel believes that the essence of arts-based interventions is that they invite people to engage with "mediating objects" that enhance communication and relationship (personal communication, August 14, 2014). Mediating objects in daily life, such as a lunch over which two people have a conversation about a personal issue, or a chess game in the park over which a group of people argue about politics, normalize human interactions and give people an object or topic through which they can relate to other people. Artistic mediating objects have the added value of being subjective and open to interpretation, so there are less absolute "right" or "wrong" ways of approaching the object, minimizing the fear of failure that can inhibit people with dementia from participation.

Zeisel speculates that it may not matter which discipline of the arts is used, or what type of cultural experience is provided. What may matter is the manner in which a person with dementia is presented with a mediating object or experience (e.g., a statue, a box of paints, a poem, or a dance movement) and is given the opportunity to use that object in the context of a relationship with other people, whether those people are peers, family members, professional caregivers, or staff at cultural institutions. If the mediating object is presented in a way that is appropriate for the person's level of functioning, and in a normalized, social setting, then relationship (and thus Kitwood's ideal of personhood) may be achieved.

Product Versus Process

In her review of the literature on art therapies in dementia care, Beard (2011) made the distinction between product-oriented and process-oriented research outcomes. Product-oriented studies focused on the quantifiable outcomes of an intervention, usually related to a reduction in behavioral symptoms. However, arts therapies tend to place more value of the process of engaging in the art activity, lending themselves to more qualitative assessments of concepts such as enjoyment, enrichment, and empowerment. In John Killick's *Playfulness and Dementia: A Practice Guide* (2013), it becomes clear that play, a central part of many arts experiences, is process-oriented by definition. The purpose of the playful activity is not to achieve an external goal, but to be present in the moment of expression and enjoyment. Perhaps the therapeutic activity could also be considered to have value not only in its outcome, but in the value of the therapeutic process itself.

Arts and the Creation of Narrative

Arts-based interventions are also uniquely powerful because they encourage the creation (and re-creation) of narrative. The narratives of dementia may sometimes be reminiscence-based, as in the oral histories created by the StoryCorps® Memory Loss Initiative, but even these factual re-tellings were made valuable by more process-oriented outcomes (e.g., being present in the moment, strengthening connections with family members, and affirming selfhood) (Savundranayagam, Dilley, & Basting, 2011).

In other programs, the narratives may be new creations of imagination and creativity. Anne Basting's creative storytelling program TimeSlips™ is a prime example of this different kind of narrative. Not only do participants become more engaged and alert during the program, but it also has an effect on the way professional staff communicate with and perceives the participants (Fritsch et al., 2009). By being open to narrative that is not necessarily factual, the practitioner or family member steps into the world of the person with dementia whose reality may seem far different from that which others are experiencing. "Narrative" and "truth" become relative and subjective experiences, letting go of previous expectations and truly "being with" dementia.

Arts-Based Interventions: Examples from the Field

Programs offering arts-based interventions are as diverse as the artistic disciplines themselves. The possibilities are endless and there are many places where high-quality work is taking place, too numerous to name and adequately describe here. In the following pages, I have selected five examples of programs to describe in detail: ARTZ: Artists for Alzheimer's®, To Whom I May Concern®, the Alzheimer's Poetry Project, Rhythm Break Cares, and connect2culture®. This is by no means a definitive list, and focuses mostly on programs in proximity to the New York City metropolitan area. The programs are simply presented as examples of quality creative arts programming for dementia in different modalities and settings. A more comprehensive list of programs and best practices in the United States can be found through the National Center for Creative Aging at http://www.creativeaging.org/programs-people/cad.

Example 1: ARTZ: Transforming Individuals, Institutions, and Communities

Kitwood (1997) called for incorporating person-centered care into daily practice not only on an individual level, but on an institutional and cultural level as well. ARTZ: Artists for Alzheimer's, an initiative of the I'm Still Here Foundation, has taken Kitwood's principles and put them into practice in the context of arts and cultural activities. ARTZ was founded in 2002 by John Zeisel and Sean Caulfield, who saw the transformative potential of the arts for people with dementia, and made it their mission for people to have cultural and creative opportunities, both in their places of residence as well as out in the community.

The philosophy of ARTZ is one of inclusion, with the aim to decrease the stigma associated with dementia amongst people with a diagnosis, their caregivers, and the community at large. ARTZ works with individual artists, art museums, and other cultural institutions to create meaningful and stimulating experiences for their participants. Although based in Massachusetts, ARTZ has contributed to dementia programs at cultural institutions around the world including the Museum of Modern Art in New York City, the Louvre in Paris, the Kohler Arts Center in Wisconsin, the National Gallery of Australia, the Big Apple Circus, and the Tribeca Film Institute. ARTZ also brings volunteer artists onsite to residential facilities to work with people with dementia on creative projects.

ARTZ museum tours may differ from tours for the general population in a number of ways. The group size is generally small, as is the number of works viewed, in order to minimize distraction and allow the group members adequate time to focus on the experience and respond as appropriate. The group facilitators focus on the visual experience and emotional content of the artwork. Touch objects can be used to enhance the experience, along with music or aromatherapy. The group often concludes with an art-making experience that is geared towards the abilities of people with dementia.

ARTZ programming works on four levels of transformation. First, it works to transform the person with dementia by offering dignified and stimulating experiences to create and observe the arts. In Zeisel's metaphor, it offers the person the opportunity to use mediating objects (art, music, poetry, etc.) to stimulate relationship and enhance personhood. Second, ARTZ works to transform the settings in which the experiences take place. The settings could be residential facilities or the cultural institutions that offer dementia-specific programming. Third, ARTZ strives to transform communities into dementia-friendly, inclusive places where people with dementia are included in cultural activities and other social aspects of daily life. This is demonstrated through the ARTZ "It Takes A Village" program in Brookline, MA, where weekly events are held at community venues around the city that welcome people with dementia and their caregivers. Lastly, ARTZ aims to transform the society, into a society where dementia is de-stigmatized, and accessibility and equal creative opportunities become the norm.

Example 2: To Whom I May Concern: Reclaiming the "I" of Their Lives

The experience of early-stage dementia is a unique one in which insight is not only possible but also potentially therapeutic. Pearce, Clare, and Pistrang (2002) found that having a supportive forum for people with dementia to discuss their experiences may help them to gain some insight about how to move forward in the context of progressive illness. Beard (2011) wrote: "when people are allowed to *live with* dementia, rather than exclusively fight against it, the condition becomes a 'manageable disability' rather than a (social) death sentence" (p. 647). Living with dementia is at the heart of To Whom I May Concern (TWIMC), a theater-based program founded by Maureen Matthews. The program provides people with early-stage dementia the opportunity to communicate their feelings and experiences in a supportive, public, and creative forum.

TWIMC is an interactive, theater-based program that uses the text of focused interviews with early-stage groups to create a script, which is then read aloud by those same individuals in front of an audience of their peers, family members, and professionals. Participants have been only recently diagnosed with dementia, so they are often actively seeking outlets for coping with the emotional trauma of the diagnosis and the slow but steady changes in their personal lives. In order to participate, they must be aware of their diagnosis and be willing to talk about it with others. They also are often interested in deepening coping skills to help them construct their evolving narratives and sense of self.

Matthews chose theater as the medium for this program because it has the potential to encompass a range of emotion and validates the stories being told by giving the performers a literal spotlight. She observed that a common complaint of people with dementia is that they often do not feel that people around them are listening to them in a meaningful way. The construct of a play normalizes the act of listening and gives the message a heightened importance above that of everyday language. It provides an opportunity for families and professionals to listen without interruptions and without the temptation to "help" the people with dementia by filling in pauses or finishing their sentences.

The program allows participants the opportunity to construct and validate their own narratives. In Matthews' words, it helps them to reclaim the "I" of their lives (personal communication, August 11, 2014). Their lives have changed, but their lives are not over. They are able to redefine themselves, moving from labels of "sufferers" and "victims" to "advocates" and "educators." They are empowered to speak out and positively impact their own care, as well as the care of others in similar situations. A talkback session follows each performance, creating dialogue between participants and audience members that further affirms the stories being told and opens communication about potentially difficult and emotional issues. A sample of performances from the program is available on the website (http://www.towhomi mayconcern.org).

Participants in TWIMC range widely in terms of age (both early-onset and late-onset) and type of diagnosis (Alzheimer's disease, Primary Progressive Aphasia, etc.). Matthews reports that across age groups and diagnoses, participants appreciate the opportunity to use language in a way that is personally meaningful. The program's structure—of building from inside the safe space of a small group setting and moving the message outwards —gives the participants the extra time and emotional support needed to express their stories confidently and articulately. Passion about the subject matter makes them more focused on the message being expressed rather than any language difficulties or mistakes that may occur. Positive feedback from the audience validates the messages and empowers participants to continue to use open communication and advocacy as outlets in managing the physical and emotional aspects of coping with an early-stage diagnosis.

Example 3: Alzheimer's Poetry Project: Poetry as Expression and Communication

To Whom I May Concern capitalizes on the abilities of people with early-stage dementia to communicate about their own stories and relationships with accuracy, given the right mix of a safe space and a skilled facilitator who can help transform those stories into a theatrical event. Gary Glazner of the Alzheimer's Poetry Project (APP) uses poetry as the medium to engage people with all stages of dementia in more spontaneous performances that involve creative expression, reminiscence, socialization, and communication. The APP was founded in 2004, a product of Glazner's skills as a professional poet and performer combined with his passion for working with people with dementia. APP originated in Santa Fe, New Mexico but has since provided programming in more than 20 states, 10 different languages, and internationally in Germany, Australia, Poland, and South Korea.

A typical APP session consists of four core elements: call-and-response poetry performance, group discussion, use of props/sensory objects, and cocreation of original poetry. The sequence and content of these elements is somewhat fluid, allowing for spontaneity and flexibility within the session's basic structure. The session can also then build upon participants' preferences and personal histories or shared cultural backgrounds. Simple themes such as "spring" or "trees" can create a more concrete, and therefore more understandable for someone with dementia, context for the selected poems and props.

Call-and-response is a simple technique in which the facilitator calls out a single phrase and invites the group or individual to repeat that phrase in unison. Call-and-response can also be used effectively in dyads, though a group experience adds a richer, if less intimate, social experience. Glazner theorizes that the call-and-response method works so well with people with dementia because it relies not on autobiographical, or episodic, memory, but instead relies on echoic memory, which only requires the brain to hold on to the information for a few seconds—long enough for one line of poetry (Glazner, 2014). People with dementia can be highly successful at this type of activity, which boosts their confidence and willingness to participate. Call-and-response poetry does not require that the audience already be familiar with the poem, though often people do recognize the classic poems and in some cases can recite the poems along with the facilitator.

Glazner describes the APP style as poetry as performance art (personal communication, July 29, 2014). As he sees it, the use of repetition, rhyme, and rhythm has been part of the human experience for so long that it is hard-wired in the brains of all people, including people with dementia. He points to examples throughout history: the great Greek poets, the Greek chorus, cultural proverbs, elements of musical traditions like gospel, jazz, and blues, as well as religious ceremonies that invoke call-and-response and use rhythmic text as a way to set prayers and sacred text to memory. Perhaps the reason that poetry seems to reach people with dementia so well is that it is innate in human beings to respond in some way to these poetic elements, despite cultural and educational differences. Even in advanced dementia, a facilitator can involve a person in a poetry session by gently holding hands and moving with the rhythm of the poem.

After presenting a poem in this call-and-response method and getting the group "warmed up," a trained APP facilitator then engages the group in a discussion of the poetry they have just recited together. This is where socialization, preference, personal history, and humor often become part of the process. There is a fine line between infantilization and playfulness, but when people feel that they are respected as adults, they often feel free to laugh and play along. Props can help to deepen the sensory experience of the verbal poetry. For example, an APP facilitator may choose a theme for the session of "Trees," selecting poems about that theme. The props could include branches, bark, and leaves that would be passed around the group for people to see, touch, and smell. In one session about "Spring," the APP facilitator brought poems about rain, gave everyone strawberries and lemonade, and gently misted the participants' cheeks with water.

Each APP session includes the group creating a poem together using an open-ended prompt question, for example: "What's the most beautiful thing you ever saw?" The facilitator goes to each person asking the question, and either the facilitator or an assistant records the answers. The answers form the lines of the group poem. The session ends with the facilitator performing the newly created poem with the group using call and response, sometimes even breaking into song. The facilitator often references or indicates each contributor, validating their creative input. Flexibility is key, as is the ability of the facilitator to approach each person with a respectful and calm energy, waiting for a response, and affirming each response whether or not it is logical. The process takes precedence over the product. Poem creation can be done on a one-on-one basis as well, with the facilitator helping to craft a poem with the person with dementia by putting line breaks into recorded reminiscence or responses to an open-ended question.

Example 4: Rhythm Break Cares: Dance as Nonverbal Communication

Beard's (2011) summary of literature on dance and movement therapy in dementia care found that this is also an area where process is generally valued above product. Movement is valuable for its expressive nature in the moment. Anecdotal evidence presents a strong case for the positive effects for this population. Once the need for verbal communication is eliminated, people with dementia can flourish in an environment where nonverbal communication reigns. In the world of ballroom dance, physical touch is normalized and accepted in a social and familiar context. Words are not needed, only eye contact, smiles, and mutual movement in rhythm to a piece of music.

Professional dancers Nathan Hescock and Stine Moen run Rhythm Break Cares (RBC) out of a dance studio in New York City, with the stated goal of bringing the benefits of music, movement, and touch to people with dementia and their caregivers. They are supported by a core volunteer group of trained ballroom dancers. Hescock began working with vulnerable elders in an adult day program as a way to translate his ballroom dancing skills into service for the community. He found that when he gave people with dementia the opportunity to engage in partner dance in a failure-free environment, he saw profound effects on their moods, levels of engagement, and motor skills. Moen, a modern dancer with dance therapy training, now works with Hescock to produce monthly social tea dances in the RBC studio as well as outside visits to adult day programs and assisted living facilities.

A typical RBC session begins when the professional dancers come into a room of assembled participants, usually seated in a circle, who may at first appear unfocused or tired. RBC staff puts on some gentle music and invites the group to warm up through actions like snapping, clapping, or kicking their legs. The staff then invites participants to come to the center of the circle and move to different types of music: from Latin, to ballroom, to 1950's rock 'n' roll. Participants can dance standing up, while seated, or in wheelchairs. Sometimes the group pairs off for partner dancing, and other times people hold hands as a larger group and move together. If a person doesn't want to dance, she may sing along, or do a small seated motion like clapping or waving. There is no "right" or "wrong" way of moving to the music.

Hescock reports that the RBC method has an organic element to it (personal communication, August 19, 2014). There is no script, simply an ability of the staff to work off of the nonverbal communication of the participants and the emotional energy of the group. The feeling is one of a social tea dance. Even if participants do not get up and dance, everyone is in the same room and listening to the same music, lending to the feeling of relationship and community generated by a group experience. The staff has witnessed participants becoming more physically confident and coordinated over the course of a 45-minute session, in addition to the benefits of physical touch and emotional expression. RBC is also a connect2culture partner of the Alzheimer's Association, New York City Chapter, who has provided dementia care training for RBC's staff and volunteers.

Example 5: connect2culture: Providing Training and Support for Cultural Institutions

The Alzheimer's Association, New York City Chapter, is one of the many local chapters of the Alzheimer's Association that has embraced the importance of arts and cultural-based activities for people with dementia and their caregivers. For example, the Memories in the Making® art program that originated in the Orange County Chapter has spread to many chapters across the country (Kinney & Rentz, 2005). The New York City Chapter has the advantage of being located in a metropolitan area with multitudes of cultural opportunities, but few of those opportunities are accessible to people with dementia. From that need has sprung the Chapter's network of cultural programming in the New York City area, known as connect2culture.

Kitwood (1997) advocated that dementia should be seen as a form of disability requiring a special level of care and accommodation, rather than a hopeless condition requiring people to be locked away with little stimulation. Museums that already offer disability access programming have begun to offer tours and activities specifically tailored to this population. The Museum of Modern Art (MoMA) was one of the first to develop such a program, piloted in conjunction with ARTZ: Artists for Alzheimer's and the New York City Chapter.

Based on the success of the ARTZ and MoMA model, more New York City museums have joined the connect2culture network by offering specialized access programs for visitors with dementia and their caregivers. These include the American Folk Art Museum, Brooklyn Museum, The Cloisters Museum and Gardens, Intrepid Sea, Air and Space Museum, The Jewish Museum, The Metropolitan Museum of Art, Museum of Biblical Art, and The Rubin Museum of Art. Arts & Minds, a local nonprofit organization, also leads dementia access tours and art-making workshops at the New-York Historical Society and the Studio Museum of Harlem. The Alzheimer's Association, NYC Chapter has played a role in providing training and support to all of these programs and continues to serve as a resource for dementia expertise and networking through connect2culture symposiums.

Moving forward, the Chapter hopes to use the connect-2culture program to provide dementia training for staff and volunteers at high-quality, accessible, dementia-friendly cultural activities. This will involve continued training and support for existing programs as well as piloting programs at other cultural institutions including, but not limited to, museums. Access programs at musical institutions, botanic gardens, aquariums, or zoos may also be enhanced by providing specialized events for visitors with dementia.

CONCLUSION

A basic tenet of social work practice is to meet people "where they are," implying that the professional is the element of the dyad or group that must adapt in order to achieve an effective therapeutic relationship. The person is seen in the context of his environment, personal history, cultural values, spirituality, and other defining characteristics. This is no less an imperative in the field of dementia care, perhaps made even more essential by virtue of the nature of dementia. The professional must not only adapt, but do so within the boundaries of disease-related limitations in cognition, behavior, and function in order to discover which adaptations are best suited to each individual. As demonstrated by the examples in this chapter, the results of this work can be highly rewarding.

This chapter has discussed research and observations on psychosocial and arts-based approaches to dementia care, in hopes that some of the basic ideas and principles may be applicable to speech-language pathology practice. Many of the themes underlying these approaches are firmly grounded in Kitwood's (1997) work: people with dementia are comprised of far more than disease-related deficits. They respond to personalized care that emphasizes emotional life and relationship over logic and reason, and they can flourish in environments where their creativity is honored. In addition, these approaches show that effective therapies do exist beyond the pharmacologic realm that result in enhanced quality of life, and that the process of engaging with a person with dementia can be worth as much or perhaps more than the quantifiable outcome of that engagement.

The five arts-based programs highlighted in this chapter are examples of how the themes above can be put into practice programmatically, and are intended as resources for further individual exploration and reflection: ARTZ: Artists for Alzheimer's provides a program model of taking arts-based transformation from an individual to a societal level. To Whom I May Concern shows how the communication abilities in early-stage dementia can be an asset for creativity and advocacy. The Alzheimer's Poetry Project demonstrates the way call-and-response poetry can compensate for language and memory limitations, and give people the opportunity for socialization, fun, and joyful expression. Rhythm Break Cares provides a reminder that movement and nonverbal communication are rich areas of exploration, and connect2culture proves that the setting for creative care can be community-based and part of the disability access programs at various cultural institutions. All these programs share goals of creative expression and increased quality of life, and those goals are achieved through different artistic modalities, care settings, and programmatic models.

Beard (2011) and de Medeiros & Basting (2013) both offer comprehensive assessments of the current state of the research in arts-based interventions, as well as future directions for the field. Both identify a need for more comprehensive research to understand the specific ways in which these interventions work, and what outcome measures are meaningful reflections of their value. Perhaps further research can identify ways in which arts-based and psychosocial intervention practitioners can collaborate with speech-language pathologists and professionals from other disciplines as well. Kitwood (1997) acknowledged that the process of changing the dominant paradigm of dementia care has been, and is likely to continue to be, very slow. With collaboration between disciplines, open-mindedness to different approaches to research, an appreciation of personhood, and a dedication to dignified, compassionate, and creative care, we can continue on the steady path of change.

REFERENCES

Algar, K., Woods, R., & Windle, G. (2014). Measuring the quality of life and well-being of people with dementia: A review of observational measures. *Dementia, 0*(0), 1–26.

Alzheimer's Association. (2014). *2014 Alzheimer's disease facts and figures.* Retrieved March 2015, from http://www.alz.org/downloads/facts_figures_2014.pdf

Beard, R. (2011). Art therapies and dementia care: A systematic review. *Dementia, 11*(5), 633–656.

Bourgeois, M. (2007). *Memory books and other graphic cuing systems: Practical communication and memory aids for adults with dementia.* Baltimore, MD: Health Professions Press.

Bowling, A., Rowe, G., Adams, S., Sands, P., Samsi, K., Crane, M., . . . Manthorpe, J. (2014). Quality of life in dementia: A systematically conducted narrative review of dementia-specific measurement scales. *Aging & Mental Health, 19*(1), 13–31.

Brush, J., & Camp, C. (1998). Using spaced retrieval as an intervention during speech-language therapy. *Clinical Gerontologist, 19*(1), 51–64.

Camp, C. (Ed.). (1999). *Montessori-based activities for persons with dementia: Volume 1.* Beachwood, OH: Menorah Park Center for Senior Living.

Camp, C. (2010). Origins of Montessori programming for dementia. *Non-pharmacological Therapies in Dementia, 1*(2), 163–174.

Camp, C., Cohen-Mansfield, J., & Capezuti, E. (2002). Use of nonpharmacologic interventions among nursing home residents with dementia. *Psychiatric Services, 53*, 1397–1401.

Camp, C., & Stevens, A. (1990). Spaced-retrieval: A memory intervention for dementia of the Alzheimer's type. *Clinical Gerontologist: The Journal of Aging and Mental Health, 10*(1), 58–61.

Castora-Binkley, M., Noelker, L., Prohaska, T., & Satariano, W. (2010). Impact of arts participation on health outcomes for older adults. *Journal of Aging, Humanities, and the Arts, 4*, 352–367.

Cohen-Mansfield, J. (2001). Nonpharmacologic interventions for inappropriate behaviors in dementia: A review, summary, and critique. *American Journal of Geriatric Psychiatry, 9*(4), 361–381.

Cohen-Mansfield, J., Buckwalter, K., Beattie, E., Rose, K., Neville, C., & Kolanowsky, A. (2014). Expanded review criteria: The case of nonpharmacological interventions in dementia. *Journal of Alzheimer's Disease, 41*(1), 15–28.

Cohen-Mansfield, J., Libin, A., & Marx, M.S. (2007). Nonpharmacological treatment of agitation: A controlled trial of systematic individualized intervention. *The Journals of Gerontology, 62A*(8), 908–916.

de Medeiros, K., & Basting, A. (2013). "Shall I compare thee to a dose of Donepezil?": Cultural arts interventions in dementia care research. *The Gerontologist, 54*(3), 344–353.

Fossey, J., Ballard, C., Juszczak, I. J., Adler, N., Jacoby, R., & Howard, R. (2006). Effect of enhanced psychosocial care on antipsychotic use in nursing home residents with severe dementia: Cluster randomised trial. *British Medical Journal*, 1–6. Retrieved from http://www.bmj.com

Fritsch, T., Kwak, J., Grant, S., Lang, J., Montgomery, R. R., & Basting, A. D. (2009). Impact of TimeSlips: A creative expression intervention program, on nursing home residents with dementia and their caregivers. *The Gerontologist, 49*(1), 117–127.

Glazner, G. (2014). *Dementia arts: Celebrating creativity in elder care.* Baltimore, MD: Health Professions Press.

Kawashima, R., Okita, K., Yamazaki, R., Tajima, N., Yoshida, H., Taira, M., . . . Sugimoto, K. (2005). Reading aloud and arithmetic calculation improve frontal function of people with dementia. *Journal of Gerontology, 60A*(3), 380–384.

Killick, J. (2013). *Playfulness and dementia: A practice guide.* Philadelphia, PA: Jessica Kingsley.

Kinney, J. M., & Rentz, C. A. (2005). Observed well-being among individuals with dementia: Memories in the Making, an art program, versus other structured activity. *American Journal of Alzheimer's Disease and Other Dementias, 20*(4), 220–227.

Kitwood, T. (1997). *Dementia reconsidered: The person comes first.* New York, NY: Open University Press.

Olazaràn, J., Reisberg, B., Clare, L., Cruz, I., Peña-Casanova, J., del Ser, T., . . . Muñiz, R. (2010). Nonpharmacological therapies in Alzheimer's disease: A systematic review of efficacy. *Dementia and Geriatric Cognitive Disorders, 30*, 161–178.

Pearce, A., Clare, L., & Pistrang, N. (2002). Managing sense of self: Coping in the early stages of Alzheimer's disease. *Dementia, 1*(2), 173–192.

Savundranayagam, M., Dilley, L., & Basting, A. (2011). StoryCorps' memory loss initiative: Enhancing personhood for storytellers with memory loss. *Dementia, 10*(3), 415–433.

Snow, T., (Actor), & Alzheimer's North Carolina, Inc. (Director). (2003). *Accepting the challenge: Providing the best care for people with dementia.* [Professional training DVD]. Raleigh, NC.

van der Ploeg, E., Eppingstall, B., Camp, C., Runci, S., Taffe, J., & O'Connor, D. (2013). A randomized crossover trial to study the effect of personalized, one-to-one interaction using Montessori-based activities on agitation, affect, and engagement in nursing home residents with dementia. *International Psychogeriatrics, 25*(4), 565–575.

Van Mierlo, L., Van der Roest, H., Meiland, F., & Dröes, R. (2010) Personalized dementia care: Proven effectiveness of psychosocial interventions in subgroups [review]. *Ageing Research Reviews, 9*(2), 163–183.

Volicer, L., & Simard, J. (2014). Palliative care and quality of life for people with dementia: Medical and psychosocial interventions. *International Psychogeriatrics.* Advance online publication.

Zeisel, J. (2009). *I'm still here: A breakthrough approach to understanding someone living with Alzheimer's.* New York, NY: Penguin Group.

Zeisel, J. (2013). Improving person-centered care through effective design. *Generations: Journal of the American Society on Aging, 37*(3), 45–52.

Zeisel, J., Silverstein, N., Hyde, J., Levkoff, S, Lawton, M. P., & Holmes, W. (2003). Environmental correlates to behavioral health outcomes in Alzheimer's special care units. *The Gerontologist, 43*(5), 697–711.

CHAPTER 10

Creating the Climate for Contact and Positive Change in the Social Adult Day Program Setting

An Interview with Elizabeth Hartowicz, Director of CARE Program at Lenox Hill Neighborhood House

Elizabeth Hartowicz

This is a unique chapter in an interview format, using the rich knowledge of an exceptional leader in compassionate and creative dementia care. The quality of life and personhood of each individual is at the forefront of the discussion in this chapter. The central notion of a person-centered approach is at the heart of many exemplary programs and can be applied in many settings for maximal benefit of all individuals.

—Linda S. Carozza

Q: It has become quite common for physicians to "prescribe" participation in an adult day programs designed for persons with dementia. How would you describe the role of such programs in the dementia care process?

A: We don't have a medical cure, as of now, which could change the course of Alzheimer's disease and other related forms of dementia, but it has been shown that socialization is a powerful, nonpharmacological form of intervention. It provides a natural, nonjudgmental, pressure free, psychologically safe setting, which helps stimulate intellectual functions and brings emotional support to both those affected by dementia and their caregivers. Although there is no definite study to confirm the reversal of the cognitive decline, we already know that the combination of nonpharmacological therapies has significant effects on the cognitive-behavioral status of the person with Alzheimer's by restoring neural functioning (Baglio et al., 2015). A variety of those interventions—including intellectual stimulation, exercise, and socialization—have been shown to have a positive impact on the overall quality of life of the person who suffers from dementia.

Losing memory is an extremely devastating fact that people with dementia face, but stigma and being addressed as children, or worse, as if they did not exist, can be the even more painful outcomes of a dementia diagnosis. In their own words, when words are still available, they frequently share disappointment and frustration of not being acknowledged as "present" in decision-making situations. Beyond safety and physical needs, which we all share, people with dementia have a tremendous need for validating and nonjudgmental relationships, a desire for continuation and autonomy, and a need for being treated the same way as they experienced in their previous, healthy lives. Unfortunately, that need is often unmet when their care focuses mostly on providing help with basic personal needs and daily activities, while neglecting individual preferences, interests, and needs. As a result, individuals with dementia frequently suffer from isolation and feelings of loneliness in the community. The social adult day centers, which were low cost and volunteer-based in their origin, were created in response to that problem, often with the help of community organizations and at their sites. They offered those individuals a chance for continuation of their social lives, through participation in accessible, comprehensive programs. Presently, there are two most common models of the adult day programs for persons with dementia in our country—a social and a medical one. In addition to a variety of therapeutic and entertainment activities, their participants are offered diverse services, which include personal care, nutrition, transportation and, in the case of the medical day model, also health monitoring. While giving the caregivers an opportunity for respite and support, the adult day programs provide an environment in which the participants affected by dementia can experience significant improvements in mood and self-confidence. Together with the sense of continuation, they bring hope to their lives.

Q: Both literature and research stress the importance of the environment in caring for persons with dementia. How do you relate this knowledge to your experience of leading a successful, creative and award-winning adult day program *(a recipient of 2004 Best Practices Award, New York State Adult Day Services Association, in recognition for outstanding and valuable innovative service to adult Day Services)* **in the middle of a part of New York City that is extremely busy and limited in terms of space?**

A: In the recent years, a lot has been done in terms of designing and improving the physical space for the individuals who suffer from memory loss (Alzheimer's Association Publications, 2014). I'd like to refer to the work of Dr. John Zeisel, a passionate advocate for nonpharmacological forms of treatment in dementia, who is also well known for his research on the impact of the environment on the well-being of people with dementia (Zeisel, 2013). Although we all share the need for comfortable and safe surroundings, for those whose feelings of security and confidence are deeply compromised by dementia, the impact of a warm, quiet, and peaceful environment is even more significant. That's why it's so important that the facility in which the program operates is safe, clean, and has a friendly feeling. Ideally, this place would consist of a sunny and warm home-like living room with a pleasant view, a sort of "spa" for personal care, and a quiet place where participants receive individual attention when needed, offering both an adequate activity space and additional rooms where caregivers might be offered a respite and an opportunity to observe those whom they care for participate in the program and to attend training opportunities whenever available. Such expectations are rarely accomplished in big, expensive cities like New York, where space is limited and costs too high. In reality, a large number of programs depend on the generosity of different community organizations, such as churches and synagogues, which often share their already crowded space. Although such a setting may differ from "the ideal" model proposed by dementia environment designers, staff running programs in space-limited sites can still be successful in creating a warm environment for contact, validating interactions for individuals dealing with dementia and who are otherwise home-bound and isolated in the community. While physical access can add significantly to a program, the success of the adult day program in facilitating positive changes in those individuals depends in much greater degree on human and cultural support than on the physical elements of a facility. Ironically, this humane element happens to be sometimes missing in some dementia centers that are "ideal" (from the architectural design perspective). In contrast, the humane element can be present and powerful in centers with significantly less fortunate financial and physical resources, thanks to the skills and personal qualities of their staff in building a humanly rich base where people, no matter their dementia status, can meet as persons. A small but humanely inviting room can achieve that. I believe that success in creating a facilitative ground that helps improve the well-being of those suffering from dementia depends on the ability of the staff to create the adequate psychological climate for contact.

Q: How do you describe the role of a program leader in building a facilitative, change-promoting atmosphere in the dementia group setting?

A: Following the example of the leading humanistic psychologist, the creator of the "person-centered approach" and my greatest inspiration, Carl Rogers (1902–1987), I have learned and believe that in any human setting in which a positive change in a person's well-being is the goal (whether it's a relationship between teacher and student, or parent and child, therapist and client, or leader and the group), there are necessary conditions that must be present. Rogers described them as: Genuineness (also as congruence, or transparency), an attitude in which the therapist is openly and truly his or her own self and "makes himself or herself transparent to the client" (Rogers 1980, p.115); Acceptance (also known as Unconditional, Positive Regard), which, in his own words, is present "when the therapist is willing for the client to be whatever immediate feeling is going on—confusion, resentment, fear, anger, courage, love, or pride. Such caring on the part of the therapist is nonpossessive" (p.116). The third and last of his so-called "core, or "principal" conditions is Emphatic Understanding, by which Rogers referred to the ability of a therapist to sensitively and accurately understand the client's feelings and his or her personal experience while communicating this understanding to him or to her. Those "core" conditions are inseparable and characterize the attitudes of a "facilitator" that greatly apply to the facilitative process in dementia care—both in an individual and a group work setting. Rogers understood congruence as the matching of experience and awareness, stating: "what is present in my awareness is present in my communication . . . At such moments I am integrated or whole, I am completely in one piece" (p. 15). Rogers was a master in the congruent, emphatic communication, which I was able to experience "first hand" while participating in the communication workshops facilitated by Rogers in the 1980s, in Europe. That experience has made me aware of the consequences of inconsistency between our messages and cues, which could be, in any given moment, contradictory to our thoughts and feelings, thus resulting in a loss of trust and in frustration. I have observed many times that even in their advanced stages of dementia, many individuals still have a very strong ability to differentiate the real, genuine communication from the false one. In that sense, as the program leader, I will not be able to build a climate of trust in the relationship with the program participants if I am false, hiding my "real self" and my true feelings behind the professional facade. By being "congruent," Rogers meant being, in a way, "transparent" to those we help. I recollect a moment when one of the group participants, Ms. D.—who was unable to express herself verbally and used to experience frequent behavior difficulties—was continuously breaking ongoing group discussions, which got the other program members frustrated and very upset. She screamed and tapped her hands against the table each time someone would try to say a word, making the continuation of that discussion impossible. The group members shared that frustration with her. The staff and volunteers attempted to "calm her down" by requesting, in a gentle, quiet voice, that she ceased her interruptions and let them continue. Behind that quiet, though congruence-lacking "intervention," there was a feeling of frustration and an inability to "handle" the situation. This conflict lasted till I looked face-to-face into Ms. D's terrified eyes and asked all the participants to grant her attention. I shared with my group members how I felt about that situation and how sorry I was for failing in giving her the attention that she needed so much. Looking at her face and holding her hands, I apologized for trying to shut her down instead of listening. I also communicated to her that I could not even imagine how hard the situation of not being able to speak, nor to be listened to, had to be for her. I sincerely felt her pain and disappointment of not being listened to and was able to emphatically communicate that feeling. Although Ms. D. was unable to verbally express herself for as long as I knew her as a group participant, I promised that I would try my very best to understand her and that I hoped the rest of the participants would help me in that as well. I meant every single word I said to her. That very moment, with a complete silence in the room and all participants listening, was followed by Ms. D's loving, articulate, and very powerful statement: "I love you Somebody." That was a powerful experience, which helped me connect not only with Ms. D., but also with all other participating members and staff. It has also played an important role in how I see myself as a dementia care professional. I know that if I did not feel the natural, unconditional, and caring acceptance for her as a person, no matter what my verbal expression had been in that very moment, I would have not been able to facilitate that process the way it happened. Such experiences confirm my trust and determination in applying Rogers's philosophy in the adult day setting for persons with dementia. Being congruent, empathetic, and accepting are the components of the way I want to be in the relationships with the program participants, their caregivers and staff, in spite of the obstacles related to everyday program operation and dynamics. Administrative demands of most dementia care programs, which in addition to programming include other tasks, including supervisory duties, can be challenging for facilitators, often distracting us from being "present" and fully focused on the relationships in a face-to-face, personally integrated, authentic setting. As a group facilitator, I have been able to experience moments that I consider the most encouraging and motivating when the world outside of the program's room seems to disappear, together with its hyper-talkativity, noisy streets, and construction sounds and when the group participants, both those who are able and unable to verbally express themselves, together with staff and caregivers, share a connection which goes far beyond words. If as the group facilitator, I am able to isolate myself from the obligations of the outside world, phone calls, and "projects," and focus on what's inside that small group circle, then I am able to more frequently contribute to and witness the real presence of caring, touch, closeness, a song, or a perfectly comfortable silence.

Q: Silence does not always happen to be a condition in which professionals, including those in different therapy settings, feel comfortable. Isn't a strongly structured day an easier approach to the program operation?

A: Allowing the concept of "silence" during the dementia group session may sometimes be perceived as a failure in activity programming. This is partly because we live in the times and the culture in which the pressure of being active, productive and successful has an impact on the way we function and are expected to be. That's why the person's inability of "doing," which is a common result of the progressing dementia, may sometimes, unfortunately, lead to disqualification from being a part of social life, by so called "healthy individuals" including family members, caregivers, and individuals associated with older adult care centers. A belief of the person being still "there," no matter how bad the cognitive damage resulting from dementia, is reflected in Dr. Zeisel's book, *I Am Still Here* (Zeisel, 2009) and in the work of Naomie Feil (1993), among others. Many of us who experience contact with dementia in daily work can easily identify with the "breakthrough" moments in communication with the persons who are considered "nonverbal" and "unreachable" which are illustrated in the documentary films like *There Is a Bridge* (2007) and more recently, *Alive Inside* (2014). As those providing care, we are reminded about our moral obligation to address the need to be acknowledged as "present" of those who cannot always advocate on their own behalf. Such acknowledgment—which could perhaps be more challenging than leading a simple, structured activity, but can be very satisfying in terms of humane connection—requires that we are open to share our presence. There are moments where, without any obligation to perform tasks, participants share their joy and comfort of expression, trusting that they won't be ridiculed or judged. In their everyday lives, persons with dementia depend, sometimes completely, on others who do all kind of things for them, including personal care, decisions about food, clothing and choice of activities. That's why it is important that the program's staff strives to create an atmosphere in which the participants can experience freedom and an opportunity to manifest their personalities as well as choices, which they often feel deprived of due to the course of dementia. That could also mean at times doing absolutely nothing but being "present" and sharing moments that seem often impossible in the outside world, like such as simply "being together" face-to-face, giving each other attention, time, and patience that allow freedom of expression. An adult day program may have a strong liberating power if we are able to open ourselves up to be real, empathetic, and present, in spite of the pressure of administrational duties that might follow group facilitation. A feeling of "presence," which Carl Rogers often spoke of and shared during his workshops, sometimes is compared to a near telepathic communication. He shared his experience of "presence" as a slightly altered state of consciousness. "I find when I am closest to my inner, intuitive self, when I am somehow in touch with the unknown in me . . . then whatever I do seems to be full of healing. Then simply my presence is releasing and helpful to the other" (p.129). While inspiring many practitioners who identified with his spiritual description of "presence," Rogers met criticism from collaborators who questioned his references to a field for which there is no empirical evidence (Brodley, 2000).

I personally find that articulating the experience of connection and the power of "presence" in professional jargon is a difficult process that often leads to missing the broad scope of feelings and emotions emerging in group sessions.

Q: The term "person-centered" seems quite common in the current literature. What is its meaning in the context of dementia?

A: For many, "person-centered dementia care" may sound self-explanatory as it's easy to imagine the other possibility—a disease, in all its forms and stages. There is a deeper history behind "the person-centered" terminology than the commonly perceived understanding of putting the person in the center of the care process (and not her or his dementia case). The wide interest in this approach started together with the publishing of the book, *Dementia Reconsidered: The Person Comes First* (Kitwood, 1997). The author of this work was a British lecturer and the Leader of Bradford Dementia professionals who inspired what is often described as "the change in dementia care culture." In the "new culture" of care, "the personhood" is a central category. By bringing the personhood of the individuals to the first plan, Kitwood opposed the simplistic biomedical psychiatric care practices of the past with their belief that dementia could be fixed with some kind of technical, medical solution. Kitwood's passionate involvement in the field brought him the reputation of a "revolutionary." It's important to remember, though, that he developed the concept of "the person-centered dementia care," following the work of Carl Rogers, the creator of the person-centered approach. Rogers believed in the absolute value and uniqueness of a person. As a clinical psychologist, he had a wide range of experience with a variety of issues and pathologies, but his holistic approach focused on health rather than illness. His choice of terminology was clear. Rather than calling his approach "patient-centered," he preferred to use the term "client-centered" and later in life "person-centered", because of its connotation with the holistic, spiritual, and psychosocial perspective. In his work with dementia, Kitwood, inspired by Rogerian trust in an absolute value of all human beings, believed that regardless of their mental disability, people with dementia can still have strong emotional and fulfilling lives. In his own words, Kitwood states: "Contact with dementia or other forms of severe cognitive disability can—and indeed should—take us out of our customary patterns of over-busyness, hypercognitivism, and extreme talkativity, into a way of being in which emotion and feeling are given a much larger place. People who have dementia, for whom the life of emotions is often intense, and without the ordinary forms of inhibition, may have something important to teach the rest of humankind" (p. 5).

Q: The belief that people with dementia can still have a fulfilling life has often been questioned. For some, quality of life is lost once the person receives the diagnosis of progressing dementia and can no longer make decisions on his or her own behalf. What is your perspective?

A: "The quality of life" concept has a different meaning for each person. The well-being of the persons suffering from dementia should be the ultimate goal of all of us who provide their care, in its different settings. In assessing the factors contributing to the quality of life of participants attending a social adult day program, we often depend on the information provided by their family members and caregivers, especially when we try to identify the needs of the individuals with advanced stages of the disease. Many dementia care providers refer to Kitwood's classification of basic psychological needs, which includes comfort, attachment, inclusion, occupation, and love (1997, pp. 80–84) and serves as a compass in building care plans and design of program activities. In addition to the assessment of basic human needs, it is our moral responsibility to learn and address our participants' individual interests as well as their preferences, strengths, and abilities, while offering activities, especially to those who due to their dementia may not be able to voice their opinions and choices anymore. Getting to know their history and background helps us design projects, which may have particular meaning for them. As an example, knowing that the adult day program may actually now be the only travel destination for those participants who in their healthy lives used to enjoy international traveling, our program staff responds by inviting the members to take part in the "imaginary trips" to the places of their choice. With the support of traveling videos, food sampling, and the music of that particular culture, we can help stimulate participants' memories and bring them a sense of continuation. Music has always played an important role in the lives of most of the program's participants. It is music, more than anything else, which helps us help our participants feel better. That's why live music sessions have been part of the daily programming and in addition to music consultants who perform and work with the program members on a regular basis, the program hosts guest performers who contribute to special events' celebration. So does the presence of art, art consultants, artists as well as the partnerships with the museums and art therapy schools.

During the group discussions, I often ask my program members questions such as: "What makes you happy?" or, "What helps you feel better, when you feel sad?" It is interesting that their answers seldom refer to economic circumstances, or living arrangements. "Meeting friends" seems to be the most common response.

Q: CARE has been acknowledged for its innovative, creative programming. How do you measure the success of the program?

A: "Creative activities" programming is often what first draws attention and makes the program look attractive to those who inquire about it. In recent years, there has been a good deal of research and literature offering ideas for dementia care program design. There are a wide variety of activities from music- and art-based therapies to intergenerational events, pet-assisted therapy, horticultural and yoga programs as well as other successful and attractive projects that are being offered now in the adult day centers and that are part of our activity calendar. "What do you do?" seems like the most common question that I am asked during initial conversations with potential clients' caregivers. They want to know our schedule, services, and specific "doing" options that the program offers. That's a natural request, in that "an adult day program" is often viewed as an "activity center" because it does offer a unique opportunity for meaningful activities for those with memory loss. The explanation of the program's success in helping improve those individuals' lives goes deeper, beyond the concept of "doing" and is closely related to the "way of being" of the team that provides care. "Doing" makes sense only when it has a meaning for those participating in an activity, while many activities and forms of entertainment often serve as a supportive tool in building the climate for connection, a real human encounter. Following Martin Buber's famous statement: "All real living is meeting," (Buber, 1937), I do believe that in spite of those perhaps most existentially challenging circumstances, it is possible to create an environment when people with dementia can experience the real meeting with others as persons, in the Buberian "I–Thou" mode and in opposition to the so common in contemporary culture "I–It" mode. Ideally, we would overcome the division between "providers" and "receivers" of care and find courage in sharing "the same boat." One of the most satisfying instances of feedback that I have received during my 16 years of experience in running the social adult day programs for persons with dementia came in the form of a question. After spending a day with the program attending the group activity along with the program staff, caregivers, and volunteers, our guests wanted to know who of all those attending was "normal" and who had dementia.

REFERENCES

Alzheimer's Association Publications. (2014). *Designing environments for Alzheimer's disease.* Retrieved from http://www.alz.org/library/downloads/designenviron_rl2014.pdf

Baglio, F., Griffanti, L., Saibene, F. L., Ricci, C., Alberoni, M., Critelli, R., . . . Farina, E. (2015). Multistimulation group therapy in Alzheimer's disease promotes changes in brain functioning. *Neurorehabilitation & Neural Repair, 29*(1), 13–24.

Brodley, T. B. (2000). Personal presence in client-centered therapy. *The Person-Centered Journal, 7*(2), 139–149.

Buber, M. (1937). *I and thou.* (R. G. Smith, Trans.). Edinburgh, UK: T & T Clark.

Feil, N. (1993). *The validation breakthrough.* Baltimore, MD: Health Professionals Press.

Kitwood, T. (1997). *Dementia reconsidered: The person comes first* (pp. 5, 80–84). Buckingham, UK: Open University Press.

Rogers, C. (1980). *A way of being* (pp. 15, 115, 116, 129). New York, NY: Houghton Mifflin.

Rossato-Bennet, M., McDouglad, A., & Scully, R. (Producers), & Rossato-Bennett, M. (Director). (2014). *Alive inside* [Documentary]. USA: Projector Media.

Verde, M. (Producer), & Kay, T. (Producer and Director). (2007). *There is a bridge* [Documentary]. USA: TMK Productions.

Zeisel, J. (2013). Improving person-centered care through effective design. *Generations, 37*(3), 45–52.

Zeisel, J. (2009). *I am still here: A breakthrough approach to understanding someone living with Alzheimer's*. New York, NY: Penguin Group.

CHAPTER 11

Color My Words: How Art Therapy Creates New Pathways of Communication

Raquel Chapin Stephenson

The use of a principled methodology such as art therapy is essential in a discussion of creative approaches to improving quality of life. The use of art as an alternative means of communication is one of the most important and rewarding of the strategies to date and has many widespread applications and successes.

—Linda S. Carozza

I found that I could say things with color and shapes that I couldn't say any other way—things I had no words for.

—Georgia O'Keefe

THE IMPORTANCE OF SELF-EXPRESSION

Long before language was formalized, early humans used visual expression to communicate: 40,000-year-old cave paintings have been found in Indonesia, and famously in Lascaux, France, vibrant cave paintings dating to 15,000 BC. Along with the development of language and sophistication of thought, we now understand the complex layering of symbols often embedded within images. Communication is a vital component of maintaining quality of life. An older person who loses the ability to communicate due to disease or illness may become isolated, lonely, or depressed. We are unsure whether individuals with dementia have the cognitive capacity to imbue imagery with complex, abstract meaning, but we do know that communication and expression are basic human needs, like eating and sleeping. When a person loses the ability to process language and words become an impossible tool for communication, that person still retains the capacity for artistic expression, whether through movement, music, or visual art.

William Utermohlen, a professional artist, recorded the progress of his decline through self-portraiture (Grady, 2006). Incredibly brave and astute, this visual recording of his journey into Alzheimer's disease reveals an increasingly fragmented ability to organize the world outside, the darkening of life around him—an increasingly frightening picture. Like Utermohlen, individuals who have dementia still have a great need to communicate with others. Despite having lost the ability to speak, they are able to share their thoughts and feelings through visual art. In this way, new windows of communication may replace verbal methods shut down by dementia. By connecting with these people through their expressions in art, along with small, nuanced forms of nonverbal communication, we are able to find new ways to unlock doors of communication and create new avenues through the art-making process. This chapter focuses on visual art as a tool that can help foster communication among individuals with dementia.

ART THERAPY AS SUPPORTIVE PRACTICE

Art therapy is a natural ally to older persons experiencing communication challenges. The visual nature of art allows individuals to bypass the exchange of words. Color, texture, line, shape, and form elicit a visceral response and can be responded to within the pictorial "language." A person does not need to be a trained or experienced artist in order to engage in art making. When understood as an alternative language, art making can be a powerful way to support the abilities an older person does have, including life experience, wisdom, and enhanced ability to solve nuanced problems (Cohen, 2005). Making a picture or a sculpture allows older persons to express feelings inside, in a visual language that has the power to convey emotion more directly and powerfully than words alone (Kramer, 1971). In this way, art therapy is person-centered (Kim, 2010).

Traditionally, art therapy was known as an approach to use visual art expression as a springboard for gaining deeper insight in psychotherapy (Kramer, 1971; Naumburg, 1950). While this may also be true in working with people who have dementia, stroke, aphasia, Parkinson's, and other illnesses causing impairment with verbal communication, the benefits of visual expression and goals for such interventions shift. For those with dementia, improving self-esteem and developing a sense of belonging trumps all. It has been shown that art therapy can enrich the daily life of an individual with Alzheimer's disease, including building relationships with others and tapping into long-term memories (Seifert, 2001), and reducing the effects of the illness and providing a sense of hope (Safar & Press, 2011). One of the powerful aspects of visual art therapy is that communication occurs in the visual realm. For people who struggle with the spoken word—whether because of cognitive or physical impairment, trauma, or language difficulties—working with art as a communication tool can be incredible liberating. For these individuals, the pressure of talking to communicate may create stress and anxiety. Given an alternative means to communicate relieves the burden of impairment or language barriers (Abraham, 2005).

The use of art therapy for people with dementia can have a lasting, positive impact on mental alertness, increased sociability, and improved physical and social engagement (Rusted, Sheppard, & Waller, 2006). While we are still seeking evidence that art therapy improves the cognitive function of patients with Alzheimer's disease, improvements in quality of life have been observed (Hattori, Hattori, Hokao, Mizushima, & Mase, 2011). In particular, art therapy improves attention, interest, emotion, and self-esteem in individuals with Alzheimer's disease. Art therapy has also been shown to reduce stress-related behaviors in people with dementia (Mimica & Dubravka, 2011), while music therapy reduces anxiety and agitation (Sung, Lee, Li, & Watson, 2012). Studies conducted with individuals with aphasia (Horovitz, 2005; Sacchett, Byng, Marshall, & Pound, 1999), showed evidence of the development of nonverbal communication skills when they were engaged in ongoing art therapy. Sacchett et al. (1999) found that drawing, when practiced and developed in structured therapy, increased participants' ability for comprehension, naming, and gesture. Likewise, with people recovering from stroke, art therapy contributed to the improvement of attention, physical coordination, visuospacial processing, and language recovery (Kim, Kim, Lee, & Chun, 2008). Wilson (2001) describes how his art therapy patient with expressive aphasia improved cognitively and emotionally, with improvements in attention, integration of form, planning, sequencing, and pictorial integration and expression. Gonen and Soroker (2000) found that art therapy helps patients address feelings around stroke and loss of functioning, as well as increase motivation and self-expression, while Symons, Clark, Williams, Hansen, and Orpin (2011) identified the social benefits of participation in art therapy. Likewise, recent studies have found that involvement in the visual arts can help older adults increase their social connections and reduce isolation and disconnection from the world (Cohen, 2006; Merriam & Kee, 2014; Patterson & Perlstein, 2011; Wikström, 2002).

Art therapy is an approach that can be used to develop introspection and self-awareness, provide the opportunity to connect with peers and other generations, facilitate the life review process, and broaden the experiences and interests of older adults. Art therapy tools and techniques can be adapted to work with individuals with Alzheimer's disease or other forms of dementia as they struggle with loss of memory and restricted ability to communicate (Abraham, 2005; Miller, 2007; Stewart, 2004). Art therapy can be useful in helping frail elders cope with physical impairments (Baumann, Peck, Collins, & Eades, 2013; Kim et al., 2008), or elderly psychiatric patients cope with depression or lifelong mental illness (Canuto et al., 2008; Orr, 1997). Community-based art therapy programs for older adults (Sezaki

& Bloomgarden, 2000; Stephenson, 2013), tend to benefit individuals who live independently. Using reminiscence techniques in art is a popular and effective tool in supporting the life review process with some older adults (Ravid-Horesh, 2004; Trueland, 2013; Woolhiser Stallings, 2010).

Art therapy can help promote communication through images and serve as means to connect with others (Abraham, 2005; Miller, 2007; Shore, 1997; Stewart, 2004; Wald, 1993). In this way, art therapists explore the ways in which art therapy tools and techniques might be adapted in working with these men and women as they struggle with loss of memory and restricted ability to communicate. Art therapists encourage those with dementia to explore their own thoughts, feelings and life experiences in their artwork. While we teach art techniques to increase their level of mastery over artistic expression, the focus is mostly on fostering sense of purpose, social connectivity, and self-esteem—factors that are supremely important in the health and well-being of older adults (Stephenson, 2013, 2014). Although it is difficult to measure these types of improvements, they are noticed at times in the subtle ways in which people expand their range of expression, take greater risks in their artwork, or develop social connections with others in the group (Alders, 2013). Occasionally, the changes are more profound.

DEVELOPMENTAL CHANGES IN CREATIVE PROCESS AND ARTWORK

Cognitive development continues to evolve throughout the life span. In late life, a person's thinking becomes more adaptable and flexible (Csikszentmihalyi, 1996; Sasser-Coen, 1993), a result of cognitive changes connected with long life experience. As the underlying thinking process evolves with age, a person's creative process and artistic style also evolve. Changes that occur include moving from culture-bound conformity to increased introspection and integration (Arnheim, 1986; Komulainen, 1985).

An older person has a wider base of knowledge and can draw from life experience. This deepened trough of resources contributes to the increased ability to define and solve problems, which are requirements for creative performance (Lubart & Sternberg, 1998; Zhang & Niu, 2013). Motivation is another important factor influencing a person's creativity, in particular the motivation to achieve a goal. Likewise, environmental issues are also at play, providing stimulation for creative ideas, involving levels of social engagement, outside stressors and health issues. Negative environmental components can have a substantial effect on the creative performance of the older person (Lubart & Sternberg, 1998).

Studies have demonstrated how older artists experience improvement in the quality and quantity of their artwork as they age (Flood & Phillips, 2007; Lindauer, Orwoll, & Kelley, 1997; Reed, 2005). Generally, the artists attributed changes in their work to maturity and motivation, becoming more creative and generating their ideas more rapidly from new sources. These artists also reported that they had achieved a higher level of self-satisfaction. They had less concern about critique from others and felt more comfortable expressing themselves, being themselves, with increased self-acceptance and motivation. More than half of the artists in the Lindauer study felt that sensory or physical changes affected their work, with sensory changes having a greater impact. For some, their techniques changed and adapted to physical changes or limitations. The characterization of the late stage of creativity as looking inward, loosening art- making style and generalizing formal elements of artwork might be a result of both psychic and physical changes. As an aging individual nears the end of life, he or she will often reflect upon life with satisfaction or regret, relishing achievements and/or regretting failures. Usually, this period of examination focuses the individual's attention inward, and begs for a harmonious consensus or at least consolidation of opinions about oneself. It is not surprising, then, that the individual's artwork during this stage would also be emotionally expressive, using a more generalized style. Many researchers (Arnheim, 1986; Cohen-Shalev, 1989; Lindauer, 1992; Simonton, 1989; Spaniol, 1997) have noted a shift in the style of art works created by older artists. This shift, or old age style, is often marked by reduced intensity and a more introspective focus. Van Buren, Bromberger, Potts, Miller, and Chatterjee (2014) found the artwork of an individual with dementia is frequently characterized by increased abstraction and use of symbols, and decreased realistic depiction of subject matter. Pictorial depth, balance, and quality of the brush stroke remained unchanged. Perhaps the changes are a visual representation of cognitive changes, with retention of the artist's personality and style.

A Few Examples of the Art-Making Process

Older adults who have lost the ability to speak can still recollect the words of a favorite song when the music begins to play (Norberg, Melin, & Asplund, 1986; Sacks, 2007). Likewise, though an older adult with dementia may not be able to execute a thematic painting or drawing, the visceral qualities of art materials often evoke an emotional response in which the individual expresses him or herself through paint strokes. Lila, a 90-year-old woman debilitated by arthritis and late stage Alzheimer's disease, could no longer speak English, her second language, and instead spoke Russian, her mother tongue. She had become isolated, with the loss of memory, language, and subsequently the ability for others to relate to her. Lila was unable to communicate with others in the way she always had. And because she had lost the ability for abstract thought, she was unable to paint a thematic picture. Had we given Lila a set of instructions to follow, she would not have been able to follow them. So much of our lives are dictated by instructions. How confusing the world must seem, then, to a person with significant dementia who cannot understand instructions. Lost in a world with words she could no longer comprehend, Lila came alive when art materials were placed in front of her. Painting for Lila was a double-handed, full experience in which she would hold and use paint brushes in both of her hands, or, sometimes, she painted only with her fingers, taking great pleasure in the feeling of the paint on her fingers as she massaged the thick, textured watercolor paper.

Kahn-Dennis (1997) found that "art can access feelings and bypass cognition through the sensual nature of the color qualities of the paint, or the way the art medium moves in concert with the client's hand" (p. 198). Lila's eyes sparkled with pride as her painting came into being, reveling in the colors that reflected back at her and the accolades she received from peers and care-givers. Witnessing her engagement in art making provided evidence of the achievement of these goals, using her strengths and developing alternate pathways of expression through visual art (Jensen, 1997).

Stewart (2004) noted that patients engaged with the colors and textures inherent in various art media, and took risks as they participated in the creative process. She found that the patients remained motivated to engage with the art materials because of encouragement from others and the safe environment of the art room. Gentle redirection is often needed to engage participants who become confused or distracted. Jacob was not self-motivated to paint; however, with the gentle encouragement of the art therapist to pick up his brush and dip it into a color, Jacob and the art therapist began a delicate dance of self-expression and soft direction. The artwork of Jacob appears rudimentary and repetitive—simple brushstrokes of bright, unmixed colors that appear nearly the same in each of his paintings, with a few splatters of paint that on first glance look like a mistake.

A fastidiously dressed 80-year-old scientist and musician, Jacob also had late stage Alzheimer's disease. Initially, at the beginning of our work together, he was mobile but limited in his verbal ability, and six years later, required a wheelchair and had lost his ability to communicate verbally. Comparing his works through the years, one might notice a decline in the precision of his brush strokes, muddier colors now mixing together unintentionally, and an overall looser appearance to his work. These changes in his artwork illustrate the parallel changes happening in his cognitive and physical functioning. But what a viewer does not see when simply looking at his work and not witnessing his process, is the rhythmic method by which he painted, and the dance between Jacob and the art therapist. Jacob was unlikely to pick up the brush and paint on his own. However, when prompted by the art therapist, "Jacob, which color would you like to use?" he would state his color choice and put the brush in the corresponding paint tray, then paint a stroke or two. This was repeated until Jacob indicated that he had finished by putting his brush down or closing his eyes. Many times, Jacob would later continue on his own, tapping the brush on the side of the table while humming, thereby splattering the remnants of paint from his brush onto his painting. While we were never certain that this was intentional, as Jacob was a musician, this movement seemed authentic and his love for music spontaneously appeared in his painting. The rhythmic/repetitive/ brush strokes seemed to be a way for Jacob to participate in the fluid task of painting, while at the same time maintaining control. While order might have been an important component of his identity as a scientist and musician, it also might have been a way for him to cope with the confusing world he now lived in, distorted by dementia.

Rylatt (2012) found improvements in self-expression, communication, and engagement of older adults with dementia who were engaged in creative arts therapy. A keen observer of the work and process of other artists around her, Ronda's work was intuitively reflective of her environment. She painted with concentration that equaled that of her observation, carefully mixing colors, often creating a diverse palette of cool blues. For Ronda, a multistep process was important to keep her engaged and stimulated. Ronda was easily distracted by those around her, getting lost in observation—probably a trait embedded in her profession as a psychologist. A gentle, inquisitive 85-year-old woman with advanced Alzheimer's disease, Ronda was keen to try painting when the materials were laid out for her. Her facial expressions became more fluid as she began to drag her brush across the thick watercolor paper, perhaps reacting to the vibrant color that appeared, or the feel of the brush in her hand, moving across the page. Ronda often paused to examine the artwork being made around her. When her neighbor used red, that same color often appeared in Ronda's painting. When an artist across the table blended blue and red together, Ronda often copied that as well. Ronda's artwork revealed her own, recognizable style, but also that she reflected the work of those around her. While she had a great deal of difficulty expressing herself verbally, struggling for minutes to release a word or two, the fluidity of communication is expressed much more fully in her paintings. The painting as an object remained as a statement of her participation in the group that day—visually communicating her active engagement as a group member who not only expressed herself but also reflected upon the expression of others.

ART THERAPY WITH DEMENTIA: FREEDOM WITHIN STRUCTURE

Person-centered care has become a common practice among many professionals who work with older adults. Person-centered care, originating with Rogers (1951) and Maslow (1962), focuses on the needs of the individual, enhancing the strengths of the individual (McCormack & McCance, 2006), rather than focusing on illness. In order to understand and communicate with an individual with dementia, the caregiver enters the world of that individual as much as possible, to see the world through that person's perspective. Person-centered care of the older adult with dementia is focused on psychosocial interventions and communication with others and the environment (Love & Pinkowitz, 2013).

From a place of person-centered care, the goals in an art therapy program for those with dementia are to: increase connection and community, increase mastery over materials, increase expression, increase self-esteem, give them a voice, and help model for caregivers. An effort should be made to encourage freedom of expression within a safe, organizing, successful structure. This includes choosing safe art materials and multistep processes that support success at each turn. Participants are offered materials that are safe and easy to use, and with limited selection, not too overwhelming. For example, semimoist watercolor paints can be offered, as they are easier to use and the color more vibrant than traditional cake sets, along with good quality paper and brushes that can stand up to excessive pressure and water (Table 11–1).

The art therapy session is divided into three parts. The first part is used for the group used to become re-acquainted with one another, and to set up and introduce the art materials, including a brief demonstration. The second, and longest part of the group is for art making. During the third and last part of the group, the artwork is hung on the wall, and the art therapist leads a group discussion of the work, giving each participant the opportunity to introduce his or her artwork, and welcome comments from others.

Table 11-1. Person-Centered Art Therapy Goals for Older Adults with Dementia

- Connecting to self and others
- Increasing mastery of art materials
- Increasing self-esteem
- Giving person a "voice"
- Improving interactions with caregiver

Dahlia, an upbeat 91-year-old woman with advanced Alzheimer's disease loved to recall several well-told stories from her childhood, but no longer had short-term memory. She was also nearly blind and though she liked to make art, struggled with the process. Giving her a thick black or red circle drawn onto thick paper, colors that she could faintly see, or a tissue paper ring glued onto the paper that she feel, helped to orient her and give her the necessary structure to make art.

She loved circles, as they were understandable. A circle is a simple, ubiquitous form that can be imagined in the mind's eye by someone without vision, as well as containing and/or orienting for someone with cognitive decline. Often, we drew a rectangular or circular outline on the paper to serve as a "frame." This helps to orient and focus the clients. A blank piece of paper can be intimidating to anyone, but the individual with mid- to late-stage dementia might also not understand what to do. Instead, offering a piece of paper with some sort of frame, template, or a partial picture already drawn on it can help dramatically to orient the individual and provide the appropriate structure and guidance needed to begin making art work.

Mary was presented with a selection of flowers and was encouraged to touch and smell them. After this multisensory interaction with the flowers—involving sense of sight, touch and smell—she was better able to make the step into painting the flowers. Simply looking at the flowers would not have engaged Mary to the same level, nor prompted deeper connection with the art materials and the overall group experience. Also, having a concrete object to focus on, and one that invokes multiple senses, helped to create some structure in Mary's art-making process.

The fluid quality of the paint also allowed for more abstraction and surprises, which often loosens the pressure to replicate the flowers, but instead encourages a creative expression of the flowers. Art making after multisensory stimulation often increases the individual's organization, motivation, and overall enthusiasm for the experience. When texture and smell are incorporated into the art-making experience, participants often have a heightened connection with memory and emotion, making visual expression more accessible. Multisensory work can be done step by step, culminating in a visual artwork, or the entire process can be multisensory.

Music can be incorporated as accompaniment during an art therapy session, helping art therapists to touch different parts of participants' memories and their present emotional states, and indicating how music can encourage or hinder their expression. Different musical styles inspire participants to paint in different ways. Elements of the group, such as painting styles, brushstrokes, colors, concentration, interaction between group members, the ideas behind pictures, the topics of conversation, and the general atmosphere can all be influenced by music. Paul, a wheelchair-bound man with advanced dementia, often shifted the way in which he made art according to the music that was playing in the background. When we played energetic jazz, his colors became bolder. With playful, classical music, his painting also became more lyrical, with softer, more fluid colors. Paul often used perseverative motions that would eventually wear a hole in the paper, but music lightened the pressure Paul asserted onto his brush. Rather than forming a dark, wet hole on his page, Paul, with music, seemed to lift his hand to skate more gently across the paper, invoking all sides and corners in his work. We noticed that softer music inspired more solitary focus, less group interaction, and a generally calmer approach to painting. For Paul, incorporating music purposefully alongside art making was another multisensory approach to stimulating creative expression. Music activated him and contributed to improved motivation and enhanced self-expression.

Remaining connected with the world relies heavily on human interaction and the ability to connect with others. Individuals with dementia have significant difficulty achieving this. When the ability to use language deteriorates, it can be difficult for individuals with dementia to communicate and interact with each other. Making art together in a group gives them the opportunity to communicate without words and encourages them to discuss their work in progress. Participants are able to sustain their connection to this small community by relating to each other through the process of art making. In one example, each participant made his or her own individual drawing on a small piece of pre-cut paper. The individual pieces were then assembled, creating a community piece, reflecting the contributions of each member. The artists were engaged in this process individually as they focused on their own work, and then connected with each other in honoring the collective artwork.

At the conclusion of the "making" art time, it is vital to bring the group to a close with a discussion about, and celebration of, the artwork. Each piece is hung on the gallery wall. The art therapist leads a discussion about the artwork, allowing each artist to speak about his or her own work, and allowing members of the group to offer their thoughts. It is important for group leaders to focus on the artwork's expression rather than its theme. This takes the pressure off of interpreting the meaning of a picture, for which there often isn't an interpretation that is discernable or with lasting intent or meaning. Instead, by celebrating the creative process, the experience of doing it together, and the joy of creating, a powerful community connection of mutual sharing can be made among individuals who might be otherwise isolated. For example, when group members were asked to give their thoughts about the work hanging on the wall, they offered the following comments: Bob, "Completely different colors that blend quite well," and Miranda, "I don't know anything about this one," and Joe, "Redundancy is helpful for this underground group. I don't comment on my art. I'm suspicious of anyone who does." Viewing the work sparked dialogue among the group, reflecting on the object presented to them, as well as to each other.

Sometimes, only moments after completing the work, individuals often forget they have made artwork. Despite this fact, taking a look at the work in this way brings the group together, focusing attention on the group's achievement, encouraging a sense of community among them. There was an especially touching moment that occurred while talking about the work as a group. Anne, a 102-year-old woman who was very depressed about losing her memory, expressed astonishment and pride at her work after a student intern had confirmed to her that, yes, in fact, she had painted it. Anne commonly disregarded and devalued herself and her work. Her reaction to seeing her work on the wall sparked reaction from other group members, namely, two individuals who rarely speak, and a third who offered a round of applause. Anne then said, "If I can do that, then maybe I haven't lost all of my mind."

ANNUAL ART EXHIBITION

Whenever possible, an annual exhibition is an important opportunity to celebrate the accomplishments of the artists as well as share their work with family, friends, caregivers, and interested people in the community. As these individuals are so often isolated and marginalized at this late stage in life, bringing forth their vitality, personalities, and contributions is an important component to reaching the goals of building self-esteem, and fostering community (Table 11–2).

Family members are often surprised by the expressiveness of the artwork that their parents or spouses create. During one exhibit, an artist's daughter was in such disbelief about what her father had created that she called her husband and asked that he immediately to leave work to come and see the show!

A culminating art show has an important and lasting affect on older adults with dementia. Celebrating the work and talents of the group with friends and family not only highlights the successes made in the art therapy program, but also builds community among participants, family, staff, and those who view the art exhibition. Artwork should be hung in a professional and aesthetically pleasing way. Signage with the artist's name, title, and medium should be visible next to the artwork, and a narrative description of the artist's process should be provided to aid in the viewer's appreciation of the artist and his or her artwork.

Table 11–2. Art Therapy Methods

Freedom Within the Structure

- Draw a frame or circle on the paper
- Provide paper with partially drawn image
- Refer to a concrete object
- Use bright, fluid paint (e.g., semimoist watercolor)

Multisensory

- Engage senses to elicit deeper experience
- Use flowers
- Use textured paper
- Provide music

Building Community

- Group art making
- Cross-table interaction
- End-of-session discussion
- Annual art exhibition

It has always been my hope to help shift the stigma of aging and dementia by celebrating the artwork of these inspiring men and women through a professional art exhibition. It is difficult to truly understand and appreciate the artwork created by individuals with dementia, which can appear childish or incomplete. It is important to educate the viewers about dementia and the ways in which the artwork displayed represents the artists' presence, participation, and inclusion in the community, rather than focusing on the losses that contribute to the "unprofessional" appearance of the artwork. Some of common terms to describe this work would be: simple, fragmented, distorted, or confused. However, the true quality of the art-making process isn't evident without witnessing it. Therefore, alongside the artwork displayed, it is helpful to have a description of how the artwork was created to help bring to light the personality of the artist to the outside viewer. For example: "A true collaborator, Bonnie is a keen observer of those around her and allows her study to inspire and influence her work. Her painting process involves periods of working carefully on her own painting, then observing other artists. She also enjoys close collaboration with students" and, "Rena's creative process is as hypnotic as her paintings. She truly enjoys the process of painting, exploring each color carefully, and pulling her brush along the paper as if it is on some great journey. All the while, Rena's outward enjoyment of the creative process inspires all those around her."

OPPORTUNITIES FOR THE FUTURE

Finding the best ways to care for older adults is an evolving process. As our world population increases, in many countries we are faced with the imminent need to find more effective health care methods and delivery systems. Often overlooked, the creative arts therapies offer an effective means to both treat illness and foster wellness in our aging population. We are learning how human development continues throughout the lifespan, and in particular, how creative thinking, motivation, and identity change with aging. As a person ages, he or she develops a greater need for self-expression and many older adults have an increased capacity for creativity through the mastery and integration of life experience (Fisher & Specht, 1999). At the same time, recent studies have begun to explore the impact of creative arts therapies as a treatment modality with older adults with dementia.

I have received reports of marked change in behavior of several participants while they were attending my art therapy program and upon their return home. For example, Ander was reportedly argumentative with his wife and at times combative at home, visibly unhappy and angry. However, while in our presence in the art therapy program, he was usually smiling, telling jokes, and seeking the friendship of others in the room.

We surmised that in part Ander's improved behavior was due to the safe, supportive environment where a person with memory impairment "fits in." Art therapy can be a significant contributor to creating that environment. Where many with dementia find it very frustrating to speak as they cannot find the words or are not sufficiently understood, through the art they may be fully expressive, drawing from ever-present emotions, but without the constraints of the spoken or written word. Family members of our participants with Alzheimer's disease remarked at how their loved one became energized and more organized as a result of the art therapy program.

It is difficult to measure impact of art therapy programs, as there are multiple factors that influence the outcome of a particular session. We intrinsically know that creative arts therapy programs bring joy to the lives of older adults with dementia, and that they often contribute to improved well-being and reduced anxiety, isolation, and dementia. However, due to the complexity of the care of individuals with dementia, and difficulty measuring changes in behavior, cognition and/or emotion, and sufficiently attributing its root, evaluating the impact of these programs has been difficult and few studies currently exist. We need to establish reliable measurement tools, including criteria for growth, improvement, and efficacy.

REFERENCES

Abraham, R. (2005). *When words have lost their meaning: Alzheimer's patients communication through art.* Westport, CT: Praeger/Greenwood.

Alders, A. (2013). The effect of art therapy on cognitive performance among ethnically diverse older adults. *Art Therapy: Journal of the American Art Therapy Association, 30*(4), 159–168.

Arnheim, R. (1986). On the late style. In R. Arnheim (Ed.), *New essays on the psychology of art* (pp. 285–293). Berkeley, CA: University of California Press.

Baumann, M., Peck, S., Collins, C., & Eades, G. (2013). The meaning and value of taking part in a person-centred arts programme to hospital-based stroke patients: Findings from a qualitative study. *Disability and Rehabilitation, 35*(3), 244–256.

Canuto, A., Meiler-Mititelu, C., Herrmann, F. R., Delaloye, C., Giannakopoulos, P., & Weber, K. (2008). Longitudinal assessment of psychotherapeutic day hospital treatment for elderly patients with depression. *International Journal of Geriatric Psychiatry, 23*(9), 949–956.

Cohen, G. D. (2005). *The mature mind: The positive power of the aging brain.* New York, NY: Basic Books.

Cohen, G. D. (2006). Research on creativity and aging: The positive impact of the arts on health and illness. *Generations, 30*(1), 7–15.

Cohen-Shalev, A. (1989). Old age style: Developmental changes in creative production from a life-span perspective. *Journal of Aging Studies, 3*(1), 21–37.

Csikszentmihalyi, M. (1996). *Creativity: Flow and the psychology of discovery and invention.* New York, NY: HarperCollins.

Fisher, B. J., & Specht, D. K. (1999). Successful aging and creativity in later life. *Journal of Aging Studies, 13*(4), 457–472.

Flood, M., & Phillips, K. (2007). Creativity in older adults: A plethora of possibilities [Electronic version]. *Issues in Mental Health Nursing, 28*, 389–411.

Gonen, J., & Soroker, N. (2000). Art therapy in stroke rehabilitation: A model of short-term group treatment. *The Arts in Psychotherapy, 27*(1), 41–50.

Grady, D. (2006, October 24). Self-portraits chronicle a descent into Alzheimer's. *New York Times.* Retrieved October 13, 2014, from http://www.nytimes.com/2006/10/24/health/24alzh.html?_r=0

Hattori, H., Hattori, C., Hokao, C., Mizushima, K., & Mase, T. (2011). Controlled study on the cognitive and psychological effect of coloring and drawing in mild Alzheimer's disease patients. *Geriatrics & Gerontology International, 11*, 431–437.

Horovitz, E. (2005). *Art therapy as witness: A sacred guide.* Springfield, IL: Charles C. Thomas.

Jensen, S. M. (1997). Multiple pathways to self: A multisensory art experience. *Art Therapy: Journal of the American Art Therapy Association, 14*(3), 178–186. doi:10.1080/07421656.1987.10759279

Kahn-Denis, K. (1997). Art therapy with geriatric dementia clients. *Art Therapy: Journal of the American Art Therapy Association, 14*(3), 194–199.

Kim, S. (2010). A story of a healing relationship: The person-centered approach in expressive arts therapy. *Journal of Creativity in Mental Health, 5*(1), 93–98.

Kim, S., Kim, M., Lee, J., & Chun, S. (2008). Art therapy outcomes in the rehabilitation treatment of a stroke patient: A case report. *Art Therapy: Journal of the American Art Therapy Association, 25*(3), 129–133.

Komulainen, S. P. J. (1985). Creative abilities as a life-span phenomenon: A cross-cut survey in Finland. *Creative Child and Adults Quarterly, 10*(3), 170–181.

Kramer, E. (1971). *Art therapy with children.* Chicago, IL: Magnolia Street.

Lindauer, M. S. (1992). Creativity in aging artists: Contributions from the humanities to the psychology of old age. *Creativity Research Journal, 5*(3), 211–231.

Lindauer, M. S., Orwoll, L., & Kelley, M. C. (1997). Aging artists on the creativity of their old age. *Creativity Research Journal, 10*(2–3), 133–152.

Love, K., & Pinkowitz, J. (2013). Person-centered care for people with dementia: A theoretical and conceptual framework. *Generations: Journal of the American Society on Aging, 37*(3), 23–29.

Lubart, T. I., & Sternberg, R. J. (1998). Life span creativity: An investment theory approach. In C. E. Adams-Price (Ed.), *Creativity and successful aging: Theoretical and empirical approaches* (pp. 21–41). New York, NY: Springer.

Maslow, A. (1962). *Towards a psychology of being* (2nd ed.). New York, NY: Van Nostrand Reinhold.

McCormack, B., & McCance, T. V. (2006). Developing a conceptual framework for person-centered nursing. *Journal of Advanced Nursing, 56*(5), 472–479.

Merriam, S. B., & Kee, Y. (2014). Promoting community well-being: The case for lifelong learning for older adults. *Adult Education Quarterly, 64*(2), 128–144.

Miller, B. (2007). *Mind alert: A joint program of American Society on Aging and the MetLife Foundation. Art and dementia.* San Francisco, CA: American Society on Aging.

Mimica, N., & Dubravka K. (2011). Art therapy may be beneficial for reducing stress-related behaviours in people with dementia: Case report. *Psychiatria Danubina, 23*(1), 125–128.

Naumburg, M. (1950). *Introduction to art therapy.* New York, NY: Teachers College Press.

Norberg, A., Melin, E., & Asplund, K. (1986). Reactions to music, touch and object presentation in the final stage of dementia: An exploratory study. *International Journal of Nursing Studies, 40*(5), 481–485.

Orr, P. (1997). Treating the whole person: A combination of medical and psychiatric treatment for older adults. *Art Therapy, 14*(3), 200–205.

Patterson, M. C., & Perlstein, S. (2011). Good for the heart, good for the soul: The creative arts and brain health in later life. *Generations, 35*(2), 27–36.

Ravid-Horesh, R. H. (2004). A temporary guest: The use of art therapy in life review with an elderly woman. *The Arts in Psychotherapy, 31*(5), 303–319.

Reed, I. (2005). Creativity: Self-perceptions over time. *International Journal of Aging and Human Development, 60*(1), 1–18.

Rogers, C. (1951). *Client-centered therapy: Its current practice, implications and theory.* London, UK: Constable.

Rusted, J., Sheppard, L., & Waller, D. (2006). Therapy for older people with dementia. *Group Analysis, 39*(4), 517–536.

Rylatt, P. (2012). The benefits of creative therapy for people with dementia. *Nursing Standard, 26*(33), 42–47.

Sacchett, C., Byng, S., Marshall, J., & Pound, C. (1999). Drawing together: Evaluation of a therapy programme for severe aphasia. *International Journal of Language and Communication Disorders, 34*(3), 265–289.

Sacks, O. (2007). *Musicophilia: Tales of music and the brain.* New York, NY: Knopf.

Safar, L. T., & Press, D. Z. (2011). Art and the brain: Effects of dementia on art production in art therapy. *Art Therapy: Journal of the American Art Therapy Association, 28*(3), 96–103.

Sasser-Coen, J. R. (1993). Qualitative changes in creativity in the second half of life: A life-span developmental perspective. *Journal of Creative Behavior, 27*(1), 18–27.

Seifert, L. S. (2001). Customized art activities for individuals with Alzheimer-type dementia. *Activities, Adaptation & Aging, 24*(4), 65–74.

Sezaki, S., & Bloomgarden, J. (2000). Home-based art therapy for older adults. *Art Therapy, 17*(4), 283–290.

Shore, A. (1997). Promoting wisdom: The role of art therapy in geriatric settings. *Art Therapy: Journal of the American Art Therapy Association, 14*(3), 172–177.

Simonton, D. K. (1989). The swan-song phenomenon: Last-work effects for 172 classical composers. *Psychology and Aging, 4,* 42–47.

Spaniol, S. (1997). Art therapy with older adults: Challenging myths, building competencies. *Art Therapy, 14*(3), 158–160.

Stephenson, R. C. (2013). Promoting well-being and gerotranscendence in an art therapy program for older adults. *Art Therapy: Journal of the American Art Therapy Association, 30*(4).

Stephenson, R. C. (2014). Art in aging: How identity as an artist can transcend the challenges of aging. *International Journal of Creativity and Human Development, 1*(3).

Stewart, E. G. (2004). Art therapy and neuroscience blend: Working with patients who have dementia. *Art Therapy: Journal of the American Art Therapy Association, 21*(3), 148–155.

Sung, H., Lee, W., Li, T., & Watson, R. (2012). A group music intervention using percussion instruments with familiar music to reduce anxiety and agitation of institutionalized older adults with dementia. *International Journal of Geriatric Psychiatry, 27*, 621–627.

Symons, J., Clark, H., Williams, K., Hansen, E., & Orpin, P. (2011). Visual art in physical rehabilitation: Experience of people with neurological conditions. *British Journal of Occupational Therapy, 74*(1), 44–52.

Trueland, J. (2013). Bringing back memories [Cover story]. *Nursing Standard, 27*(26), 16–18.

van Buren, B., Bromberger, B., Potts, D., Miller, B., & Chatterjee, A. (2013). Changes in painting styles of two artists with Alzheimer's disease. *Psychology of Aesthetics, Creativity and the Arts, 7*(1), 89–94.

Wald, J. (1993). Art therapy and brain dysfunction in a patient with a dementing illness. *Art Therapy: Journal of the American Art Therapy Association, 10*(2), 88–95.

Wikström, B. M. (2002). Social interaction associated with visual art discussions: A controlled intervention study. *Aging & Mental Health, 6*(1), 82–87.

Wilson, L. (2001). Symbolism and art therapy. In J. Rubin (Ed.), *Approaches to art therapy: Theory and technique* (pp. 40–53). Hove, UK: Brunner-Routledge.

Woolhiser Stallings, J. (2010). Collage as a therapeutic modality for reminiscence in patients with dementia. *Art Therapy: Journal of the American Art Therapy Association, 27*(3), 136–140.

Zhang W., & Niu, W. (2013). Creativity in the later life: Factors associated with the creativity of Chinese elderly. *The Journal of Creative Behavior, 47*(1), 60–76.

CHAPTER 12

Music Therapy in Neurologic Dysfunction to Address Self-Expression, Language, and Communication

The Impact of Group Singing on Stroke Survivors and Caregivers

*Joanne V. Loewy, Jamée Ard,
and Naoko Mizutani*

*The notion of music and medicine is one that is
complementary in the field of alternative strategies
to life participation and enhancement. Socially and
scientifically, many applications of music-based
approaches are found in the research literature and are
key in maintaining and developing selfhood as well as
partnership with the environment and those around
us. The creative approaches to communication-assisted
strategies are greatly enhanced via the incorporation
of music therapy as a central program component in
meaningful service delivery throughout the lifespan.*

—Linda S. Carozza

INTRODUCTION

The potential efficacy of music applications and music therapy approaches in medicine and rehabilitation has been the subject of a growing number of clinical trials spanning the past several decades. The treatment of neurological dysfunction is gaining public interest, particularly as limitations of speech and language, and/or movement, are often accompanied by vulnerable mood states, threatening the quality of life for so many, and with rising frequency. The results of traumatic brain injury, Parkinson's, Huntington's, and Alzheimer's diseases, cerebral palsy, and afflictions affecting cognition, movement, and communication are increasing in part because our general population is living longer.

Neurologic Music Therapy (NMT) provides a comprehensive rehabilitative model of therapeutic application that has been developed as a specialization in the field of music therapy. It is designed to meet the needs of people who have neuro-dysfunction. Music therapists working in this specialized field incorporate behavioral and rehabilitative applications of music therapy, movement, and speech techniques involving sensory, gait trainings combined with rhythmic, auditory, and physiological aspects of function.

While treatment of functional deficits caused by neurological diseases has been a primary focus of NMT, in addition there is an increased focus on the need to address the psychological and psychosocial impact on those affected by such diseases, and within a format that informed by music's implicit functionality. Music memory remains notably intact, and at times, exclusively intact, amidst uniform collateral loss of language and movement function. A focus on the healthy aspects of music, and its "ensemble" mechanisms can dictate aesthetically-emergent resilient properties of expression that influence neurologic function. NMT has informed new and emerging developments in some new models of music therapy in neurologic dysfunction. A research study on the evaluation of music therapy, for instance, in German neurorehabilitation centers (as cited in Jochims, 2004) reveals the importance of addressing the integration of various needs in those affected by acquired brain damages, including not only physical, sensory, cognitive, and communicative areas, but social, and emotional areas as well. Furthermore, including caregivers and addressing ways to collaborate within musical community domains is a growing treatment strategy receiving increasing attention, as an aspect of marked clinical focus is the global music therapy field of neurology. This chapter will outline some of the general applications in which music and music therapy have been used in the treatment of neurodysfunction before delving more specifically into music therapy treatment for stroke survivors and their caregivers. The chapter's final focus will present the authors' treatment of people who have survived stroke, and integration of their caregivers, as well, in describing an intervention that is part of a unique model of community music psychotherapy entitled Singing Together, Measure by Measure.

As a foundational orientation similar to other allied disciplines designed to impact neurologic function, music therapists are trained in human physiology and neuroanatomy, addressing cognitive and motor functions through a focus on speech, movement and mood. Inclusion of caregivers in the treatment of those with neurologic dysfunction may have unique advantages where music's potential in people who have lost their retention and communicative competence can be addressed in an "ensemble" moment of singing or playing together. The impact may be most meaningful for all members (patients and caregivers) because there is no leveling of context based on solely verbal expression and/or retention, but rather a combination of cognitive mechanisms at play, which are inclusive of psychosocial domains of functioning such as incentive, spontaneity, and risk-taking, which are integral parts of the musical-expressive experience. These areas are psychotherapeutic aspects of dynamic function that can be tweaked or elicited within a music-making experience. Components of the music neural pathways are recognizably preserved, often through neurologic dysfunction. When dynamic function of musical expression is fostered and activated through a singing experience, in the moment, between two or more people, it can enhance feelings of trust, safety, inclusion, and bonding. At the same time, the content of the music may help activate a memory or a context for how and when a recovered or retrieved melody or song was first elicited, because memory is contextually dependent.

Music is part of our everyday lives, be it in our frequent singing of the national anthem or our meaningful wedding song; or perhaps in a nursery rhyme preserved from our childhood and then repeated with our own children and grandchildren; or in repeatedly listening to a favorite symphony; our capacity to access tunes and associated lyrics comes easily, at no cost. Music is associative, connecting us to others and to intricate parts of most people's life stages. In many cases, songs serve as a marker to many historical periods that weave together components of peoples' lives, similar to a photo album or scrapbook. In this way, music can encapsulate meaningful moments not only for people facing neurological dysfunction, but for those who care for them as well. In this chapter, we will provide an orientation for music and music therapy in neurologic function, providing a few examples of how music therapy has been effectively used in specific neurological treatment areas.

LITERATURE REVIEW

The brain houses the neural substrates that govern communication, memory, mobility, sight, and emotions, functioning through the work of two types of cells, neurons and glia. Each neuron has two projections from the cell body, one that receives information from the neighboring neuron (dendrite) and one that transmits the information (axon). The area of the brain where the dendrite of one neuron meets the axon of the adjacent neuron is called the synapse. Glial cells govern the properties of neurotransmission and are key to the repair of neurons in the event of injury, as neurons do not have the capacity for self-repair.

As we think about the mechanisms of language and music—particularly recognizing, though current neuroscience research, the significant role that music takes in neural pathway preservation of unique "music memory"—a world of possibility unfolds. Because song is a mechanism in which lyrics, composed of language, are attached to sequences or phrases of melodies and histories and contexts therein, the capacity to retain, recover, and retrain expression through sung language presents the possibility of a significant tool, especially when used within a therapeutic course of treatment. As investigations through scientific approaches (brain imaging), behavioral approaches (speech therapy, neurologic music therapy) as well as music psychotherapy approaches (incentive, mood, motivation) are used with patients with neurologic dysfunction throughout clinics and university labs worldwide, we are learning. Increasingly, our understanding is heightened through the explosion of research in a variety of neurologic diseases, with each trial or project undertaking a unique way of addressing how music can affect neurologic function.

Recent advances in neurological imaging have dramatically transformed our understanding of both the organization and functioning of the brain. Research focusing on the impact of music and musical study of the brain has unlocked some of the most elusive aspects of this fascinating organ. For example, the long-held belief in the right–left functional dichotomy in the brain was dispelled over 30 years ago (Bever & Chiarello, 1974) when we learned that musical training promoted hemispheric lateralization, which, in turn, facilitated the brain's elasticity in the face of injury or trauma. Two decades later, Schlaug and his colleagues (1995) found that the anterior corpus callosum, an area of the brain essential to hemispheric communication, is larger in musicians than in nonmusicians. And more recently, Lappe, Trainor, Herholz, and Pantev (2011) found that short-term musical rhythmic training produced recognizable changes in the plasticity of the auditory cortex.

MUSIC THERAPY IN NEUROLOGIC FUNCTION

Parkinson's Disease

Parkinson's disease is a chronic, progressive, neurodegenerative disorder that destroys neurons in the brain, in the area known as the substantia nigra. People with Parkinson's disease experience neuron expiration and are subjected to a loss of motor control throughout the body. Music therapy can be effective in addressing motor control impairment in these patients (Elefant, Baker, Lotan, Lagesen, & Skeie, 2012). For example, weekly group music therapy sessions improved 5 of 6 outcomes for singing and voice range, as measured by a KayPentax Multi-Dimensional Voice Program. Furthermore, participation in the music therapy group helped to maintain speaking quality.

Deficits in persons with Parkinson's disease also can be related to speech. A biweekly choir that used a "Group Music Therapy Protocol (G-MTP)" consisting of physical, facial, and vocal warm-ups, conversation, and singing choral music increased the intensity of conversational speech in ten subjects, offsetting the effects of Parkinson's, which can include a "jitter" to the voice and diminishing vocal frequency (Yinger & Lapointe, 2012).

An integrative approach of weekly joint music and physical therapy resulted, after 3 months, in enhanced gross motor control, particularly with bradykinesia, in which movements are slowed to an extreme rate as a result of Parkinson's disease. The sessions included choral singing, as well as rhythmic and free body movement to music (Pacchietti et al., 2000). The music was improvised by the therapist's encouragement of participants to take an active role—to use their voices and/or instruments. Instruments included piano, organ, and percussion instruments: woodblock, metallophone, and so forth.

Individuals who have experienced brain injury have also benefitted from playing and listening to music. After 20 weeks of one-hour music listening and playing sessions consisting of 30 minutes of listening to music and 30 minutes of playing instruments, there was a sizable improvement in mood and reduction in anxiety (Guétin, Soua, Voiriot, Picot, & Hérisson, 2009). The music listening section consisted of patient-selected recorded music. The researchers used a method they call "U-based" which entailed slowing the rhythm of the music chosen by patients, and reducing the number of instruments, all to promote relaxation. In the active music portion, the therapist improvised and encouraged the patient to sing or play an instrument. There were no specific instruments mentioned.

The effects of a neurologic music therapy protocol on individuals with brain injury found that executive function improved after four sessions, which included vocal and instrumental warm-ups (Thaut, 2009). For each session, the improvisation focused on the area studied, that is, executive function, attention, memory, or emotional adjustment. For example, in the session on executive function, the improvisation involved problem-solving as it related to improvisation. Thaut has developed a protocol for Neurologic Music Therapy, which will be briefly addressed later.

Alzheimer's Disease

Alzheimer's disease is the most common of dementia and was discovered by a German psychiatrist and neuropathologist Alois Alzheimer in 1906. Alzheimer's disease is a degenerative neural illness and largely affects people over age 65. Plaques and tangles in the brain affect the short-term memory and impede language function. Throughout its course of development there is a notable increasing impairment of learning and memory as well as distortions of perception and it can result in apraxia. Music can have a profound affect on memory recall and enhance interactive function in the moment, particularly emotional expression through singing.

In a recent music therapy review of treatments worldwide for Alzheimer's disease, a group of investigators noted benefits of music therapy existing primarily through emotional and psycho-physiological pathways. In Alzheimer's, perhaps as much as memory and language limitations, are also observable difficulties with frustration tolerance leading to generalized agitation. Studies reflect that music psychotherapy, using favorite songs, can reduce anxiety, alleviating periods of depression and aggressive behavior. Over time, autonomy of these patients might increase. Music therapy can significantly improve socialization and mood (Guétin et al., 2013).

The effects of music therapy have focused on elevating mood and reducing agitation in patients with Alzheimer's disease. A pre-post study (Zare, Ebrahimi, & Birashk, 2010) addressed frustration tolerance of not only patients but caregivers as well.

Stroke

One of the most prevalent causes of neurologic trauma is stroke, which is caused by an interruption in the flow of blood to the brain, by an artery being either ruptured or blocked. In the

United States, a stroke occurs every 40 seconds and is the leading cause of disability in adults (National Stroke Association, 2013). A stroke is a cerebrovascular accident (CVA), where there is threatened neurologic function due to a temporary arrest of blood supply and/or flow to the brain. A hemorrhage or block results in cognitive impairment, restrictions of gross motor function, and/or visual and speech deficits that may be temporary or permanent, depending on the severity of the stroke. The pathological symptoms of apoplexy from bleeding or blockage of blood to the brain, as is so frequent in stroke was noted in the mid-1600s by a Swiss doctor named Johann Jacob Wepfer. Although men have a higher risk of having a stroke, more women die from stroke, once diagnosed.

Aphasia is a common complication after a stroke affecting the left middle cerebral artery, and is recognized as a major impairment by patients and their family members (Wade, Wood, & Hewer, 1985). The types of aphasia can be roughly divided into fluent and nonfluent. Fluent aphasia reduces understanding of language and nonfluent aphasia reduces expressive skills of language (Walker-Batson & Avent, 2007). Broca's aphasia is known as a nonfluent aphasia because there is auditory understanding but difficulty in expression. Most of these patients can speak in short sentences or mixed descriptive nouns or verbs. Nonfluent aphasia is caused by injury to the left frontal lobe including Broca's area, and is the result of injury to the subcortical area of the brain.

Since the beginning of the 20th century, researchers have used music to address the impact of stroke, noting that stroke survivors who could not speak were still able to sing (Hurkmans et al., 2012). Some researchers have identified what is believed to be a "golden period" for stroke rehabilitation. The thinking is that treatment should be rendered within the first six months post onset (Huang, Chung, Lai, & Sung, 2009). However, this is often a difficult time of adjustment for not only stroke survivors, but their caregivers as well. The predominant research in music and music therapy has occurred at all phases of recovery.

Music and music therapy's rehabilitative influence are notable as therapeutic tools focusing on neuromotor-related activation of brain structures and regions related to movement in stroke. However, research addressing the effects of music, and singing in particular, on psychological and social well-being is limited in stroke treatment (Raglio, Fazio, Imbriani, & Granieri, 2013) compared to the research related to music in neuromotor rehabilitation.

A critical study investigating the impact of emotional perceptual difficulties and relatedness to social participation and quality of life following stroke (Cooper et al., 2014) assessed 28 stroke survivors on three emotional perception tasks; visual, auditory, and multimodal, using (1) Facial Expressions of Emotions: Stimuli and Test (FEEST; Young, Perrett, Calder, Sprengelmeyer, & Ekman, 2002); (2) Florida Affect Battery (FAB; Bowers, Blonder, Slomine, & Heilman, 1996); (3) and the Awareness of Social Influence Test (TASIT; McDonald, Flanagan, Martin, & Saunders, 2004). The Modified Functional Limitation Profile (mFLP) was used for the measurement of activity limitation and social participation restriction (Pollard & Johnson, 2001). The World Health Organization Quality-of-Life measure (WHO-QoL BREF) was employed to assess multiple domains of quality of life, including physical health, psychological well-being, social relationships, and functioning in the environment (The WHO-QOL Group, 1998). A strong correlation between emotional perception performance and social participation indicated a reduced level of social engagement related to difficulties in emotional perception after stroke. This seminal study points to the need for greater understanding of the emotional, psychological, and psychosocial aspects of stroke recovery and their influence on individual social functioning.

Among various music therapy interventions, the use of singing is recognized as one of the most powerful tools in enhancing emotional, psychological, and psychosocial aspect of well-being (e.g., mood, quality of life) in normal function (Clift & Hancox, 2010; Livesey, Morrison, Clift, & Camic, 2012). Singing in groups is also notable as beneficial for individuals living with chronic illness, including strokes (Särkämö, Tervaniemi, & Huotilainen, 2013; Sun & Buys, 2013; Talmage, Ludlam, Leão, Fogg-Rogers, & Purdy, 2013). The existing literature in music therapy focusing on the interrelationship of communal/group singing and health is limited to several studies, each of which has proven efficacy in promoting emotional, psychological, and psychosocial well-being (Clift & Hancox, 2010; Clift & Morrison, 2010; Livesey et al., 2012; Sun & Buys, 2013; Talmage et al., 2013)

A baseline cross-national survey of 1,124 choral singers conducted in England, Australia, and Germany investigated the possible effects of singing on well-being and health (Clift & Hancox, 2010). Participants consisted of choral singers from 21 choral societies and choirs in England (n = 633), Germany (n = 325) and Australia (n = 166). The large part of the repertoire was from major choral works from the Western classical music from the 15th to the 20th century, whereas some choirs sang a more eclectic repertoire, including songs from musical shows and films. Participants completed two questionnaires: the WHO-QoL BREF measuring physical, psychological, social and environmental well-being, and a 12-item scale for assessing perceived well-being and effects of choral singing. The results indicated the benefits of choral singing on well-being and health, and psychological function. The results also showed that 85 participants who had been initially assessed as relatively low psychological being on the WHO-QoL BREF had higher scores on the singing scale post intervention. Moreover, four categories of significant personal and health challenges—enduring mental health problems, family/relationship problems, physical health challenges, and recent bereavement—improved as indicated from written comments by participants in relation to the effects of choral singing. The comments from participants suggested that singing might have an impact on well-being and health, such as increased mood, focused attention, deep breathing, social support, cognitive stimulation, and regular commitment.

A second qualitative study based on the previously mentioned cross-national survey research (Clift & Hancox, 2010) showed that 178 out of 1,124 participants selected, based on their score on the WHO-QoL-BREF, could be divided into two groups, a high mental well-being group and a low mental well-being group. Participants were then asked to answer open-ended questions regarding the effects of singing. Thematic and content analysis were conducted to generate the results from participants' responses to the questionnaire. The results indicated multiple benefits to health and well-being from choral singing, including social benefits, emotional benefits, and adding meaning and purpose to life (Livesey et al., 2012)

To examine the effects of group singing on the recovery and social inclusion of individuals with a history of serious and enduring mental health issues, researchers employed a mixed method, longitudinal, observational design where a total of 137 individuals participated in a choral singing group conducted by trained facilitators over a period of eight months from September 2009 to November 2010 (Clift & Morrison, 2010). The choir met weekly over three terms with breaks for Christmas and Easter. They also participated in two public performances, in February and June 2010. The repertoire was selected upon group members' agreement, learned by ear, and sung without accompaniment.

Among the 137 participants (age: 27–81 years old) a questionnaire that assessed feelings and behaviors related to mental distress calculated results by the CORE outcome measure (CORE-OM, CORE Information Management Systems, 2014). The measurements were taken at the end of each term, and outcomes from the end of the first term (November 2009) and the third term (June 2010) were compared. Significant changes were observed in participants' responses to particular items (11 out of 34 items), which indicated a decreased level of mental distress in some categories indicating a general improvement with 11 out of 42 participants reporting a significant decrease in mental distress.

The therapeutic effects of communal choral singing on stroke survivors and individuals with Parkinson's disease was a randomized control trial consisting of weekly choral singing therapy sessions with eight stroke survivors, six individuals with a history of Parkinson's disease, and nine significant others for 12 weeks. Choral Singing Therapy was designed to facilitate communication rehabilitation and improvement in quality of life for individuals with neurological conditions (Talmage et al., 2013).

In this approach, a sense of membership in the group was an important factor in facilitating the maximum therapeutic outcomes. Choir members were encouraged to actively participate in selecting songs and a public performance was included. The participation of significant others, caregivers, and volunteers seemed to play an important role in what the researchers thought created a positive and inclusive atmosphere.

Each session, led by a certified music therapist, was 90 minutes, and consisted of greetings, warm-up exercises, vocal exercises, and singing songs, with one break at the midpoint of the session. Songs chosen by group members included simple, repetitive lyrics. Music rounds and echo songs were used as a bridge between exercises and repertoire singing of cultural and traditional songs of relevance to the group, show tunes, holiday songs, popular music from the 1950s to 1970s, and songs with positive and affirming lyrics. The result of the study, obtained through the interviews with choir members, their significant others or caregivers, and the wider community revealed positive outcomes of the social and therapeutic benefits of choral singing therapy. Performance is an aspect of singing that relates to an important component of speaking. When we speak, we are "performing" a prosodic expression of content (Loewy, 2004, 1995).

Another study included 291 participants who sang for 2 hours per week for 12 months. Five mixed-age groups were formed, each consisting of Aboriginal and Torres Strait Islander Australians (ages 18–78), 90% with chronic conditions, such as stroke, depression, heart disease, diabetes, hypertension, and schizophrenia, with the aim of promoting the social and emotional well-being at both individual and collective level (Sun & Buys, 2013). The study focused on the promotion of resilience and prevention of chronic disease in these populations, based on the rationale that well-being and health were related to resilience.

This study was designed with an emphasis on the cultural and social aspects of music that enhanced the participants' capacity to maintain their identity and culture (Shapiro, 2005). Singing songs has been considered a musical tradition for people in this community and has been integrated in their everyday life as a way for them to express and identify with the cultural, social, and historical connectedness in their country. Therefore, choosing and singing songs that were deeply rooted in their life and culture was an important part of the process for group members. The research was nonrandomized and employed mixed methods, including both quantitative and qualitative data analysis. The Singing Activity Participation Questionnaire was employed to assess perceived benefits of singing-related activities on psychological health, physical health, and spiritual health on a Likert scale. Resilience was assessed using a questionnaire adopted from the resilience measures developed by Sun and Stewart (2007). The data from focus group interviews were analyzed using grounded theory procedures, and initial coding was conducted with distinct themes emerging. Assessments were conducted at the beginning and the end of a 12-month trial.

The results from the quantitative data revealed outcomes in three areas: (1) the number of stressful life events reported; (2) feelings of connectedness to the community; and (3) quality of life. When the pre- and postintervention assessments were compared, there were no significant differences in the number of stressful life events reported by the study groups (singing groups) and control groups at the preintervention assessments, whereas there was a significant increase in the number of participants in study groups (singing groups) reporting no occurrence of stressful events at the postintervention assessment. The participants in the singing groups reported feelings of connectedness to their community and quality-of-life improvements at their postintervention assessments.

The qualitative data obtained from the focus group interview questions revealed three main themes that had developed within the singing groups: individual resilience characteristics (e.g., learning, confidence, self-esteem, purpose of life, coping); social interaction and social capital (e.g., sense of connectedness, collective experience, developing friendship, trust, equality); and use of community health services (e.g., increased access to counseling services, increased undertaking health checks). Researchers reflected that experience in these three themes/ areas facilitated their development of support systems when experiencing stresses related to their illness, which indicates the effectiveness of community singing in promoting resilience, increasing social interaction, and developing social capacity.

The integration of music as a therapeutic modality and its effectiveness in neuromotor rehabilitation for those with neurological conditions, including stroke, has been investigated and widely accepted in U.S. society (Raglio et al., 2013). Current research investigating the effectiveness of communal/group singing on individuals living with chronic illness such as stroke and other neurological conditions shows effectiveness in not only physical and cognitive aspects of rehabilitative treatment, but also in the emotional, psychological, and psychosocial aspects of well-being and health. As has been shown by recent research studies (Clift & Hancox, 2010; Clift & Morrison, 2010; Livesey et al., 2012; Sun & Buys, 2013; Talmage et al., 2013), communal/group singing promotes the recovery process on both an intra-and interpersonal level by providing the experience of self-worth, positive coping, learning, connectedness to others, support, encouragement, trust, and joy. Furthermore, the collaborative and sociocultural nature of communal/group singing facilitates members' ownership of the group and respect for one another in the supportive environment, one in which people can come together on the basis of a shared interest, not their health conditions or diagnosis.

Beyond the application of singing and music therapy, music itself has been used to address the consequences of stroke in a method entitled music-supported therapy (MST). This program uses musical instruments, an electronic piano, and an electronic drum set emitting piano sounds to retrain fine and gross movements of the paretic upper extremity (Rodriguez-Fornells et al., 2012, p. 282). The MST protocol was also used by Amengual et al. (2013) with 20 chronic stroke patients who had a slight hand paresis. In their study, participants were given twenty 30-minute sessions of MST over a period of 4 years; that resulted in improved motor performance.

Singing was used to address physical impairments resulting from stroke—such as dysphagia, difficulty in swallowing—in 8 patients over 12 music therapy sessions of 30 minutes, including breathing exercises, singing, and a laryngeal elevation exercise. "Significant improvements across reflex, respiration, and laryngeal categories showed increased control" (Kim, 2010, p. 117).

Thirty-nine stroke survivors who were asked to listen to their choice of music an hour a day for the first 2 months after stroke were found to have increased motor activity (Forsblum, Särkämö, Laitinen, & Tervaniemi, 2010). Patients were interviewed pre- and postintervention. In addition, they were asked to keep logs. Giorgi's phenomenological research model was used to analyze the narrative data (Forinash, 2005).

Jungblut (2009) has developed a music therapy protocol, called SIPARI®, that has proven to be effective in the rehabilitation of long-term impairment from stroke. The sessions using SIPARI® include singing, intonation, prosody, breathing, rhythm, and improvisation. The singing is described as "ritual songs, familiar songs, newly composed songs developed together with the patient, voice training exercisers . . . vocal improvisation" (p. 103). Jungblut used this music therapy intervention with individuals who had experienced aphasia from 4 to 26 years and found that they improved their "expressive linguistic skills as an overall profile score on the Aachen Aphasia Test" (p. 197).

Stroke survivors' disruption of mood and behavior impacted social interaction and cooperative behavior—improving with music therapy in 18 individuals with either traumatic brain injury or stroke. There were 3 weekly sessions for up to 10 treatments "for the duration of their stay in the hospital" (Nayak, Wheeler, Shiflett, & Agostinelli, 2000). The music therapy sessions included a variety of procedures, including opening song and instrumental improvisation (using simple percussion and melodic instruments). The therapist would often structure the improvisation by asking the participants to play in a way that depicted the emotions they might be experiencing. The instruments included drums, tambourines, maracas, xylophones, tone bars, bells, and chimes. A study by Särkämö et al. (2008) illustrated that daily music listening to patient-selected music improved mood after middle cerebral artery stroke in the 19 subjects studied.

A rhythmic auditory stimulation (RAS) protocol (Thaut et al., 2007) was compared with a neurodevelopmental therapy (NDT)/ Bobath-based approach in the treatment of gait in hemiparetic stroke patients. Subjects were studied over 3 weeks, during which they received daily training (43 received rhythmic auditory stimulation and 35, the NDT/Bobath). The results showed that improvements were significantly higher for RAS compared to NDT/Bobath training in the area of gait training (p. 455).

Cohen's studies (Cohen, 1988, 1992, 1995; Cohen & Ford, 1995; Cohen & Masse, 1993) were among the first to use music therapy (singing of songs and vocal exercises) to facilitate improvements in speech after brain trauma. Her 1992 study looked at 8 subjects who were neurologically impaired as a result of either traumatic brain injury or cerebrovascular accident. Each received singing instruction three times a week for 30 minutes over three weeks. "The singing instruction format was adapted from Lucia's vocal skills model (1987), and included physical exercises, vocal exercises, rhythmic speech drills, and the singing of premorbidly learned songs" (p. 92). In 67% of the treatment group, improvements were seen in rate of speech and intelligibility. The speech was assessed by 6 judges who listened to recordings of the participants, played back on a Nakamichi BX-II cassette deck and two Bang and Olufsen S45 speakers. The assessments are based on the number of words each judge had correctly understood.

NEUROLOGY AND MUSIC THERAPY: ASSESSMENT/TREATMENT FOCUS

Medical neurological examinations include a mental status exam, and evaluation of the cranial nerve response function, tendon/motion reflex, sensory nervous system, cerebellum, and sensation. When combined, these examinations identify and locate any lesions in the central or peripheral nervous system, and whether a lesion is diffuse or specific.

Neurologic music therapy applications focus on rhythmic auditory stimulation (RAS) that is meant to facilitate rehabilitation, or reinstitute movements that are organic and biologically rhythmically oriented. When one considers the system and sounds of the body, including respiration and cardiac function, for example, we realize that these movements and operations work as a duet where each solo system must coordinate and rely on the other system's part. It may also be useful to apply this thinking to the neural systems, the firing of neurons, interspersed with pathways that are preserved with music memory and previous patterning involving rhythm, melody and sensory stimulation.

A critical aspect of our capacity to learn tasks of music and speech occurs in our brain's tendency to bundle rhythmical movement in patterns. This can assist in the recovery and relearning of gait and applicable movements. Neurologic music therapy (Thaut et al., 2009), including the RAS program, assists gait disorders of stroke patients, Parkinson's patients, and those with traumatic brain injury. Some early studies observed how conscious entrainment or patterning monitored by an externally pulsed rhythm, such as a drum beat that repeats, enables the listener to predict and move in sequence to the driven sound whereas without a "groove" or cued beat, this would be less possible (Haas & Distenfeld, 1986; Miller, Thaut, McIntosh, & Rice, 1996).

In Neurologic Music Therapy (NMT) as designed by Thaut et al. (2009), rhythmic patterns serve as the timing sequences of the movement, and pitch patterns can facilitate shifting spatial positions, where harmonic and dynamic patterns simulate applications of force and muscle tone. Other NMT work has included goals of patterned sensory enhancement, and motor rehabilitation that are strengthened by the playing of musical instruments to stimulate movement and build endurance through performance that at the same time builds flexion/extension, digit dexterity, and limb coordination.

Cognition with psychosocial behavior training is part of the NMT focus where specific techniques of music psychotherapy and counseling are applied. However, the deeper context of linking therapeutic outcomes to an expansive model of music psychotherapy treatment is perhaps more effective when it is not entirely religated to a necessarily behavioral model of treatment.

In such cases, particularly where a strong musical memory is notably preserved and indicated upon assessment, it may be useful to incorporate a nonbehavioral approach to music therapy treatment whereby explicit methods of meaningful memories are employed into a song-meaning-recall approach to music therapy treatment.

In adapting methods of cognitive psychology to neuropsychology, one study examined the relationship between memory and familiar abilities in music in relation to emotion and presented data illustrating how emotional content related to stimuli can influence the memory for music. Such an inference supports the need for a detailed music psychotherapy assessment which might lead to significant aspects of the neurologic dysfunction onset, exploring the level of trauma for the patient and those involved, assessing aspects of both the former (preonset, healthy) and current life world status (personal history) (Loewy, 2000), and the reports of others and caregivers. The culmination of this leads to a plan for a contextual model of music decision-making based on cultural preference and individual as well as group treatment (Samson, Dellacherie, & Platel, 2009).

While treatment of functional deficits caused by neurological diseases has been a primary focus of NMT, there has also been increased focus on the need to address the psychological and psychosocial impact on those affected by such diseases. The research study on the evaluation of music therapy in German neurorehabilitation centers (as cited in Jochims, 2004) reveals the importance of addressing the integrative needs of those affected by acquired brain damages, including physical, sensory, cognitive, communicative, social, and emotional areas.

As NMT is based largely on neuroscience models of music perception and production, music-centered approaches have emerged as an alternative way to enhance the specialization of music therapeutic neurologic treatment. Music-centered approaches have been used with a variety of populations, and have more recently been initiated in a broadened scope of treatment options for neurologic dysfunction. This approach focuses on the aesthetics of music that develops through the actual experience of "being" in music, and the intra- and interpersonal processes that can occur in the here and now. Aigen (2007) emphasizes the fundamental value of the therapeutic use of music as a primary role in its aesthetic process within music therapy. He argues that music itself and its aesthetic value can be the mechanism whereby health can be optimized. From a music-centered point of view, the aesthetic is not only referred to as an objective means, but rather it is its gestalt phenomenon that occurs within the experience of music making, a phenomenon which is "a three-way interaction: the truth of the human experience embodied in the music, the commitment of the client to giving expression to this truth, and the therapist being open to hearing this truth" (Aigen, 2007, p. 120). Individuals who seek music therapy may be in need of integrating such "aesthetic experiences" into their everyday life through person-to-person interplay in music, where they have opportunities for self-exploration, self-actualization, transformation, and a sense of connectedness to the self and one's surroundings.

A recent study investigated the efficacy of a music-centered music therapy intervention. Music therapy/upper limb therapy-integrated (MULTI-I; Guerrero, Turry, Geller, & Raghavan, 2014) is a prime example of how a music-centered approach was integrated into the treatment of stroke survivors (ages 21–65, $n = 15$). Subjects received 45-minute sessions of MULT-I treatment twice a week for 6 weeks. Sessions were facilitated by an interdisciplinary team consisting of two music therapists and an occupational therapist. With an approach emphasizing the aesthetic of music, the Nordoff-Robbins music therapists involved in the study emphasized on the various elements of music—including rhythm and tempo, melody, harmony, timbre, and dynamic—as well as a variety of musical styles, idioms, and tonalities in improvised and precomposed live music. All sessions were video recorded and analyzed. MULTI-L sessions consisted of movement within musical activity, as well as physical exercise supported by music. The upper-limb exercises were led by the occupational therapist while the music therapist supported the session by providing improvisational music that was tailored to the clients' moment-to-moment experiences in the music. The qualitative data were collected through in-depth analysis of session recordings and showed significant emerging themes, such as enriched peer support, overall improvement in physical functioning, restoration in sense of self, and improved emotional awareness and expression. Moreover, in one-year follow-up interviews, some participants expressed developments in their relation to music in the year following the therapy.

This approach explicates a focus on the therapeutic process in which people have opportunities to create their own paths toward healing and recovery in regaining their sense of self. Such an approach reflects music's potent function within its capacity to instill a sense of an integrated being, in contrast to an exclusive focus on the treatment of one's impairments. The interventions described in this treatment were designed to address the various needs of clients, including physical, psychological, and social domains. The goals pertaining to psychological and social well-being were particularly important, because it was the capacity of music that enabled spontaneous and collective experiences in the here and now.

Each of the varying music therapy approaches available in the treatment of neurological diseases employs a specific concept and/or method, depending on the targeted therapeutic goal(s). However, focusing on only one aspect of patient's needs might possibly compromise the need to treat a patient as a whole person. Therefore, integration of functional and psychotherapeutic approaches may prove necessary in optimally treating all aspects of the individual's needs, from physical, sensory, cognitive, communicative, social, and emotional domains (Jochims, 2004).

COMMON MUSIC AND MUSIC THERAPY TREATMENT OF STROKE

In 1973, researchers Sparks, Helm developed a protocol known as melodic intonation therapy for the treatment of aphasia, a common speech disorder that occurs after stroke. MIT is "designed to lead nonfluent aphasic patients . . . from intoning (singing) simple, 2 to 3 syllable phrases, to speaking phrases of 5 or more syllables" (Norton, Zipse, Marchina, & Schlaug, 2009, p. 431).

Melodic intonation therapy (MIT) developed as a protocolized intervention for language rehabilitation in people with Broca's aphasia. In learning to speak, use of exaggerated morphemic, intoned speech, and expressive language has improved speaking in some patients with aphasia.

In an interesting article on MIT that viewed the combined elements of rhythm and pitch, researchers noted that the combination adds a redundant cue to rhythmicity in the intoned-speech technique. Their proposed idea that pitch shifts assist the processing of rhythmic patterns is notable for music therapists who design interventions. Because if we believe what these authors call the "classical Hebbian axiom 'neurons that fire together wire together,'" then the way we implement rhythm and pitch would accordingly influence our song choices and the techniques that we implement in fostering the design of song phrases into sentences. The reactivation of the rhythm and language combination on generalized language recovery after stroke is one important goal of effective music psychotherapy. The combination of rhythm and pitch was found to account for the beneficial effect of melodic intonation therapy on connected speech improvements in patients diagnosed with Broca's aphasia (Zumbansen, Peretz, & Hébert, 2014).

THE SINGING SPEECH CONNECTION

In an effort to explore the effects of group singing for people with aphasia, a recent study measured the effects of singing in a community choir on mood and social engagement for people living with aphasia following a stroke. In recognizing the communication deficits resulting from aphasia that negatively impact stroke survivors' relationships and social participation in general, Tamplin, Baker, Jones, Way, and Lee (2013) found singing to be an accessible and enjoyable forum for treating aphasia (*n* = 13) before, and at 12 weeks and 20 weeks after singing.

Results from the 12-point General Health Questionnaire suggested a trend toward reduction of psychological distress and qualitative analysis showed increased confidence, peer support, enhanced mood, increased motivation, and changes within communication patterns.

Music therapy at Centerlight, where Connie Tomaino and her colleagues have treated patients with stroke for many years, includes breathing and articulation exercises, melodic phrasing, and rhythmic vocalization leading to conversational phrases that are embedded into melodic phrases to support speech. Centerlight's innovative music therapy programs have resulted in enhanced communication skills that allow individuals to speak more clearly and fluently. This has increased their confidence in communication attempts and enhanced verbal expression (Centerlight website, personal communication, 2013).

SINGING TOGETHER—MEASURE BY MEASURE

There are a multitude of music therapy interventions addressing symptoms of stroke and ways in which to use music interventions that may help movement or encourage speech and/ or language function. Most of these interventions do not attend to the continuum of care in the stroke survivors' life world and these people gravely affect the outcomes of how the many daily interventions are implemented and digested.

The research indicating that singing may have an impact on language development is encouraging. The Musical Stages of Speech is a developmental model of sound-making developed by Loewy (1995) to enhance emotional expressive speech in a developmental context beginning with the primal cry at birth. This model formulates ways in which music therapists may playfully enhance mechanisms (Loewy, 1995) that are intrinsic to both improvisational singing and play, in tandem with the principles of the well-known speech and language pathologist Charles van Riper who developed a model of speech sound development (from crying-lalling-parallel play-phoneme construction-interactive-cooperative play-morphemes).

Music's noted potential to assist in the mechanisms of language, specifically fostered through song memory seem significant. Loewy (2004) noted three models of vocal music psychotherapy that, when integrated with movement and language, would take into account the unique qualities of the individual lifeworld of each human being, individually, within the context of a particular musical element. According to Loewy "one person may be more receptive to melody, and another to harmony, for instance."

> Emphasizing songs with a focus on significant periods and events in time may lead to the most optimal retrieval capacity. Such research may be further expanded when we consider the emotional context and history of the patient's lifeworld as revealed through a comprehensive psychotherapeutic analysis of the voice. (https://normt.uib.no/index.php/voices/article/view/140/116, 2004)

An important aspect of the "Singing Together, Measure by Measure" is the hypothesis that the quality of life will be not only enhanced for patients who have had a stroke and who sing, but in many cases, for their caregivers, as well. At Mount Sinai Health Systems, we have invited stroke survivors to participate with or without their caregivers in a choir that meets weekly.

Examining the effects of music therapy on language and quality of life experienced by patients during their poststroke recovery period seems to present a prime opportunity. Initial pilots indicate that patients who participate in group singing as part of their stroke treatment show improved speech and language, and experience mood enhancement when music therapy is part of their group choral intervention rehabilitation treatment plan. We suspect that other effects might include increased motivation and reduced anxiety. This singing group presents potential outcomes that may reflect that scientifically, music therapy may help stroke patients' affect, and speech and language expressive functions. It may also enhance other therapies (PT, OT) as well, and critical factors such as attendance and resilience, which are received as part of stroke treatment, may lead to better results from overall treatment in general.

COMMUNITY MUSIC THERAPY: NAMING OUR PARTICIPANTS

As our interdisciplinary team was preparing a brochure to share with our community of patients, families, and staff, we had a series of meetings to ensure that the language and photographs we were developing would be accurate and appealing to all involved. We wanted to include patients, families, and professional staff as well. We had assumed that the terms: "patients," "personal caregivers," and "professional caregivers" would encapsulate the constructive composites of our group and we thought that we were being politically sensitive.

We soon learned that this was not the case for our patients and families. They informed us of their preferences for the term "survivors" and "carers." In discussing this further, it became apparent that the term "survivor" implied that they had endured a horrific episode and many had felt they had done so, with resilience.

Where "caregiver" had once seemed sufficient to represent of "one who gives care"—to some of the staff and families involved with survivors, *caregiver* implied a function or necessary duty, whereas *carer* was an empathic person who was sensitive not because it was a job to give care, but rather because it was heartfelt instinct.

Our decision to include *carers* was reflected in review of studies reflecting a growing understanding of the difficulty in the integration of community re-entry post stroke for both survivors and their families. Research reflected caretakers of those with strokes "suffer from an alarming amount of depression and psychological morbidity, with estimates ranging from between one-third to one-half of caregivers" (Bhogal, Teasell, Foley, & Speechley, 2003 p. 127). When we relate this information to patient health, it is also found in research that with higher-level adaptation and supportively strong functioning families, including circumstances where emotional/social support mechanisms are in place, there tend to be better outcomes.

The health of those who care for stroke victims is inextricably linked to a survivor's level of emotional, physical, cognitive, and psychological functioning in the recovery and rehabilitative processes. The likelihood of caregiver compassion fatigue and stress increases to higher levels of burden, and pervasive depression when support systems are not available. The Bakas Caregiving Outcomes Scale is a unique instrument, developed specifically for carers of stoke survivors. It measures how caregivers adapt to providing care and validated the assessment of such provisions of care at about 18 months poststroke time.

PUTTING IT TOGETHER: COMMUNITY MUSIC THERAPY

Community music therapy, as defined by Ansdell, Pavlicevic, Procter, and Venrey (2002) is an approach to working musically with people in the context of their society and natural environment, where social and cultural factors of their health, illness, relationships, and music are taken into consideration. In 2001, as part of a community concern for those personally and professionally affected by the events of September 11, 2001, our team had coordinated training in which we studied for 9 months of experiential music processing aspects of what it meant to be using music through the aftermath of our tramumatic experiencing (Scheiby, 2002).

Although our experience of using music therapy in the community was limited to treating children and teens with asthma in groups in the NYC public schools and working with the resulting effects of human-vindicated trauma, the lessons we learned relating to medical regimens and considerations of physical and emotional ailments related to disease, and the necessity of medical and psychosocial inclusion were imperative to our organization. Furthermore, the blending of survivors, "carers," and professional caregivers hold unique factors requiring sensitivity, advanced prowess in therapeutic leadership, and embracing an approach whereby leadership may best be set forth through a "leader-as-participant" model.

STROKE SURVIVORS AND "CARERS"

Upon completion of an initial assessment and measuring mood and horomones through saliva samples before the day of a stroke survivor's first choir rehearsal, we provide a consultation with the music therapist and speech therapist, where a full assessment takes place. It is imperative for us to explain to all of the participants the details of the music therapy choir sessions and what the therapy may provide for them. In addition to the Western Aphasia Battery and a series of other quantitative measurements we are also seeking to understand the desired music, and its effect when sung, to help us understand each survivor's personal music preferences, particularly those that have with associational contexts. Bruscia discussed the releveance of a song and its meaning in detail (Bruscia, in Loewy, 2000).

Based on the assessment, musical selections for the choir are prescribed, with songs based on the members' musical tastes. Familiar arrangements of songs are preferred, so that enjoyment is enhanced and, furthermore, so that participants are able to sing during the rehearsal, as they become emotionally and socially integrated, as part of the treatment.

We are using Figley's (1995) compassion fatigue scale to evaluate the stress and impact of trauma in personal "carers" and professional caregivers who participate in the weekly rehearsals.

SINGING TOGETHER MEASURE BY MEASURE: THE GIG AS MUSIC THERAPY

Our warm-ups and songs are carefully processed in a personal and dynamic way. Typically, we routinely warm up with some kind of blues, and name game, prompting recall to promote socialization with a touchstone that musically drives interaction at the start of each rehearsal. We have spaces for improvisation within the structure of many of our tunes, where scat singing and call and answer music therapy interventions provide non-morpheme, purely musical play, and where many opportunities for leadership occur.

The group decided that they preferred a mix, of projected lyrics to songs on a screen, while other songs might be sung in-the-moment, as a challenge to their recall. Most prefer not to read and hold music or even to have the music at an individual music stand in front of them. Looking straight ahead altogether at the same lyric slide on a large lit screen provides for more communal active recitation, similar to watching a movie together.

The songs we sing are based on the music therapy assessment and include favorites from the group members. Several tunes have been arranged in two- and three-part harmony. We sing in a variety of musical genres and idioms including rounds, Broadway, classical, light rock, hard rock, country, and jazz. Our closing song each week is the same and selected to represent the unity and positive attitude of the group: "What a Wonderful World." This developed from our first rehearsal, where the first two members, survivor and wife-"carer" proclaimed that this song was their wedding song and, thereafter, it became our ritual.

We hope that community music therapy and projects including research opportunities can expand the growth and opportunities for both survivors and caregivers of those who experience the difficulties of neurological dysfunction. Through participation, with the efforts of music therapists and professional caregivers, patients will grow in vitality, and creativity, and through the vocal expression that is kindled by community involvement. A chorus of "carers" and professional caregivers will prevail and the static schism that once separated patients, caregivers, and professionals will fade and meld into a realized symphony of sounds that witnesses the voices of all of our communal concerns through the effortless power of song and the fortitude that can be most effectively recovered through singing together, measure by measure.

REFERENCES

Aigen, K. (2007). In defense of beauty: A role for the aesthetic in music therapy theory. *Nordic Journal of Music Therapy, 16*(2), 112–128. doi:10.1080/08098130709478181

Amengual, J. L., Rojo, N., de las Heras, M. V., Marco-Pallarés, J., Grau-Sànchez, J., Schneider, S., & Rodriguez-Fornells, A. (2013). Sensorimotor plasticity after music-supported therapy in chronic stroke patients revealed by transcranial magnetic stimulation. *PLoS ONE*, *8*(4), e61883. doi:10.1371/journal.pone.0061883

Ansdell, G. (2002). Community music therapy and the winds of change: A discussion paper. In C. Kenny & B. Stige (Eds.), *Contemporary voices of music therapy: Communication, culture, and community.* Oslo, Norway: Unipub forlag.

Bakas, T., & Champion, V. (1999). Development and psychometric testing of the Bakas caregiving outcomes scale. *Nursing Research*, *48*(5), 250–259.

Bever, T. G., & Chiarello, R. J. (1974). Cerebral dominance in musicians and non-musicians. *Science*, *185*, 537–539.

Bhogal S. K., Teasell, R. W., Foley N. C., & Speechley, M. R. (2003). Community reintegration after stroke. *Topics in Stroke Rehabilitation*, *10*(2), 107–129.

Bowers, D., Blonder, L. X., Slomine, B., & Heilman, K. M. (1996). *Nonverbal emotional signals: Patterns of impairment following hemispheric lesions using the Florida Affect Battery.* San Francisco, CA: American Academy of Neurology.

Clift, S., & Hancox, G. (2010). The significance of choral singing for sustaining psychological well-being: Findings from a survey of choristers in England, Australia and Germany. *Music and Health*, *3*(1), 79–96.

Clift, S., & Morrison, I. (2010). Group singing fosters mental health and well-being: Findings from the East Kent "Singing for Health" network project. *Mental Health and Social Inclusion*, *15*(2), 88–97. doi:10.1108/20428301111140930

Cohen, N. S. (1988). The use of superimposed rhythm to decrease the rate of speech production in a brain-damaged adolescent. *Journal of Music Therapy*, *25*(2), 85–93.

Cohen, N. S. (1992). The effect of singing instruction on the speech production of neurologically impaired persons. *Journal of Music Therapy*, *29*(2), 87–102.

Cohen, N. S. (1995). The effect of vocal instruction and Visi-pitch® feedback on the speech of persons with neurogenic communication disorders: Two case studies. *Music Therapy Perspectives*, *13*(2), 70–75.

Cohen, N. S., & Ford, J. (1995). The effect of musical cues on the nonpurposive speech of persons with aphasia. *Journal of Music Therapy*, *32*(1), 46–57.

Cohen, N. S., & Masse, R. (1993). The application of singing and rhythmic instruction as a therapeutic intervention for persons with neurologic communication disorders. *Journal of Music Therapy*, *30*(2), 81–89.

Cooper, C. L., Phillips, L. H., Johnston, M., Radlak, B., Hamilton, S., & MaLeod, M. J. (2014). Links between emotion perception and social participation restriction following stroke. *Brain Injury, 28*(1), 122–126. doi 10.3109/02699052.2013.848379.

CORE Information Management Systems. (2014). Retrieved from http://www.coreims.co.uk/index.html

Elefant, C., Baker, F. A., Lotan, M., Lagesen, S. K., & Skeie, G. O. (2012). The effect of group music therapy on mood, speech, and singing in individuals with Parkinson's disease: A feasibility study. *Journal of Music Therapy, 49*(3), 278–302.

Figley, C. F. (1995). Compassion fatigue as secondary traumatic stress disorder: An overview. In C. F. Figley (Ed.), *Compassion fatigue: Coping with secondary traumatic stress disorder in those who treat the traumatized* (pp. 1–20). New York, NY: Brunner/Mazel.

Forinash, M. (2005). Phenomenological inquiry. In B. L. Wheeler (Ed.), *Music therapy research* (pp. 321–334). Gilsum, NH: Barcelona.

Forsblom, A., Särkämö, T., Laitinen, S., & Tervaniemi, M. (2010). The effect of music and audiobook listening on people recovering from stroke: The patient's point of view. *Music and Medicine, 2*(4), 229–234. doi:10.1177/1943862110378110

Guerrero, N., Turry, A., Geller, D., & Raghavan, P. (2014). From historic to contemporary: Nordoff-Robbins music therapy in collaborative interdisciplinary rehabilitation. *Music Therapy Perspectives, 32*(1), 38.

Guétin, S., Soua, B., Voiriot, G., Picot, M. C., & Hérisson, C. (2009). The effect of music therapy on mood and anxiety-depression: An observational study in institutionalised patients with traumatic brain injury. *Annals of Physical and Rehabilitation Medicine, 52*(1), 30–40. doi:10.1016/j.annrmp.2008.08.009.

Haas, F., Distenfeld, S., & Axen, K. (1985). Effects of perceived musical rhythm on respiratory pattern. *Journal of Applied Physiology, 61*(3), 1185–1191.

Huang, H., Chung, K., Lai, D., & Sung, S. (2009). The impact of timing and dose of rehabilitation delivery on functional recovery of stroke patients. *Journal of the Chinese Medical Association, 72*(5), 257–264.

Hurkmans, J., de Bruijn, M., Boonstra, A. M., Jonkers, R., Bastiaanse, R., Arendzen, H., & Reinders-Messelink, H. A. (2012). Music in the treatment of neurological language and speech disorders: A systematic review. *Aphasiology, 26*(1), 1–19. doi:10.1080/02687038.2011.602514

Jochims, S. (2004). Music therapy in the area of conflict between functional and psychotherapeutic approach within the field of neurology/neurorehabilitation. *Nordic Journal of Music Therapy, 13*(2), 161–171. doi:10.1080/08098130409478113

Jungblut, M. (2009). SIPARI®: A music therapy intervention for patients suffering with chronic, nonfluent aphasia. *Music and Medicine, 1*(2), 102–105. doi:10.1177/1943862109345130

Kim, S. J. (2010). Music therapy protocol development to enhance swallowing training for stroke patients with dysphagia. *Journal of Music Therapy*, *47*(2), 102–119.

Lappe, C., Trainor, L. J., Herholz, S. C., & Pantev, C. (2011) Cortical plasticity induced by short-term multimodal musical rhythm training. *PLoS ONE*, *6*(6), e21493. doi:10.1371/journal.pone.0021493

Livesey, L., Morrison, I., Clift, S., & Camic, P. (2012). Benefits of choral singing for social and mental well-being: Qualitative findings from a cross-national survey of choir members. *Journal of Public Mental Health*, *11*(1), 10–26. doi:10.1108/17465721211207275

Loewy, J. V. (1995). The musical stages of speech: A developmental model of pre-verbal sound making. *Music Therapy*, 13(1), 47–73.

Loewy, J. V. (2000). Music psychotherapy assessment. *Music Therapy Perspectives*, *18*(1), 47–58.

Loewy, J. V. (2004). Integrating music, language and the voice in music therapy. *Voices: A world forum for music therapy*, *4*(1). Retrieved October 13, 2014, from http://www.voices.no/mainissues/mi4000 4000140.html

McDonald, S., Flanagan, S., Martin, I., & Saunders, C. (2004). The ecological validity of TASIT: A test of social perception. *Neuropsychological Rehabilitation*, *14*(3), 285–302. doi:10.1080/09602010343000237

Miller, R. A., Thaut, M. H., McIntosh, G. C., & Rice, R. R. (1996). Components of EMG symmetry and variability in parkinsonian and healthy elderly gait. *Electroencephalography and Clinical Neurophysiology*, *101*, 1–7.

National Stroke Association. (2013). Retrieved from http://www.stroke .org/site/DocServer/STROKE101_2009.pdf?docID=4541

Nayak, S., Wheeler, B. L., Shiflett, S. C., & Agostinelli, S. (2000). Effect of music therapy on mood and social interaction among individuals with acute traumatic brain injury and stroke. *Rehabilitation Psychology*, *45*(3), 274–283.

Norton, A., Zipse, L., Marchina, S., & Schlaug, G. (2009). Melodic Intonation Therapy: Shared insights on how it is done and why it might work. *Annals of the New York Academy of Sciences*, *1169*, 431–436. doi:10.1111/j.1749-6632.2009.04859.x

Pacchiettei, C., Mancini, F., Aglieri, R., Fundarò, C., Martignoni, E., & Nappi, G. (2000). Active music therapy in Parkinson's disease: An integrative method for motor and emotional rehabilitation. *Psychosomatic Medicine*, *62*, 386–393.

Pollard, B., & Johnson, M. (2001). Problems with the Sickness Impact Profile: A theoretically based analysis and a proposal for a new method of implementation and scoring. *Social Science & Medicine*, *52*, 921–934.

Raglio, A., Fazio, P., Imbriani, C., & Granieri, E. (2013). Neuroscientific basis and effectiveness of music and music therapy in neuromotor rehabilitation. *OA Alternative Medicine, 1*(1), 1–8.

Rodriguez-Fornells, A., Rojo, N., Amengual, J., Ripoll, P., Altenmüller, E., & Münte, T. F. (2012). The involvement of audio–motor coupling in the music-supported therapy applied to stroke patients. *Annals of the New York Academy of Sciences, 1252,* 282–293. doi:10.1111/ j.1749-6632.2011.06425.x

Samson, S., Dellacherie, D., & Platel, H. (2009). Emotional power of music in patients with memory disorders. *Annals of the New York Academy of Sciences, 1169*(1), 245–255.

Särkämö, T., Tervaniemi, M., & Huotilainen, M. (2013). Music perception and cognition: Development, neural basis, and rehabilitative use of music. *Wiley Interdisciplinary Reviews, 4*(4), 441–451. doi:10.1002/ wcs.1237

Särkämö, T., Tervaniemi, M., Laitinen, S., Forsblum, A. Soinila, S., Mikkonen, M., . . . Hietanen, J. (2008). Music listening enhances cognitive recovery and mood after middle cerebral artery stroke. *Brain 131,* 866–876. doi:10.1093?brain/awn013

Scheiby, B. B. (2002). Caring for the caregivers: Trauma, improvised music, and transformation of terror into meaning through community music therapy training. In J. Loewy & A. Frisch-Hara (Eds.), *Caring for the caregiver: The use of music, music therapy in grief and trauma.* Silver Spring, MD: AMTA.

Schlaug, G., Jäncke, L., Huang, Y., Staiger, J. F., & Steinmetz, H. (1995). Increased corpus collosum size in musicians. *Neuropsychologia, 33,* 1047–1055.

Shapiro, N. (2005) Sounds in the world: Multicultural influences in music therapy in clinical practice and training. *Music Therapy Perspectives, 23*(1), 29–35.

Sun, J., & Buys, N. J. (2013). Improving Aboriginal and Torres Strait Islander Australians' well-being using participatory community singing approach. *International Journal on Disability and Human Development, 12*(3), 305–316. doi:10.1515/ijdhd-2012-0108.

Sun, J., & Stewart, D. (2007). Development of population based resilience measures in the primary school setting. *Health Education, 107,* 575–599.

Talmage, A., Ludlam, S., Leão, S. H. S., Fogg-Rogers, L., & Purdy, S. C. (2013). Leading the CeleBRation choir: The choral singing therapy protocol and the role of the music therapist in a social singing group for adults with neurological conditions. *New Zealand Journal of Music Therapy, 11,* 7–50.

Tamplin, J., Baker, F. A., Jones, B., Way, A., & Lee, S. (2013). "Stroke a chord": The effect of singing in a community choir on mood and social engagement for people living with aphasia following a stroke. *NeuroRehabilitation, 32,* 929–941. doi:10.3223.NRE-130916

Thaut, M. H., Leins, A. K., Rice, R. R., Argstatter, H., Kenyon, G. P., McIntosh, G. C., . . . Fetter, M. (2007). Rhythmic auditory stimulation improves gait more than NDT/Bobath training in near-ambulatory patients early post-stroke: A single-blind, randomized trial. *Neurorehabilitation Neural Repair, 21,* 455–459.

Thaut, M. H., Gardiner, J. C., Holmberg, D., Horwitz, J., Kent, L., Andrews, G., . . . McIntosh G. R. (2009). Neurologic music therapy improves executive function and emotional adjustment in traumatic brain injury rehabilitation. *Annals of the New York Academy of Sciences, 1169,* 406–416.

Wade, D. T., Wood, V. A. & Hewer, R. L. (1985). Recovery after stroke: The first three months. *Journal of Neurology, Neurosurgery and Psychiatry, 48,* 7–13.

Walker-Batson, D., & Avent, J. R. (2007). Adult neurogenic communication disorders. In R. L. Braddom (Ed.), *Physical medicine and rehabilitation* (3rd ed., pp. 49–62). Philadelphia, PA: Saunders.

The WHOQOL Group. (1998). Development of the World Health Organization WHOQOL-Bref QOL assessment. *Psychological Medicine, 28,* 551–559.

Yinger, O. S., & LaPointe, L. L. (2012). The effects of participation in a group music therapy voice protocol (G-MTVP) on the speech of individuals with Parkinson's disease. *Music Therapy Perspectives, 30*(1), 25–31.

Young, A. W., Perrett, D., Calder, A., Sprengelmeyer, R., & Elkman, P. (2002). *Facial expressions of emotions: Stimuli and test (FEEST).* Thurstone, UK: Thames Valley Test Company.

Zare, M., Ebrahimi, A., & Birashk, B. (2010). The effects of music therapy on reducing agitation in patients with Alzheimer's disease, a pre-post study. *International Journal of Geriatric Psychiatry.* Advance online publication. doi:10.1002/gps.2450

Zumbansen, A, Peretz, I., & Hébert, S. (2014) The combination of rhythm and pitch can account for the beneficial effect of melodic intonation therapy on connected speech improvements in Broca's aphasia. *Frontiers in Human Neuroscience, 8,* 592. doi:10.3389/fnhum.2014.00592. eCollection

Afterword

Linda S. Carozza

Communication and Aging: Creative Approaches to Improving Quality of Life is an outgrowth of interdisciplinary collaboration between and among professionals in the medical rehabilitation community, including neuroscience specialists, speech-language pathologists, audiologists, cognitive scientists, social workers, psychologists, as well as creative arts interventionists. Concerns for the care of the aging population is high on the worldwide agenda of health care priorities: increasing needs for models of effective and efficacious community programs, in-home, and nursing home placements.

To provide a context and background for this vast array of information, the book offers descriptions of theories of aging and normal changes that take place through the lifespan, with emphasis on healthy aging followed by discussions of medical conditions affecting independence, well-being, and quality of life. These topics include cognition, communication, sensory processing, and physical and biological changes in human voice and swallowing. It is also during the later life cycle, that the onset of comorbid neurogenic communication disorders may occur. These wide-ranging conditions, from stroke-related aphasia to Parkinson's disease and dementia are at the forefront of many research, clinical, and educational initiatives. In the past, approaches to individual and group interventions have relied heavily on medical models and less on adjustment and "living successfully" with aging and health-related conditions. It is our view that communication-oriented strategies that emphasize social adjustment will provide the best long-term effect for aging individuals with chronic medical conditions that compromise communication and interaction with their environment. This book provides a window of opportunity for families and professionals to gain insight into the nature of some of these chronic conditions, and many opportunities to learn about quality of life outcomes as the ultimate intervention measurement. Communication and aging issues can be supported best through programs and strategies that emphasize "can-do" versus "can't-do" behaviors and form a gateway to maintaining personal identity and dignity. Individuals may attain benefits from programs via psychosocial recovery that can be objectively measured in reports of quality of life and successful community reintegration. Creative, functional, and effective programs are described and illustrated throughout the book, drawing on different disciplines. Service delivery, outcome management, and planning can all be enhanced via the creative approaches and adaptations described in the book. With the insights from programs such as social model communication groups, person-centered approaches, and art- and music-infused strategies, professionals can gain tools to assist individuals by focusing on personal-social adjustment, support, and return to community integration.

Communication and Aging: Creative Approaches to Improving Quality of Life describes changes in the communication systems during the aging process, and outlines creative approaches to increase life participation for the aging disabled populations. The concept of healthy aging or wellness is related to the needs of all individuals, and most particularly those who may have suffered with the comorbidities of stroke or dementia but who may not have access to traditional programs. Models that emphasize individual personal interests and history and "non-verbal" modalities such as creative arts can have a strong impact on the measured quality of life of the participants, and can provide an array of rich research-building opportunities to develop integrative medicine modalities for special populations in the future. Creative approaches to quality of life and social model interventions are proposed as a long-term care option for the graying population that is living longer with chronic medical disease and related communication disabilities. This clinical philosophy, and related strategies and methodology, ultimately will provide a more meaningful context for individuals living with chronic communication disorders, and consequently will also benefit families and society in general. Creative approaches to quality of life programming underscores an exciting and expanded horizon for "aftercare" interventions for patients who would otherwise potentially decline. It is hoped that this book will serve as an inspiration to those seeking a new and deepened understanding of the power of community reintegration as the ultimate goal of rehabilitation and wellness.

Index

A

AAC. *See* Alternative and augmentative communication devices
Abbreviated Profile of Hearing Aid Benefit, 141–142
Academy of Neurologic Communication Disorders and Sciences, 107
Acceptance, 237
Acetylcholine, 170
Acetylcholinesterase inhibitors, 193
Active Communication Education (ACE) program, 143
AD. *See* Alzheimer's disease
Adler Center, 112
Adult day programs, for dementia, 234–236, 242
AFA. *See* Alzheimer's Foundation of America
A-FROM. *See Living with Aphasia: Framework for Outcome Measurement*
Aftercare, 176
Age-related hearing loss. *See* Hearing loss

Aging
cognition-related changes secondary to, 6, 15
creative processes affected by, 251
definition of, 13–14
discourse processing declines secondary to. *See* Discourse processing, age-related declines in
hearing loss related to, 15
neurobiological changes associated with, 40
preserved skills in, 35–41
crystallized intelligence, 36–37
gist-based processing, 37–38
situation modeling, 38–40
psychological aspects of, 21
swallowing function affected by, 163–166, 171
theories on, 20
visual deficits secondary to, 15
working memory affected by, 130–131, 178
Aging population. *See also* Older adults
demographic changes in, 4–5, 121–122

Aging population *(continued)*
geographic differences in, 5
growth of, 68, 122, 168
racial/ethnic diversity of, 5
Aging voice, 72–74
Alcohol-induced dementia, 97
Alpha-synuclein, **99**
Alpha waves, 127
ALS. *See* Amyotrophic lateral
sclerosis
Alternative and augmentative
communication devices, 85
Alzheimer, Alois, 275
Alzheimer's Association
description of, 226
Working Group on
Technologies, 192
Alzheimer's disease
characteristics of, 42–43, 97
cognitive-linguistic changes in,
41–44
definition of, 275
discourse difficulties in, 43
early-stage, 42–43
future projections for, 6
life expectancy of, 209
music therapy for, 275
semantic memory impairment
associated with, 97, 100
symptoms of, **98**
Alzheimer's Foundation of
America, 96
Alzheimer's Poetry Project, 219,
222–224, 228
American Speech-Language
Hearing Association
aphasia and, 102
clinician responsibilities
according to, 6
Guidelines for Audiology
Service Delivery in
Nursing Homes, 136
research by, 88

Amplification systems
binaural, 140
cochlear implants, 139–140
hearing aids, 138–141, 143,
146
summary of, 147
surgically implanted, 139–140
types of, 138
Amyotrophic lateral sclerosis,
169–170
Anarthria, 80
ANCDS. *See* Academy
of Neurologic
Communication Disorders
and Sciences
Anterior corpus callosum, 273
APHAB. *See* Abbreviated Profile
of Hearing Aid Benefit
Aphasia
"after-care" social conversation
group for, 106–107
art therapy for, 114
assessment of, 105–108
Broca's, 103, 276
case study of, 194–196
CEASRS tool for, 111, 182
community groups for, 110,
112
community reintegration for
patients with, 181–184
coping skills for, 106
creative aftercare for, 111–112
definition of, 102
fluent, 276
functional communication
approaches to, 105
global, 104
group therapy for, 108–110
indirect interventions for, 111
life adjustments for, 106
Life Participation Approach to
Aphasia, 106
long-term management of, 114

management of, 114
melodic intonation therapy for, 288
mixed, 104
nonfluent, 276
post-stroke, 276, 288
pragmatics evaluation, 107–108
primary progressive, 104
receptive, 104
response therapy for, 109
right hemisphere damage as cause of, 104
social and life-participation approaches to, 112–113
social communication approach to, 183
social communication evaluation, 107–108
social language enhancement in
  caregiver supports, 182–183
  community re-entry, 182–183
  community reintegration as goal of, 181–184
  poetry used for, 185–187
  quality of life approach, 184–185
  social networks, 182, 184
speech-language pathology treatment effects on, 180, 192
symptoms of, 103–105
trends in, 113
types of, 103–105
VAST for, 78
Wernicke's, 103
AphasiaAccess, 180
"Aphasia Needs Assessment," 108
Apraxia of speech
  causes of, 75
  characteristics of, 74–75, **76**
  classification of, 75

dysarthria versus, 75
melodic intonation therapy for, 78–79
motor reconnect apraxia program for, 79
phonetic placement approach for, 77–78
PROMPT for, 77
traditional treatment approaches to, 77–78
treatment of, 75, 77–79
VAST for, 78
AR. *See* Audiologic rehabilitation
Art-based interventions, for dementia
  Alzheimer's Poetry Project, 219, 222–224, 228
  ARTZ program, 219–220, 226, 228
  benefits of, 216–217, 259
  connect2culture® program, 219, 226–227
  dance, 224–226
  description of, 213, 216, 228
  field examples of, 218–227
  mediating objects, 217
  narratives, 218
  process-oriented, 217–218
  product-oriented, 217–218
  research in, 228
  Rhythm Break Cares program, 219, 224–226, 228
  summary of, 227–228
  To Whom I May Concern program, 219–222, 228
Articulation, 84
Art therapy
  aphasia managed with, 114
  art exhibition, 260–262
  art-making process, 253–255
  benefits of, 249–250, 259, 262
  case studies of, 253–255, 257–258

Art therapy *(continued)*
  communication through, 249,
    251
  community-based programs in,
    250–251
  creative process, 251–253
  in dementia patients, 255–260,
    262–263. *See also*
    Art-based interventions
  description of, 9
  future opportunities for,
    262–263
  goals of, 256
  introspection through, 250
  measuring the impact of, 263
  methods of, **261**
  music incorporated into, 258
  nonverbal communication
    during, 250
  reminiscence techniques in,
    251
  self-awareness through, 250
  self-expression through,
    247–248, 262
  self-satisfaction from, 252
  sessions in, 256
  stress reduction through, 250
  as supportive practice, 248–251
ARTZ program, 219–220, 226,
  228
ASHA. *See* American Speech-
  Language Hearing
  Association
Aspiration pneumonia, 169
Association for Frontotemporal
  Degeneration, The, 115
Ataxic dysarthria, **81**
Audiologic acuity and function
  assessments, 136–138
Audiologic rehabilitation
  Active Communication
    Education program, 143

caregiver involvement in,
  145–146
communication outcomes, 144
community reintegration as
  goal of, 175
components of, 138
counseling as part of, 146
family involvement in,
  145–146
Listening and Communication
  Enhancement program,
  143
narratives, 144
person-centered approach to,
  142–143
spouse involvement in,
  145–146
strategies for, 142–145
summary of, 147
Auditory comprehension, 27
Auerbach's plexus, 159
Axons, 272

B

Background knowledge, 37
Background noise, 126–128
Balanced Budget Act of 1997, 7
Bilingual adults, task set shifting
  in, 22
Binaural amplification, 140
Biofeedback, 88
Bourgeois, Michelle, 214
Brain
  alpha waves of, 127
  frontal lobe hypothesis of, 26,
    32–35
  musical training effects on, 273
  music therapy for injuries of,
    274
  neural recruitment, 40–41
Broca's aphasia, 103, 276

C

Call-and-response technique, 223
Camp, Cameron, 214–215
CARE Program, 233, 243–244
CEASRS, 111, 182
Cerebrovascular accident. *See also* Stroke
  dysphagia after, 166–168
  music therapy for, 275–284
Cerumen impaction, 136–137
Choral singing, 278–279, 293
Closed questions, 176
Cochlear implants, 139–140
Cognition
  age-related changes in, 6, 15, 44
  hearing loss effects on, 135
  speech rate affected by declines in, 73
Cognitive development, 251
Cognitive slowing, 18, 26–27, 128, 135, 177
Communication
  age-related changes in, 15
  facilitation tips for, 45
  Gerontological Society of America tips for, 15, **16**
  with hearing loss patients, 143
  importance of, 96
  nonverbal, 224–226
  with older adults, 15, **16**
Communication breakdowns
  in dementia, 191
  description of, 177–179
  stress caused by, 191
Communication disabilities
  aphasia. *See* Aphasia
  dementia. *See* Dementia
  long-term strategies for, 179
Communication Rings, 144

Communicative Effectiveness and Stress Rating Scale. *See* CEASRS
Community-based art therapy programs, 250–251
Community groups, for aphasia, 110, 112
Community music therapy, 291–292, 294
Community reintegration, for aphasia patients, 181–184
Compensation hypothesis, 40
Conductive hearing loss, 136–137
connect2culture® program, 219, 226–227
Context, linguistic, 131–132
Conversational analysis, 176
Creative activities programming, 243
Creative therapies
  art therapy. *See* Art therapy
  definition of, 8
  drama therapy. *See* Drama therapy
  music therapy. *See* Music therapy
  poetry, 185–187
Creutzfeldt-Jakob disease, **99**
Crystallized intelligence, 36–37
Cueing systems, 214

D

Dance, 224–226
Dedifferentiation hypothesis, 40
Deep brain stimulation, 86–87
Dem@Care project, 188
Dementia
  adult day programs for, 234–236, 242
  alcohol-induced, 97

Dementia *(continued)*
    Alzheimer's. *See* Alzheimer's
        disease
    art-based interventions for
        Alzheimer's Poetry Project,
            219, 222–224, 228
        ARTZ program, 219–220,
            226, 228
        benefits of, 216–217
        connect2culture® program,
            219, 226–227
        dance, 224–226
        description of, 213, 216, 228
        field examples of, 218–227
        mediating objects, 217
        narratives, 218
        process-oriented, 217–218
        product-oriented, 217–218
        Rhythm Break Cares program,
            219, 224–226, 228
        To Whom I May Concern
            program, 219–222, 228
    art therapy for, 255–260
    behavioral symptoms of, 213,
        215, 262–263
    cognitive interventions for, 188
    communication in
        breakdowns in, 191
        medications to enhance, 193
        strategies for, 188–192
    Creutzfeldt-Jakob disease as
        cause of, **99**
    definition of, 96–97
    diagnosis of, 97, 188–189
    dysphagia in, 168
    frontotemporal, 97, **99**, 100,
        115
    future projections for, 6
    hearing loss and, 132–133
    Huntington's disease as cause
        of, **99**
    increases in population with,
        192

Lewy body, 97, **98**
memory loss associated with,
    234
mixed, **98**
multi-infarct, 97, 100
nonpharmacologic
    interventions for, 211–213
nonverbal communication in,
    224–226
normal pressure
    hydrocephalus as cause
    of, **99**
Parkinson's disease as cause
    of, **99**
person-centered care for, 210,
    236, 241–242, 256
personhood in, support for,
    210–211
psychosocial interventions for
    cueing systems, 214
    in environment, 215
    overview of, 213–214
    personalization of, 214
    spaced retrieval, 214–215
psychotropic medications for,
    212
quality of life in, 208, 242–243
signs and symptoms of, 97,
    98–99
social language enhancement in
    overview of, 187–188
    quality of life strategies for,
        189–190
spaced retrieval for, 101
speech loss secondary to, 73
subcortical, 100–101
summary of, 101–102
swallowing disorders in,
    168–169
treatment of, 101
vascular, 97, **98**
wandering associated with,
    215

Wernicke-Korsakoff syndrome
as cause of, **99**
*Dementia Reconsidered: The
Person Comes First,* 241
Demographics, in United States,
4–6, 121–122
Dendrites, 272
Digit memory span test, 130
Discourse processing
age-related declines in
cognitive slowing hypothesis
of, 26–27
domains affected by, 27
inhibitory efficiency
discourse hypothesis of,
30–31
processes involved in, 34
summary of, 44–45
working memory discourse
hypothesis of, 27–30
deficits in, 19
description of, 27
time required for
background knowledge
effects on, 37
situation modeling effects
on, 39
Distractions, 178
Distractors, 31
Drama therapy, 9
Dual-sensory impairments, 134
Dysarthria
adult-acquired, 79
apraxia of speech versus, 75
ataxic, **81**
causes of, 80, **81–82**
characteristics of, 84
classification of, 80, 83–84
definition of, 79
flaccid, **81**
hyperkinetic, **82**
hypokinetic, **81**, 85
Mayo system for, 83

mixed, **82**
motor speech disorder versus,
80
prevalence of, 79
progressive neurological
disease as cause of, 80, 83
spastic, **81**
treatment of, 84–85
Dysphagia. *See also* Swallowing
disorders
after cerebrovascular accident,
166–168
definition of, 157, 159
in dementia patients, 168
esophageal manometry
evaluation of, 170
evaluation of, 159–160
in myasthenia gravis, 170
neurogenic, 166–168, **167**
in Parkinson's disease, 169
prevalence of, 171
referrals for, 171
signs of, 158
summary of, 170–171

E

Ear canal collapse, 136–137
Early stage Alzheimer's disease,
42–43
EF. *See* Executive function/
functioning
Emphatic understanding, 237
Error theory, 20
Esophageal manometry, 162–163,
170
Esophageal phase, of
swallowing, 158–159
Executive function/functioning
abilities associated with, 32
frontal lobe and, 32
memory and, 33
in mild cognitive impairment, 42

Executive function/functioning
(continued)
processes involved in, 34
role of, 32–33
External auditory canal, 123

F

FEES. *See* Fiberoptic endoscopic
evaluation of swallowing
Feil, Naomie, 239
Females
hearing aid fitting in, 139
males versus, life expectancy
differences in, 5
Fiberoptic endoscopic evaluation
of swallowing, 161–162
Flaccid dysarthria, **81**
Fluent aphasia, 276
Fluent speech, 71
Fluid intelligence, 36
FM systems, 140–141
Frontal lobe, 32
Frontal lobe hypothesis, 26,
32–35
Frontotemporal dementia, 97, **99**,
100, 115
Functional disorders, 70

G

GABA, 124
Gender
hearing aid use and, 138–139
hearing loss differences based
on, 125
life expectancy differences in,
5
presbycusis differences based
on, 125
Genuineness, 237
Gerontological Society of
America, 14–15

Gist-based processing, 37–38
Glazner, Gary, 222–223
Glial cells, 272
Global aphasia, 104
Group singing, 278–279, 281, 288
Group therapy, for aphasia,
108–110
GSA. *See* Gerontological Society
of America
Guided rehearsal, 182

H

Hartowicz, Elizabeth, 233–244
HAT. *See* Hearing assistive
technology
Hearing aids, 138–141, 143, 146
Hearing assistive technology
description of, 136, 138, 146
FM systems, 140–141
hearing aids and, 140
types of, 140–141
Hearing loss, age-related
amplification systems for. *See*
Amplification systems
anatomic and physiologic
auditory alterations
caused by, 123–125
audiologic acuity and function
assessments, 136–138
auditory stimulation reductions
associated with, 128
caregiver education about, 142
cognitive decline and, 135
communication strategies for
patients with, 143
dementia and, 132–133
description of, 15
diagnostic tools for, 137–138
family education about, 142
gender differences in, 125
hearing aids for, 138–141, 143,
146

onset of, 122
prevalence of, 122
psychosocial implications of,
    134–135
sensorineural, 122
summary of, 146–147
visual impairment and, 134
Hescock, Nathan, 225
Huntington's disease, **99**
Hyoid bone, 166
Hyperkinetic dysarthria, **82**
Hypoglossal nerve, 158
Hypokinetic dysarthria, **81**, 85

I

I Am Still Here, 239
IC. *See* Inferior colliculus
Inferior colliculus, 124
Inhibition
    language function affected by,
        178
    lexical retrieval deficits and, 18
    by older adults, 30–31, 178
    purpose of, 30, 178
    working memory effects on, 29
Inhibition deficit hypothesis, 6
Inhibitory efficiency discourse
        hypothesis, 30–31
Interpersonal communication, 95

K

Kay Pentax, 88
Knowledge
    background, 37
    object, 42

L

LACE program. *See* Listening
        and Communication
        Enhancement program

Language
    age-related decline in, 14–20
    cognitive underpinnings of,
        177–178
    social use of, 176
Language comprehension, 15
Language development, 289
Language function
    age-related decline in, 14
    inhibition effects on, 178
    neural basis for, 21
Language performance declines
    conditions associated with, 34
    inhibitory efficiency discourse
        hypothesis of, 30
    working memory discourse
        hypothesis of, 28
Language processing, 178
Language rehabilitation, poetry
        for, 185–187
Lee Silverman Voice Technique,
        86, 88
Lewy body dementia, 97, **98**
Lexical processing
    deficits in, 18
    lifespan changes in, 19
Lexical retrieval impairments, 18
Life expectancy, 5, 14
Life Participation Approach to
        Aphasia, 106
Linguistic context, 131–132
Linguistic knowledge, 131–132,
        145–146
Listening and Communication
        Enhancement program,
        143
*Living with Aphasia:
        Framework for Outcome
        Measurement,* 106
Loudness, 70–71
Lower esophageal sphincter, 159
LPAA. *See* Life Participation
        Approach to Aphasia

LSVT. *See* Lee Silverman Voice
Technique

M

Macular degeneration, 134
Males
females versus, life expectancy
differences in, 5
hearing aid fitting in, 138
MCI. *See* Mild cognitive
impairment
Mediating objects, 217
Medicare, 7
Melodic intonation therapy
for aphasia, 288
for apraxia of speech, 78–79
Memory
contextual support for, 131
executive function and, 33
external strategies for, 35
limitations in, language
processing affected by,
178
source, 33
temporal, 33
working. *See* Working memory
*Memory Books and Other
Graphic Cuing Systems:
Practical Communication
and Memory Aids for
Adults with Dementia*, 214
Memory span tests, 130
mFLP. *See* Modified Functional
Limitation Profile
Microvascular disease, 125
Middle ear
description of, 123
implants of, 139
Mild cognitive impairment
cognitive-linguistic changes in,
41–44
criteria for, 42

definition of, 41
executive functioning
difficulties in, 42
MIT. *See* Melodic intonation
therapy
Mixed aphasia, 104
Mixed dysarthrias, **82**
Modified Functional Limitation
Profile, 276
Moen, Stine, 225
Monoloudness, 71
Monopitch, 70
Montessori, Maria, 215
Motivation, 252
Motor reconnect apraxia
program, 79
Motor speech
multidimensionality of, 83
research about, 68
Motor speech disorders
apraxia of speech. *See* Apraxia
of speech
dysarthria. *See* Dysarthria
overview of, 74
Parkinson's disease as cause
of, 85–87
MRAP. *See* Motor reconnect
apraxia program
Multi-infarct dementia, 97, 100
Multilingual adults, task set
shifting in, 22
Music
brain affected by, 273
literature review on, 272–273
neural pathways of, 272
Musical Stages of Speech, 289
"Music memory," 272, 285
Music psychotherapy, 285, 290
Music-supported therapy, 282
Music therapy
for Alzheimer's disease, 275
art therapy and, 258
benefits of, 8–9, 250

for brain injury, 274
community, 291–292, 294
definition of, 8
description of, 293–294
efficacy of, 270, 286–287
literature review on, 272–273
neurologic, 270, 274, 284–286
in neuromotor rehabilitation,
    281
for Parkinson's disease, 273–275
research of, 270–271
rhythmic auditory stimulation,
    283–284
singing as, 277–282
SIPARI® program, 282
speech improvements after
    brain trauma through, 283
for stroke, 275–284, 288, 293
studies of, 286–287
Music therapy/upper limb
    therapy-integrated,
    286–287
Myasthenia gravis, 170

N

Narratives, 144, 218
Neural atrophy, 21
Neural cell bodies, 124
Neural plasticity, 6, 124
Neural recruitment, 40–41
Neurogenic dysphagia, 166–168,
    167
Neurolinguistics, 190
Neurological examinations, 284
Neurologic music therapy, 270,
    274, 284–286
Neuron, 272
NMT. *See* Neurologic music
    therapy
Nonfluent aphasia, 276
Nonverbal communication,
    224–226, 250

Normal pressure hydrocephalus,
    99
Nursing homes, 136–137

O

Object knowledge, 42
Older adults. *See also* Aging
    population
cognitive slowing in, 18
communication with, 15, **16**
educational level of, 5
geographic differences in, 5
health conditions in, 5
inhibition in, 30–31, 178
speech recognition by,
    background noise effects
    on, 126
technology use by, 5–6
word-finding issues in, 17
workforce participation by, 5
Olfaction impairments, 164
Open-ended questions, 176
Oral language, poetry therapy
    for enhancement of, 186
Oral phase, of swallowing,
    158–159, 164
Organic disorders, 70
Otolaryngologist, 73
Otoscopy, 136
Outer ear, 123
Outer ear canal, 137
Outer hair cells, 123–124

P

Parkinsonism, 85
Parkinson's disease
aspiration pneumonia in, 169
characteristics of, 85–87, **99**
definition of, 273
dysphagia in, 169
music therapy for, 273–275

PCQuirer software, 89
PD. *See* Parkinson's disease
Perceptual slowing, 128, 135
Person-centered dementia care,
    210, 236, 241–242, 256
Pharyngeal phase, of swallowing,
    159, 165–166
Pharynx
  aging changes in, 171
  musculature of, 159
Phonemic regression, 123
Pitch, 70–71
Pneumonia, 169, 171
Poetry, for language
    rehabilitation, 185–187
Pragmatics, 107–108
Presbycusis. *See also* Hearing
    loss, age-related
  anatomic and physiologic
    auditory alterations
    caused by, 123–125
  gender differences in, 125
  speech perception affected by,
    126–128
  summary of, 146–147
Presbyesophagus, 158
Presbyphagia, 163
Presbyphonia, 72
"Presence," 240
Primary progressive aphasia,
    104
Program theory, 20
Progressive neurological disease,
    80, 83
PROMPT, 77, 88
PROMPTing, 77
Pronoun usage, working memory
    capacity effects on, 29
Prosody, 84, 132, 146
Psycholinguistics, 190
Psychological needs, 242
Psychotropic medications, 212
Pure-tone threshold testing, 137

Q

Quality of Communication Life
    Scale, 184
Quality of life
  definition of, 208
  in dementia, 208, 242–243
  description of, 142
  functional communication
    ability and, 185
  post-stroke, 290
  singing effects on, 290
  strategies involving, social
    language enhancement
    uses of
  in aphasia, 184–185
  in dementia, 189–190
Quick Speech-in-Noise test, 140

R

Reaction times, 21
Recall
  age-related declines in, 28
  discourse processing declines
    effect on, 27
Receptive aphasia, 104
Reimbursement for treatment, 7
Rhythm Break Cares program,
    219, 224–226, 228
Rhythmic auditory stimulation,
    283–284
Right hemisphere damage-
    induced aphasia, 104
Rogers, Carl, 210, 236–237,
    240–241, 256
Role-play, 183

S

Satisfaction with Amplification
    in Daily Life (SADL),
    141–142

Self-expression
art therapy as, 247–248, 262
importance of, 247–248
Semantic priming, 178
Sensorineural hearing loss, 122, 140
Sentence comprehension, syntactic prosody for, 132
Silence, 239
Singing
aphasia affected by, 288–289
language development affected by, 289
as music therapy, 277–282
quality of life affected by, 290
Singing Activity Participation Questionnaire, 280
SIPARI®, 282
Situation modeling, 38–40
Slowing hypothesis, 6
SNHL. *See* Sensorineural hearing loss
Social and life-participation approaches, to aphasia, 112–113
Social communication
description of, 107–108
evidence-based approaches in, 193
Social communication approach, 183
Socialization, 234
Social language enhancement in aphasia
caregiver supports, 182–183
community re-entry, 182–183
community reintegration as goal of, 181–184
poetry used for, 185–187
quality of life approach, 184–185
social networks, 182, 184

in dementia
overview of, 187–188
quality of life strategies for, 189–190
Social networks, for aphasia, 182, 184
Solid-state intraluminal manometry, 162
Sounds, neural coding of, 124
Source memory, 33
Spaced retrieval, 101, 214–215
Spastic dysarthria, **81**
Speech
apraxia of. *See* Apraxia of speech
background noise effects on recognition of, 126–128
clear, acoustic parameters of, 144
fluent, 71
motor. *See* Motor speech
perception of, presbycusis effects on, 126–128
singing and, 288–289
temporal characteristics of, 68, 71
Speech hygiene, 73
Speech intelligibility
creative approaches to improving, 87
environmental supports to promote, 84
"slowing down" to improve, 87
summary of, 89
technologies for improving, 85
Speech-language pathologists
for aphasia treatment, 105, 180, 192
group therapy led by, 109
therapy cap for, 7
Speech production
age-related changes in, 69–70
functional disorders and, 70

Speech production *(continued)*
  muscles involved in, 69
  organic disorders and, 70
  summary of, 89
Speech rate
  cognitive decline effects on, 73
  description of, 69, 71, 129
  fluent, 71
  linguistic knowledge used to
    compensate for, 131
  motor speech declines
    suggested by decreases
    in, 72
Speed of processing
  cognitive slowing hypothesis,
    26–27
  declines in, 27, 129, 177
Spontaneous speech, 42
StoryCorps® Memory Loss
  Initiative, 218
Stress
  art therapy for reduction of,
    250
  communication breakdowns as
    cause of, 191
  reaction times affected by, 21
Stria vascularis, 124–125
Stroke
  aphasia after, 276, 288–289
  caregivers for victims of, 292
  description of, 275–276
  dysphagia after, 166–168
  emotional perceptual
    difficulties after, 276
  "golden period" for
    rehabilitation of, 276
  music therapy for, 275–284,
    288, 293
  prevalence of, 276
  quality of life after, 290
Subcortical dementias, 100–101
Supraglottic larynx, 165
Suprahyoid muscle, 166

Surgically implanted
  amplification systems,
    139–140
Swallowing
  aging effects on, 163–166, 171
  clinical evaluation of
    description of, 160
    esophageal manometry,
      162–163, 170
    fiberoptic endoscopic
      evaluation of swallowing,
      161–162
    videofluoroscopic swallow
      study, 160–161, 165, 169
  esophageal phase of, 158–159
  hyoid bone elevation in, 166
  oral phase of, 158–159, 164
  pharyngeal phase of, 159,
    165–166
  stages of, 158–159
Swallowing disorders. *See also*
    Dysphagia
  after cerebrovascular accident,
    166–168
  in amyotrophic lateral
    sclerosis, 169–170
  in dementia patients, 168–169
  in myasthenia gravis, 170
  in Parkinson's disease, 169
  prevalence of, 168, 171
Synapse, 272
Syntactic prosody, 132

T

Task set shifting, 22
Technology
  older adults' use of, 5–6
  speech production uses of, 87
Temporal memory, 33
TimeSlips™, 218
TimeSlips Storytelling program,
    190

"Tip-of-the-tongue" phenomenon, 179
Tongue
  in bolus propulsion, 164
  hypertrophy of, 164
  innervation of, 158
  maximum isometric pressure of, 164
  muscles of, 158, 160
To Whom I May Concern® program, 219–222, 228
Transmission deficit, lexical retrieval impairments caused by, 18
Treatment
  Medicare limitations effect on, 7
  reimbursement for, 7
Trigeminal nerve, 158
TWIMC. *See* To Whom I May Concern® program

U

United States, demographic changes in, 4–6, 121–122
Upper esophageal sphincter, 159, 163, 166
Utermohlen, William, 248

V

van Riper, Charles, 290
VAST, 78
VFSS. *See* Videofluoroscopic swallow study
Video assisted speech technology treatment. *See* VAST
Videofluoroscopic swallow study, 160–161, 165, 169
Visual deficits, age-related, 15

Vocal loudness, 70–71
Vocal pitch, 70–71
Vocal quality, 70–71
Voice, aging, 72–74
Voice hygiene, 72–73

W

Wepfer, Johann Jacob, 276
Wernicke-Korsakoff syndrome, **99**
Wernicke's aphasia, 103
WHO-Qol. *See* World Health Organization Quality-of-Life measure
Word boundaries, 129
Word memory span test, 130
Word recognition
  impairments in, 18
  linguistic context used for, 36
Workforce, 5
Working memory
  aging effects on, 130–131, 178
  definition of, 27–28, 130
  inhibition affected by, 29
  pronoun usage affected by, 29
  storage capacity in, 28
Working memory discourse hypothesis, 27–30
Working memory hypothesis, 6
World Health Organization Quality-of-Life measure, 277
Written language, poetry therapy for enhancement of, 186–187

Z

Zeisel, John, 235, 239